MAKING *more* WAVES

MAKING

NEW WRITING

more

BY ASIAN AMERICAN WOMEN

WAVES

EDITED BY ELAINE H. KIM, LILIA V. VILLANUEVA,
AND ASIAN WOMEN UNITED OF CALIFORNIA

WITH A FOREWORD BY JESSICA HAGEDORN

BEACON PRESS / BOSTON

Beacon Press
25 Beacon Street
Boston, Massachusetts 02108-2892

Beacon Press books
are published under the auspices of
the Unitarian Universalist Association of Congregations.

03 02 01 00 99 98 97   8 7 6 5 4 3 2 1

Text design by Iris Weinstein
Composition by Wilsted & Taylor Publishing Services

Library of Congress Cataloging-in-Publication Data
Making more waves : new writing by Asian American women /
edited by Elaine H. Kim, Lilia V. Villanueva, and Asian Women
United of California; with a foreword by Jessica Hagedorn.
p.   cm.
"Published under the auspices of the Unitarian Universalist
Association of Congregations" —T.p. verso.
Includes bibliographical references (p.   ).
ISBN 0-8070-5913-7 (paper)
1. American literature—Asian American authors.
2. Asian American women—Literary collections.
3. Asian Americans—Literary collections.
4. American Literature—Women authors.
5. American literature—20th century.
I. Kim, Elaine H.   II. Villanueva, Lilia V.   III. Asian Women
United of California.   IV. Unitarian Universalist
Association of Congregations.
PS508.A8M35 1997
810.8 '09287'08995073—dc21   96-52670

CONTENTS

4 CONTESTATION

5 MOVEMENT

FOREWORD: "THERE ONCE WAS A WOMAN . . ."

"There once was a woman," Anu Gupta writes in "Storytime." "She was the daughter of fire; fury and anger incarnate. She would be the cause of the destruction of the universe and the beginning of a new era, a darker era, the era in which we now live." The female fury Gupta alludes to so ominously and yet lovingly in her piece is very much present here in *Making More Waves: New Writing by Asian American Women*, the latest anthology edited by the collective known as Asian Women United of California.

Making More Waves: New Writing by Asian American Women continues in the inclusive, generous tradition of the first volume. History and memory, sexuality and repression, cultural, spiritual, artistic, and generational conflicts are explored in various ways by another dynamic group of women. The works of established and respected writers, poets, journalists, and scholars such as Chitra Divakaruni, Kimiko Hahn, Helen Zia, Lisa See, Marilyn Chin, Lisa Lowe, Yen Le Espiritu, Mitsuye Yamada, Elaine Kim, and Trinh T. Minh-ha are presented alongside the works of emerging voices such as Susan Ito, Anu Gupta, and the precocious sixteen-year-old Filipino American poet Juno Parreñas. The editors clearly believe in creating a forum for us to keep telling our stories, exploring what it means to be Asian, to be American, and to be female. They took the exhilarating risk of setting out without a typical editorial "agenda," utilizing an open-door policy in their call for submissions to women all over the country. Stories, memoirs, essays, and poems poured in. *Making More Waves* is a continuum, a celebration and acknowledgment of our unique artistic visions, our differences, our often painful histories and complex experiences. Our ethnic roots can indeed be traced to Asia, but the ties to America are just as binding. The English language and the American landscape are reclaimed, reinvented, and transformed by many of the women in this anthology.

In the nineties, we seem to be enjoying a modest boom in Asian American literature. Many women, in particular, have broken their silence to produce powerful and exciting work. The hardwon success of the first *Making Waves* anthology, published by Beacon Press in 1989, came as no surprise to many Asian American women and writers of my generation. At last! The mainstream publishing industry was finally catching up to what we'd known all along. The universe does not run on testosterone alone. The need and the audience for ethnic women's literature definitely exists. But does being tagged an "ethnic" or "woman" writer help or hinder us? Nowadays, even with the publication of many more books by Asian American women and other people of color, our presence and concerns remain marginalized in this society. The editors of Asian Women United have taken independent action by gathering our stories—determined to make and distribute literature out of our lives and our writings, with or without the support and cachet of a commercial publisher.

The growing audience of readers for writing by and about Asian American women will not be disappointed by the rich and diverse selections in *Making More Waves*. There are timely essays examining domestic violence within the immigrant community, and essays dealing with race, class, and gender. There are poignant stories about gang girls and Hollywood icons, inspiring profiles of "bad-ass" contemporary visual artists, and a compelling interview with an amazingly brave and forgiving Korean comfort woman. Last but not least, there are poems. Multilayered, sensual, funny, and tragic poems. Marilyn Chin's "A Portrait of the Self as Nation, 1990–1991" could serve as an ironic manifesto for this anthology, her poem a subversive and witty deconstruction of the ongoing colonization of body and soul by the West. The final stanza is a bitter, breathtaking lament: "History has never failed us. / Why save Babylonia or Cathay, / when we can always have Paris? / Darling, if we are to remember at all, / Let us remember it well— / We were fierce, yet tender, / fierce and tender."

The self as battleground and as defiant nation, the self as illuminating poem and story, the self as dark song of memory and resistance remains a profound and eloquent metaphor for the writers of this empowering collection.

Jessica Hagedorn

PREFACE

Asian Women United of California (AWU) is a nonprofit organization founded in 1976 to promote the socioeconomic and general welfare of Asian American women. AWU's changing membership is composed of women from various Asian ethnic backgrounds. The group now focuses primarily on producing print and visual educational materials.[1]

Frustrated by what we saw as a lack of voice and visibility in all walks of American life for the rapidly growing community of Asian American women, members of Asian Women United had been talking about producing a book since the late 1970s. We did not want a medley of personal memoirs about women of various Asian ethnicities growing up as daughters of immigrant mothers. We were not interested in stories that moved characters along a linear continuum from Asian immigrant to American citizen to a happy ending suggesting the superiority of the latter over the former. We wanted to produce something that had nothing to do with exotic Orientalism and that was not necessarily reassuring to an audience accustomed to thinking about Asian Americans as a harmless "model minority," an immigrant success story demonstrating that racism has vanished from the U.S. social landscape, replaced by a cheerful Disneyesque "we are the world" multicultural pluralism.

In 1984, we received a federal education grant to do a book project. We were able to hire a project director and an editor, as well as to pay small stipends to members of the editorial board, although only for the beginning of the project. It took us almost five years to bring *Making Waves: An Anthology of Writings By and About Asian American Women* into publication.

When we began working on *Making Waves* in the mid-1980s, we expected to produce a sheaf of curriculum materials that would be listed under "A" for "Asian" in a Washington, D.C. clearinghouse. We had not been successful in finding ways to disseminate our earlier materials in the public schools, although the videos were shown on public television and the books were sold to individuals. By the late 1980s, many public funding sources for nonprofit organizations like ours had been phased out, and dissemination of our materials was becoming even more difficult. Then, at the very moment when the *Making Waves* manuscript had been completed, an editor from Beacon Press visited the Asian American Studies program at U.C. Berkeley to ask if there were any publishable materials about Asian American women.

Because it was published by a commercial press, *Making Waves* found its way into many college course reading lists across the country. We were astonished by the response to the book. We never dared to imagine that our work would earn enough revenue to really support a new project. But when royalty checks for *Making Waves* did begin to accrue, we put these funds together with proceeds from rentals and sales of our videotapes and with revenue from the sale of *With Silk Wings: Asian American Women at Work*, a book for high school students that had generated almost $20,000 for the organization by the time it sold out in the mid-1980s.

In 1991, we had accumulated enough for a modest budget to produce a thirty-minute video documentary on Asian American women visual artists, so we sent out a call to potential directors. The treatment we liked best was submitted by visual artist Valerie Soe, who proposed a video in four segments, directed by four different filmmakers about four different visual artists, all women of various South, Southeast, and East Asian American backgrounds. *Art to Art: Expressions by Asian American Women* was screened at the San Francisco Asian Art Museum in 1993.

At about that time, members of Asian Women United began working in earnest on a sequel to our 1989 anthology. *Making Waves* had laid an important foundation by tracing the histories of women of various Asian nationalities in the U.S., providing something of an international political context for these histories, and introducing some pivotal issues facing Asian American women, such as those related to work, family, sexuality, racial injustice, social movement. But *Making Waves* was in the end an introductory book. Given the increasing body of work published about Asian American women since 1989, we wanted the new collection to either delve deeper into already addressed topics or to broach untapped subjects. While we wanted to acknowledge the rapid diversification and expansion of Asian American communities since the mid-1980s, we also wanted the new book to go beyond simply representing the various Asian ethnic groups, away from our old smorgasbord approach (one Chinese, one Japanese, one Korean, one Filipina, and so forth).

We envisioned an anthology that would include writings by septuagenarians and teenagers, that would deal with mixed racial identities, sexuality and sexual orientation, relationships between Asian American women and other Americans of color, and other asymmetrical and surprising subjects. At the same time, we liked the idea of just allowing what was being felt and thought about among Asian American women in the 1990s to emerge on our pages. Therefore, just as with *Making Waves*, we did not ask for writings on particular topics or themes. Instead, we sent a general announcement to Asian American Studies programs, as well as to Asian American news media and community groups around the country, saying that we wanted to publish what we tentatively called *Making Waves II*. Then we waited to see what would happen.

During the next year, we received almost one thousand submissions from all over the country. Drawing on our local community of Asian American writers, educators, students, community workers, and cultural critics, the board of Asian Women United assembled an editorial advisory board that met regularly over the course of about eighteen months, reading and discussing submissions. The result is a collection of writings that touch on a number of unexpected topics, sometimes in unexpected ways. While *Making Waves* was meant to break silences, particularly about the dispossession and exclusion experienced by many Asian Americans over the decades since Asian immigration to the U.S. began, *Making More Waves* is an attempt to weave history and memory with desire and possibility in such a way that multiple identities emerge as irregularities and discontinuities, beautiful and unpredictable, in the pattern. This attention to multiple identities and subjectivities in no way signifies a waning of commitment to collectivity and to social justice. On the contrary, deepening the commitment requires widening the circle of inclusion. We hope that readers will find *Making More Waves* filled with surprises that open spaces for speaking about the past in new ways, as well as for dreaming of alternative practices in the present and future.

PART 1

MEMORY

*twists
of wash
in the
starched
sunlight*

THE BOX OF ABANDONED WHITE BUTTONS

Kimiko Hahn

for Tomie

*f*ound on the sidewalk three years ago
have come in handy for pajamas and dolls' eyes.
Today I choose a dozen to sew on Rei's crew socks
annoyingly indistinguishable from Miya's.
Cuffing each sock, I sew one on the left side
then to the mate, sew one on the right.
I wish mother were alive to see this handiwork.
She'd be pleased I took the time
from correcting exams and scouring real estate classifieds
to solve this small dilemma. I wish
she could see Rei turn her delighted ankles.
I remember the blue and pink stars she stitched
on my slips and Tomie's, that I saw
her own mother had sewn when we visited Maui
and I handed them the twists of wash in the starched sunlight.

JEAN AND ME

Linda Nishioka

*a*rms linked for the class picture.
Jean in her blond Dutch Boy
me, sporting a China Doll bob
our eyes peering coyly
into the camera
under full, straight bangs
color the only difference.

Naptime and we scoot deep
into our sleeping mats.
We lie tented
in the twilight leaking
through the woven threads.
Under us, the concrete floors
seep cool relief
from sweaty necks
and matted hair.

The teacher patrols
the rows of kids pretending sleep.
Her heels clomp past
signal for Jean and me
to begin backstroking
up to the mouths
of our swelling mats.

We break through
to daylight
plunge again
into the dark-blue denim,
folding the tops
over our heads,
we seal ourselves
in navy envelopes
licked shut from the inside
face each other
sapphire-skinned.

The envelopes puff
and collapse
with exchanges of
our voiceless debate:
where to hide
the Indian head nickel
sifted from white sands
under the swings
during morning recess
no longer safe now
tucked in the crotch
of the giant panax hedge.

That humid afternoon
we even kissed
once-on-the-lips
me and Jean
deep inside
the cool, dark-blue denim
of fourth grade.

MOURNING THE BLOOD THAT SPILLED TO MAKE THIS STEW AND LAUGHING LOUD,
OR
WHY I HATE MY COUSIN PUCHA

Maria Sarita Echavez See

*f*irst of all Pucha could dance and that's always the favorite in family gatherings unless you can croon cherished Spanish ballads, play Liberace favorites on the piano, or strum a guitar. The only thing ugly about her was her nasal out-of-tune New York accent which, of course, impressed the whole of Bulusan Street once a year when the Americano kids arrived in Manila for Christmas. Gangs of caroling children straggled from house to house, banging on the gates and howling Bing Crosby's "White Christmas," Pat Boone's "Silver Bells," or Johnny Mathis's "Hark the Herald Angels Sing," until a face flushed with drink, anger, or both, appeared and threw a few coins onto the street. Usually "Jingle Bells," with its potent trademark genericism and potential to repeat indefinitely, got the quickest response. Especially if accompanied with jangling tin cans.

Delighted at the throng of visiting cousins, the streetwise local children snatched at this once-a-year-only chance to make an easy peso. With saintly smiles, my older cousins approached all mothers within range and offered to take care of their babies—"more babies, more sympathy, more money" was our slogan—and we had our own caroling troupe. Formation was important. The chinky cousins ("you look rich") were in the back, the dark ones up front and holding the babies, and everyone else in the middle. All Americanos were given strict instructions not to say a word and give the game away with our suspiciously wealthy accents. Pucha, with her shades of Rican accent, passed as a lowly one-and-a-half generation spic in New York City, but in Manila she reigned.

～～～

In the days leading up to Noche Buena, more and more relatives from the provinces arrived at my Lola's door on Bulusan Street. Ging-Ging and Cherry, the maids, washed and rinsed yet another basket of rice, fried yet another dozen lumpia, and rushed into the street to halt the vegetable peddler trundling by. Tito Ding, Pucha's father, opened suitcases and boxes of presents from the U.S.: red crispy apples, packages of nuts, chocolate, and toys. "Still thinking like colonials," he mumbled. Pursing her lips, Lola smacked at the children's hungry hands, and squirreled the food away, as she did in the war, rationing it out sparingly—stingily if you asked my cousins—making it last months until the brown chocolate got white spots and went bad.

Furnished with two plain, almost ugly, narrow wooden beds and cheap built-in cupboards that reached the high ceiling, Lola's bedroom never changed. Even so, I was surprised every time I stepped into the tiny room in the back of the house. I had always pictured Lola—the Dona of Bulusan Street—as surrounded by ebony, lace, jewelry, and scented wood. But her bare walls displayed not a hint of luxury or frivolous decoration, save a battered picture of the Virgin Mary shrouded in her usual blue and white. Nothing was ever left out on the aging mattress or on the floor, so everyone always exclaimed at Lola's tidy habits and Spartan lifestyle. But her room did not look neat; it looked bare and lifeless. Pucha once said that it looked like a nun's cell. Tita Binky, our youngest and favorite aunt, laughed when she heard Pucha's sacrilegious observation, then looked at us with glittering eyes, "My bedroom may look like that soon." Pucha and I saw the sadness in Tita Binky's face, but we shrugged disbelievingly and ran away.

The Bulusan kids—the ones who still lived in the Philippines—never discovered Lola's secret hiding spots. Emboldened by the arrival of Americanos and province cousins and desperate for the already decaying chocolates, they convinced all of us to enter the forbidden attic above her sacred bedroom. One afternoon, surrounded by grinning cousins, Pucha and I stacked chair upon chair on Lola's creaking bed. We forgot to first remove the sagging foam mattress, and the chairs gently rocked back and forth as we climbed up and tried to reach the small covered hole in the ceiling. The younger kids gave muffled screams of excitement as the chairs threatened to topple down. Coughing from the dust that drizzled down into our open mouths, we slowly pushed aside the wooden plank that served as entrance to the attic. A suffocating, gray smell of cloves and moist grime drifted down the ladder of chairs. Pucha and I crawled up into the cramped storage space,which could only fit the two of us, and cautiously gazed around at Lola's treasure. She had hidden everything important and useless there. Lolo's now-silent, unused violins, crinkled sheet music, framed photographs delicately sprinkled with threads of white fungus, hampers of gaudy t-shirts "for the province." And letters. Stacks of letters, partially wrapped in brown paper and tied with pink plastic raffia, as if resigned and ready to be mailed back to their original writers. Pucha untied one of the stacks and the letters fell dustily into her hands, threatening to dissipate into ancient confetti. Browning with age, they were all addressed to our grandfather Manuel in the same unpracticed, almost childish, handwriting. Some letters were still sealed, yet some had opened from the moist heat of the attic. Chinese handwriting was scrawled on the back of each envelope. Neither of us could read the strange writing, though, and we were too disappointed at the absence of chocolate to pay much attention to our finding. Our cousins below whispered urgently and we scrambled back down again. Later, after tidying Lola's bedroom and fleeing next door to Tita Binky's house, I remembered to ask Tita Binky about the letters because I knew she would not tell Lola about our adventure. She smiled and said she would tell me soon when I was ready to hear a long story about my grandfather, but right now there was too much work to be done in preparation for the festivities.

More and more people gathered in the dusty high-ceilinged living room with the old grand piano, one electric fan, black-and-white television, and the blinking plastic Christmas tree in the corner. The visiting strangers shuffled hungrily around the buffet spread on the dining table until they staggered to the living room with sighs and burps, while Ging-Ging and Cherry tiredly washed dishes and stored leftovers in the wheezing refrigerator. Below the chatter and laughter, the sounds of the daily soap opera crackled softly from Ging-Ging's kitchen radio and wafted towards the nearby living room.

The evenings after dinner were time for relaxation and entertainment. The grown-ups, mostly the extended relatives that magically appeared every Christmas, sprawled around the living room and gossiped about the latest scandals in Bulusan. Tita Binky's name always came up.

"She should marry him!" hissed a complacent matron, and everyone murmured agreement.

Fanning herself slowly, she continued, "She was always too pretty. Too *mestiza*. The boys always flocked around her." More nods.

"Uncontrollable," added another, shaking her head regretfully. She leaned forward, her gold crucifix dangling sweat. "I tell you, it's *in the blood*."

That was enough to explain everything, and everyone looked at one another knowingly.

The flickering television displayed the usual beauty and talent contests, blaring out the name of the new Miss Everyone's Christmas Sweetheart: "Miss Dolores Tolentino, a sweet sixteen from Pangasinan!!" But the Holy Infant's birthday was not a time for television, and this was where the children came in for official scrutiny and exhibition.

We eyed the presents piling up daily under the tree that never shed pine needles, but we had to pay homage to all the Santa Clauses sitting on the couches every night. On entering the dreaded living room, every child asked the blessing of each adult, taking up the adult's hand and pressing it devoutly to one's forehead, before moving on to the next outstretched wrinkled hand. The usual round of compliments and astonished, "You're so big!

Ay, maganda!" were exchanged by proud parents, and then the requests, threats, wheedling, and finally stern orders to dance, sing, act, or play piano, began.

Pucha had joined her Mama's dance troupe when she was four years old. American though she was, Pucha knew the village dances, Spanish dances, the *tinikling*, Igorot dances, the samba, the waltz, the tango, and all the latest disco moves. At eleven, she was the prepubescent star of Lola's living room, twirling sexily on the floor, a thin glittering polyester band tied around her curving forehead. Sort of the budding *artista* of the family. Pucha could understand Tagalog, and talk if she had to. She could imitate anything! One night she put on a show of New York city life—from a ghetto-blaster-toting black guy strutting down to the corner bodega, to the flip FOB lost and piteously asking for directions in the big bad city. She was smart-alecky, tough, funny, and pretty: the genuine article.

I played piano. But classical only, no corny Spanish love songs or Pilita Corales favorites so everyone could sing along. "Mina! Come and play for Lola!" But I stubbornly refused to budge from my mother's side, even when she began to plead with me. Baffled by my ugly behavior—no one ever declined to perform—all the grown ups smiled pityingly at my mother and complimented her on her daughter's modesty. "So shy, naman." No one could persuade me to touch the sticky yellowing keys of my dead Lolo's piano and then listen to the silence of polite indulgent applause. Classical piano is classical after all: dead, worshiped, laminated, and expensive. And the uselessness of that kind of music is nowhere more obvious than on Bulusan Street, where music is still for everyone who can hear it.

~~~~

But it really came down to the *mestiza* versus the Chinese. Pucha was unconditionally beautiful. There were never any split-second silences hastily filled by superfluous modifiers tacked on like "*Chinese* beauty"—the most frequent phrase for me. Pucha's hair was long and curly, almost frizzy. Everyone pitied her admiringly because she had to get her hair straightened out once in a while at the hairdresser's to keep the curls in check. My Chinese hair frizzed just the tiniest bit at the top of my forehead when the typhoons came. I always forgot that nobody else noticed. Light-skinned, big eyes with of course double folds, and a not-too-Anglo, but not-too-flaring, perfectly *mestiza* nose, she got her period when she was ten and coached our dark-skinned, flat-nosed cousin Ponggay through her first bleeding. Pucha was confident and comforting. She grabbed Ponggay's trembling wrist with one hand and a couple of pads with the other, and they disappeared into my Lola's bathroom for hours, it seemed. No one else except for the maids found out, and Ponggay emerged a woman. Thirteen at the time, I still hadn't started to bleed.

We were all playing as usual in the streets. The older cousins yelled, "Koche!" once in a while. All the girls grabbed the babies and dragged them off the street onto the pavement while the boys shouted and slapped the car that dared to drive down our street. That was when I found out about mistresses in Taiwan, and Lola shut her mouth firm and angry and strode back into the house. My *other* Taiwanese Lola and my half-Taiwanese, half-Filipina Tita. I learned about them in between a joke and a hush-hush whisper.

"Who?"

"Lolo Manuel."

"You're lying."

"No, I'm not."

"We have another Tita?"

"Yeah. That's what my Ma said."

Pause.

"You're lying!"

"No, I'm not!"

"Well, your mom's lying!"

"No, she isn't!"

"Uh huh. If she knows so much, how come she doesn't know where your daddy is?"

Chests heaved and the crying started.

"My father went to America to make lots of money. . . . And at least my Pa isn't Chinese! *Pangit!*"

"Stupid!! I hate you!"

It would kill Lola to have "that woman" talked about even though Lolo died twenty-five years ago.

Nobody knows the names of all our ancestors, so I guess it really is in the blood. Bored with the mores of a too-early motherhood that kept her captive in the shadows of Lola's dusty parlor, Tita Binky used to yell out all our crazy nicknames in her raucous, dusky timbre, callously ignoring Lola's disapproving glances. Lola screwed up her face, pursed her lips, and squinted her eyes. Too young and too pretty to be imprisoned, Tita Binky brought the outside world inside, "Mikey! Baby! Carlito! Pucha! Get inside!" A sexy, pregnant Santa Claus called for her delinquent pack of reindeer, she shouted for each of us rapidly and perfectly, just enough space between each name as if each mattered ever so much. "Junior! Beck-Beck! Greg! Ponggay! Mina! Where are you?!" And we elbowed and pushed one another inside faster than lightning and thunder, eager to see what new game she had invented. Blinking and wriggling from the sudden darkness, we lined up, as always, according to age, and faced Tita Binky as she grandly announced, "Let's have a competition!" Everyone wriggled a little more. Tita Binky loved the suspense and so did we. She marched importantly up and down, inspecting our faces on parade, "First prize for the cousin with the chinkiest eyes!" Jumping up and down, we began giggling and pointing at one another. Screaming accusations, the fingers began to wave vaguely in the direction of Carlito, me, and my brother, so I edged over to Pucha's side and laughed and pointed along. It had come down to Carlito and my brother. Nobody ever won the competition, though, because everyone broke from the line-up and began running aimlessly round and round the piano, the plastic Christmas tree, and even Lola's sacred chair. "Too much noise!" scolded Lola. But the admonition was not serious enough, and it lost its way in our circle of howls and shrieks of laughter. Frowning, she began waving the almighty wooden clothespin at our noses but it no longer struck fear into our hearts. All of us could have used a little work on our flaring nostrils, even Pucha, but Lola never made good on her threats to make us wear clothespins at night while we slept. Lola suddenly rose from her chair and gave us her Most Serious Dona Glare through terrifying eyes that slanted ever so slightly and almost disappeared into her brown wrinkled cheeks. Tita Binky threw back her head and laughed and laughed, and we ran back outside to play in the street, hesitating and blinking again at the threshold, paralyzed momentarily by the harsh, blazing sunshine.

GIFTS OF THE MAGI

Grace Elaine Suh

*t*he day my father died my mother said to me, "He loved you. Don't think that he didn't."

My brother Peter stood by the water fountain, his red ski jacket on and zipped up. He held his gloves in his hands, and squinted through his glasses to watch my mother and me. The corridor ran endlessly on either side, blue-lit and hushed, like a museum empty on a weekday afternoon.

I saw that my mother was waiting, that she wanted an answer of some kind. A number of things occurred to me to say, but my mother was crying, and I have never been a very brave person. I was fifteen years old and idealistic and wanted to believe that I was not capable of cruelty. And so, although I would have liked to say more, in the end I simply told her, Yes.

It was all she wanted. My mother wept, she reached out to hug me, and in her arms I said it again—I could not stop myself—Yes, mother, yes.

Since that time I have come to face the cruelty we humans inflict on each other every day. Tiny holes of pain perforate the surface of our lives. Millions die of hunger, their mouths crusty from lack of use; governments attach electrodes to the tongues and testicles of their prisoners; at parties people gossip about others' failed children and marriages.

I myself have done my part. In addition to everyday cruelty to cabdrivers, old friends, and random strangers, in two years I have neither called my mother nor visited her. When sometimes she calls me, to her hesitant questions I respond shortly: "I'm just fine. Listen, Mom, I have to go now." And, "No, sorry, I already have plans for Thanksgiving," although, in truth, both years, I didn't. Our phone conversations don't last long. I make no effort to fill in the long gaps of silence. I am not a monster. But I have become addicted to the sharp thrill that comes with the knowledge of having caused her pain.

When Peter and I were ten and fourteen, my father spoke at a conference in Dallas a couple of weeks before Christmas. My mother came home one night from her friend Vilma Canella's house with a large, rectangular box in her arms. Peter jumped for the TV and pushed the Power button in with his big toe. We were watching a *M*A*S*H* rerun and she hated the show, having lived through that war and not found it funny. We headed for the stairs to our rooms.

"Wait, kids," she said. "Look what I have."

She thrust the box at Peter. It was an old cardboard box, beat-up and warped and frayed fuzzy at the corners. The ends were heavily crisscrossed with old tape. The side of the box said "Holiday Cheer."

"What's in it?" Peter asked.

"Open it up. No—" she changed her mind, "Guess."

I look at her then. She was different. Her eyes were alive and her face glowed pink from the cold. Her heavy wool coat exhaled fresh cool evening air like a radiator breathing out heat. It felt good. My head felt pushed in at the temples from watching TV and reading all day.

She went to sit on the couch with her coat still on. She smiled at us in a funny way and watched my brother unpeel the orangey strips of tape. His fingernails were chewed to the quick; it was hard for him to begin each strip.

"Here, let me," I said, and wondered at my impatience even as I began pulling up bits of tape and felt them disintegrate, gritty, between my fingers. I didn't care what was in that box.

Finally we'd undone enough for Peter to rip off the rest. He held the box upside down and shook. Nothing at first, and then, a tangle of dark green wires.

"What is it?" I asked dully.

Peter was already fitting the end of a big branch into a two-inch thick pole. My mother sorted wires into sizes and fluffed out the plastic needles.

"What are they?" I asked again, as if I could not understand.

"Vilma found it the other day in her basement. Their first tree. She thought we might like it."

I had one of the branches in my hands. It was flexible, it bent easily at any point. I ran my fingers down the wire, and flipped the needles one way, and then all back the other. "What about Dad?" I asked.

Our father didn't allow a Christmas tree or decorations or presents. It was all crass, gaudy materialism. It obscured the true meaning of Christmas.

I knew he was right. I went over to friends' and saw the wreaths on their front doors and the six-foot-tall fresh Douglas firs flanked with brightly wrapped presents. Their mothers handed me candy-cane-shaped cookies and mugs of mulled cider and I said, "Yes, well, in my family we find all the trappings distracting. We celebrate very simply."

Every year our relatives in New York and California sent us big packages that we opened right away. Every year they gave us the same things: Metropolitan Museum wall calendars, sweaters, nightgowns and pajamas and slippers, mufflers and gloves for Peter and my father, scented lotions and silk scarves for my mother and me.

The relatives were my mother's sisters and their families. I had only seen them a couple of times. The way I kept them apart were the boxes: Aunt Edith's said B. Altman's, Aunt Nancy's said Lord & Taylor, Aunt Sue's said Saks Fifth Avenue, and Aunt Mathilda's in California said I. Magnin. We had pictures of the aunts, but to me they all looked the same, middle-aged Asian women with short black hair. They were strangers. I would have been embarrassed if they'd known how grateful I was to them. A little jar of Estée Lauder White Linen cream (to: Karen, Merry Christmas, love: Aunt Edith) made me feel connected to the decent, normal world.

My father snorted. "Let them send presents," he told us, "but you kids remember, they don't even know what Christmas is really about. Christmas isn't presents and parties and merry merry ho ho Santa Claus, or Satan Claus or whatever. That's *X-Mas*. You know what they did when your mother married me? Do you know? They disowned her, that's what they did. Disinherited her. Did you know that, huh, did you?" He glared at us over his glasses, his arms folded across his chest. "I'm asking you kids a question, did you know or didn't you know?"

We'd heard the story a hundred times. "No," we whispered.

But he didn't notice, he'd started talking again: "They can send their nice gifts, but they have rejected the true gift, the only gift that's worth a cent of all their money. Their hearts are closed to the true message of Christmas. Christmas is about Jesus coming down to the filthiness of this world to die for you and me and our stinking, dirty sins. And as long as they reject that message, they are headed straight for hell. Isn't that right?"

"Yes."

"What? I can't hear you!" He put his cupped hand to his ear, like kindergarten teachers do to shy students. "What? I asked you a question. Speak up, shout out the message of God!"

Against our wills, our throats tight and scratchy, like automatons we yelled, "Yes!"

"What?"

"Yes!"

"*What?*"

"YES!"

"Good, that's right," he beamed at us, nodding his head.

It was then, when I felt beaten, crushed somehow, that I hated him. I felt my muscles clench and ossify, my blood was volcanic. Afterward the inside of my chest felt empty and raw, like after you've screamed.

I did a lot to avoid feeling that way. That's why that night, as we sat on the floor, our laps filled with plastic pine branches, I asked again, "What about Dad?"

My mother and brother didn't bother answering. Peter was screwing the trunk onto the base, and then the little tree was done. We cleared the piles of papers and books off the corner end table, and stood the tree in the center. Peter brought down the red plaid car blanket from his room and draped it around the base. I fluffed the needles so that they all went the same way and untwisted some of the wires. My mother got out a bag of those shiny cellophane bows, the kind you stick onto presents in the car on your way to baby showers and weddings. We got the bows to stay on the branch tips with lots of Scotch tape. It turned out we didn't have enough for the whole tree. We put them on the front, where it showed.

When we were done, we sat down and looked at the tree. I'd never seen my mother acting this way. She seemed carefree, reckless. The skin on her face looked filled out. She smiled at Peter and me. She was beautiful. But I couldn't give in. I kept thinking how the bows were ruined. They had so much tape on them they could never be used. It was a waste. I couldn't look at the tree, it made me embarrassed. I didn't meet my mother's eyes. The whole thing was too corny, like an episode of *Little House on the Prairie*: Ma makes Christmas festive with a jar of canned peaches and some dried fat pork.

But the tree *was* pretty. The beat-up plastic throw-out tree looked nice. Peter stood up and cracked his knuckles, he stepped one-two, one-two back. I thought he would help me, say something. He looked at me out of the corner of his eye. He raised his eyebrows, questioning, and then it was like a little door opening up in my chest. Something hot was pouring, filling, and I had to smile back, smile at him and my mother, because I was happy, we were happy, all of us, Peter, my mother, and I.

We meant to take down the tree before our father came back. We were only going to keep it up for a couple of days. But one afternoon, my mother came home with a package, a single string of little white lights, and after that, it didn't seem possible to pack the tree back up—it was plugged into the wall.

Something made us shy, we couldn't talk about it. We revolved around each other as if we'd just met. Eating dinner together in the black winter evenings, we felt full, bursting, brave. We talked quietly—please pass the corn, I had a test today, do you think it'll snow tomorrow?—it felt good to talk, it didn't matter about what. We talked and ate, and we couldn't stop smiling. At ten, when my mother went to bed, Peter and I went upstairs with her. We left our homework, undone, on the dining room table. We turned the downstairs lights off, but the little tree we left blinking in the corner. We stood in the hall, awkward, each standing in front of our bedroom doors, and said goodnight. We waved to each other as if we were blocks apart.

My father came home two days before Christmas. My mother picked him up from the airport after work. Peter and I stood in the living room, waiting, stiff, not moving, our hearts ticking like alarm clocks. I couldn't seem to breathe. By five-thirty it was totally dark. Cars whizzed by in the slush.

"Do you think maybe he'll like it?" Peter asked. We stared straight out the big living room window, our hands clasped behind us.

"Shut up," I said. My brother never knew when it wasn't any use talking.

"Maybe he will."

"Shut up, shut up!" I screamed it.

A car swooped into our circle. My heart clutched. Headlights flashed us for a minute, an engine rumbled to a stop. We breathed out. It was okay. Mr. Kennard's Lincoln.

Then it was Mom and Dad. The garage door was gliding up, the car roared in. Peter and I looked at each other then. His eyes were wide, nervous, hopeful. I couldn't get over how dumb he was.

"Hey, where's everyone, isn't anybody home?" our father called out. He sounded like he might be in a happy mood. I began to set my face to smile. Then he was at the living room doorway, and he wasn't.

"What are you two doing standing in the middle of the room in the dark?" He flicked on the switch. My eyes squeezed shut from the sudden glare. We'd forgotten to turn lights on.

"Huh? I asked you a question. What's the problem, you two can't speak?" My mother appeared at the doorway behind him, her face tensed up and tired. My father turned to her over his shoulder. "What's wrong with the kids, what's been going on here?" He was turning back to us, "No one's even going to say 'Hi Dad, Welcome home' or . . ."

His head swiveled, he saw the tree behind us. "What's that?"

Then he asked more slowly, "What is that doing here? Somebody tell me right now."

Nobody said anything. My father began again, his voice was reasonable and flat, "I said, what . . ."

Mom and Peter started at the same time.

"It's my fault, Vilma thought that . . ."

"A Christmas tree."

Dad ignored her. He looked at Peter out of the corner of his eyes and then after a moment, his chin lifted and followed slowly, like it was a tray he was carrying. "A Christmas tree, is it?"

Peter nodded.

"A Christmas tree? Well, Peter, Karen, you Mom, all of you, let me tell you something: I knew that." He smiled and repeated, "I knew it was a Christmas tree. So what were you thinking, Daddy's so mean he won't let us have a Christmas tree? Is that what you were thinking?"

He crossed his arms high on his chest and smiled down at us like the jolly green giant. I was afraid, but more—I was angry, so angry at Peter and my mother.

"That's fine," my father said. "You all want a Christmas tree, and Christmas and everything, that's what you want, well, let's do it."

He stood there for a full minute, looking not at us, but over our heads to the tree. My legs began to crick, I'd been standing in one place for a long time. My mother still stood in the doorway, my father's big suitcase on the floor by her feet, the handle of his overnight bag still gripped in her hand. At Peter I didn't look at all.

Then my father spun on his heel, he spread his arms out wide in the air above his head, and he yelled, "DO IT! Do-you-hear-me, I said, You want Christmas, we'll have Christmas RIGHT NOW!"

He bent down and with one calm movement of his long, straight arm, he swept everything off the top of the coffee table. The pile of magazines spilled onto the African violet. My mother yelled, "No!" but his arm kept going, going, as inevitable as slow motion. The ceramic pot tipped over, clumps of black soil tumbled out, and his white-shirted arm kept going, bright and clean as a blade, unstoppable, into a mug, into a shoehorn and a bottle of lotion, it swept it all onto the floor, the whole mess: the unpotted plant and the bottle of Jergens on its side, covered with the last dregs of coffee from the mug, and over it all, face up, a *National Geographic*: "Wildlife in the Bay of Fundy."

"Now," my father said as he gathered himself up. His eyes looked calm. He smiled at us; his voice was quiet, "Now, clean this up." He gestured at the table, the shirt was stained and clung to his arm, "Clean this whole thing up, the whole room, the entire house, it's all filthy! The whole house is a mess, it's disgusting, clean it now! None of you are going to go to bed until the house is clean, until it's all clean."

My mother had scurried to the coffee table; she scooped dirt with her fingers back into the flower pot. Peter knelt beside her, stacking the magazines, turning them around so that they were all upright and facing the same way.

"Stop," my father said to my mother. "You stop cleaning. That's for the kids to do." My mother looked up, her cupped hands black with wet dirt. I hated her surprised mouth and the way she pleaded so humbly with her eyes. She crumbled so easily. She was no help. She never protected us at all.

"You," my father said, "go to the grocery store and buy a turkey and dressing and yams and a pie and everything. We're going to clean the house and then we're going to eat Christmas dinner, just like you wanted."

"Charles, please," she whispered.

She stood up, she walked to the door without looking at any of us. Peter was crying. He cried like a child, fat tears rolling down his cheeks, his knees grinding plant soil into the carpet.

My father saw me glaring. "Get going," he said.

That night we cleaned for hours, the kitchen, the dining room and living room, the bathrooms. I remember that when I was young, my mother kept everything immaculate. I'd go over to friends' or neighbors' and be shocked by the newspapers on the couch and the dying plants. But somehow, through the years, our house got to be that way too. There started being piles of things, drawers full of odds and ends. We were always tired, it was hard to keep up. Entropy was like a tidal wave, it overcame us. Now, there was dirt everywhere, places you wouldn't have thought. Of course the top of the refrigerator was unbelievable, not just dusty, but slick with a film of black. But even its front doors, which we saw every day, turned the paper towels grey almost instantly.

We vacuumed and dusted, we swept off the dusty tops of footboards, we wiped fingerprints off light switch panels, we mopped the kitchen and bathroom floors, we ran a duster in the corners where the walls met the ceilings for dust and webs. With piles of old magazines and papers in our arms, we ran out coatless in the freezing dark to pile them by the mailbox for the garbage men.

Peter followed me from room to room, and now he stood polishing the faucet, his head heavy, his shoulders drooping. I realized how little he still was. He could lean his elbows on the vanity top without bending down. I heard my mother in the kitchen running the sink. She was trying to thaw the turkey. The label said it needed eight hours or overnight. My father had gone down to his study in the basement. He had us scurrying, he'd beaten us again, it was no use, and that's all he'd wanted us to know.

By three-thirty in the morning, the food was done. My mother had cut off the breast meat and roasted it. She'd made yams, cooked stuffing in a casserole in the oven, and warmed the apple pie. My father was maniacally, elaborately cheerful. "Mmmm, that smells delicious!" he said. "Come on kids, go put some nice clothes on, can't eat Christmas dinner in sweatpants." He grinned at us like the devil.

My mother's face was dead. She leaned back against the refrigerator and closed her eyes. We were all exhausted. As we climbed the stairs to our rooms to change, Peter began to cry. I slapped him, hard. We'd never hit each other before, not even as little kids. But he didn't look at me. He bumped me away with his shoulder and turned into his room with his face toward the wall.

None of us had eaten anything. My stomach rumbled, but I didn't feel hungry. My mother offered Peter and me things in a soft voice, would we like some yams, there were peas in the freezer, did we want those, she could just microwave them. Her voice was concerned, as always, that we eat, but her eyes didn't care at all. The turkey was roasted to a suspiciously hard and shiny pink. My mother put a slice on my plate, and I avoided the stuffing that touched it.

Peter's head bent low over his plate, his fingers went limp, and his knife fell clattering to the floor. He jerked awake, startled from the noise, his face blank and open, like a baby's right before it cries, and then he saw everything, my father, my mother, me, the food on the table, and his eyes went small, and he pulled both his hands into his lap.

As soon as we could Peter and I asked to be excused, and we started upstairs to our beds. I left the dishes to my mother, I didn't care. I hoped it took her forever to clean up. We trudged up the stairs, one two three four five, as my father watched, Peter one step behind me, our backs feeling vulnerable, and just as we reached the top, he called us—"Kids, wait." It was like heartbreak.

I didn't turn around.

"Kids."

"What," I said, my eyes closed.

"Come back down, let's take a picture of Christmas." His jovial voice was forced. He was tired too, but it was like he couldn't stop.

"Where are some of those boxes your sisters' presents came in?" he asked my mother.

"In the basement." Her voice was so distant, she just wasn't there with us anymore. She came back up carrying a large, square box in her arms. Inside were many small ones. She knew what to do without being asked. She got out wrapping paper and scissors and Scotch tape, and sat down and began to wrap one of the little boxes. She did it meticulously, matching corners and ends, taping neatly, as if it were a wonderful gift she were giving to someone she loved. Peter and I began to help her. My fingers fumbled. Cutting the paper to the right size seemed like some kind of difficult puzzle.

We covered the boxes, while my father watched. It didn't occur to us to only do some. One by one, we covered them all. By the time we finished, the sky was beginning to grey. Peter moved like he was sleepwalking. Even my father didn't talk anymore. We did everything automatically. We put the tree on the floor, settled all the covered boxes around the tree, and sat around it. My father set the timer on his camera, put it up on the coffee table, and we took pictures. He counted the time out aloud, "Four three two kim-chee!" We did it again and again, until the film was out. We kept taking pictures, changing positions, ripping paper off boxes like we were opening gifts, all the time smiling, smiling.

At last the film ran out. We were done. We went upstairs to bed. It was six in the morning on Saturday. I brushed my teeth and put on a fresh t-shirt and sweatpants. I waited till I heard Peter and my mother and father settle into their beds.

In the wan morning light, the tree looked cheap and pathetic. It drooped to one side, the little plastic-covered wires bent at weird angles. I pulled out the plug, tugging on the wire, like my mother always told me not to do. I shook Peter's blanket off the base. I picked up the tree by its trunk, and dumped the whole thing, lights and bows, into the one big box, and threw all the little boxes and the litter of shiny paper in after it. I carried the box out into the frozen morning, my bare feet stinging on the crunchy, frost-bitten grass, and dropped it beside the stacks of magazines for the garbage men to take away.

FOR MY LOLA

Juno Salazar Parreñas

Mahal kita

*t*he clock by the virgin mary says it is 9:06 P.M.
   Lola lies in bed
        while I sit on the floor

I hold her soft wrinkled
            orange hand
       it is the same color of the mangoes
            i ate as a baby in the philippines
the scent of Agua de Previa
        on her wrist

tomorrow she will leave
        for our homeland

tita baby and tito boy
can't afford her expenses
mama and papa
can't look after her

her bedroom is the
        closest to the garage
the night chills easily flow through the room
the sun's intense heat penetrates through the walls

I can feel her pulse
    soft
        but even and flowing

i let go of her hand
i feel my fingers
        and touch the smoothness
            of gold
        and the sharp cut
            of rubies

Lolo gave her this ring
    before he left
this ring has been in my family
    for 500 years

    she took it off
        her wrinkled finger
     and put it in my hard
         young hands
      before she fell asleep.

REMEMBERING MA-MÁ

Jessica Oliver

This essay won first prize (ages six to eleven) in the San Francisco Bay Area
"Growing Up Asian in America" contest in 1996.

*A*hhh . . . The sweet aroma of incense . . .

It beckons my memory to when I was little, watching my great-grandmother burning incense and praying to Quan Yin (the Chinese Goddess of Mercy), Sahm Bo Fut (the Three Gods), and for the loss of her husband, Chung. She would put a little tiny spoon of cooked rice in three tiny bowls, and she would put tea in three other tiny cups. Also, she would put fruits and steamed chicken on the altar to pay her respects to the gods and goddesses of the kitchen. Gracefully, she would lean down and chant these words over and over again, holding her prayer beads: "Na Mo Au Lae Tau Fut." These words tingled in my ears so peacefully, and they sounded like a soothing lullaby.

I was determined to understand what she was doing. So I asked her what those peaceful words meant: the enlightenment and energy within. Also, she said that she was praying for me to have health, happiness, and a good education.

What I love about Ma-Má (the Chinese name for great-grandmother in a respectful way) was that not only was she my great-grandmother, but she had a good sense of humor. Sometimes Ma-Má would make funny faces that would just make me hysterical. Whenever Ma-Má was mad at someone, she would make a face at them when they weren't looking. She would scrunch her nose closer to her eyes like a wrinkled raisin and tighten her mouth like she just ate a super lemon (sour candy). Then she would stick out her two fingers and point at him/her. When the person turned to look at Ma-Má, she would smile like an innocent angel.

What makes Ma-Má so special to me is that she would always explain about how she came from China, about my ancestors, and my Chinese heritage. Ma-Má told me lots of stories. She also told me about her life in China. This is what she told me:

Ma-Má was born in 1907 in Canton. She had nine brothers and sisters. Her family was very poor and always had to share whatever they had with each other. When Ma-Má was twenty-one, her father arranged a marriage, and she was very mad. She wanted to stay and help her mother to work and support her family, but she couldn't disobey her father, so she married Yèa-Yèa (great-grandfather), and they fell deeply in love. After that, she had three sons, but two died from lack of food.

Shortly after, Yèa-Yèa had to go to San Francisco for a business trip because he was an opera star. But they never realized that they would be separated for thirty-two years! Every day Ma-Má grieved. They couldn't contact each other. Also, it was during wartime, so there was hardly any food for Ma-Má and her son. She was always really thoughtful about her son (my grandfather, Gong-Gong). Sometimes she wouldn't eat anything and give it all to Gong-Gong and to her nieces. One of Ma-Má's brothers died, and he had a little girl whom nobody wanted because they thought she was too much trouble. Ma-Má didn't want to see her little niece, Sau Ying, die so she adopted her. Ma-Má had to knit sweaters and make matchboxes to buy food. Her neighbors were eating dead human babies and rats to survive. But Ma-Má didn't have the heart to eat babies and rats, so she cut down trees and boiled the insides of tree trunks for food.

After twenty-two years, Ma-Má, Gong-Gong, and Sau Ying finally found a way of escaping from China to go to Hong Kong. Yèa-Yèa would always send money to Ma-Má, but her brothers would always steal her money. She would never know because she didn't know how to read or write.

Many years passed. One day, Yèa-Yèa finally contacted Ma-Má's brother (in Hong Kong) and he found out that Ma-Má, Gong-Gong, and Sau Ying were staying there. Yèa-Yèa tried for ten years to bring her to the United States. Finally, in the summer of 1966 they were once again reunited!

Without her great love and encouragement, many lives, such as those of my aunts and uncles, would have been lost. She kept on telling them to stay strong through the war and communism. I remember she would encourage me to bear through my problems, especially when my parents were divorced and my dad wouldn't come to see me. When my cousins made fun of me because I wasn't full-blooded Chinese, and I didn't look Chinese, Ma-Má would sing to me and tell me that it was okay to be a multicultural person. She would cry with me and tell me to keep my head high and be proud of who I am. She also told me not to follow her and be an illiterate. An education could take me anywhere I wanted, and that I couldn't be cheated by others with my money.

Ma-Má's dream was to be reunited with her husband, Yèa-Yèa. Their love stayed alive even though they were separated from each other for thirty-two years. Yèa-Yèa could have easily forgotten about Ma-Má and married someone else in America, but their love kept them strong. They never forgot the hope of one day seeing each other again. She also dreamed of living in a place with no war, communism, or starvation. She hoped one day to see her son married, and she wanted to live long enough to see her grandchildren born. I will fulfill the rest of Ma-Má's dreams as much as I possibly can. She dreamed for me to be the best person I could be and to respect my mother with dignity.

My dream is to become a singing star and follow in Yèa-Yèa's footsteps. I also hope I can become as patient as Ma-Má and never give up on my dreams, exactly the way she never gave up for thirty-two years!

People in China expected Ma-Má to marry a rich person who had a good education and was a doctor, instead of an opera singer. They doubted that she would survive the war. They expected she would remarry.

People expect me to be an all-American person, to know nothing about the Chinese culture, and speak only English. I'll never be just an all-American. I want to learn all there is to know about Chinese culture.

It is beneficial for me to be an Asian American growing up in America. Not only do I know the American culture, but I know my Chinese cultural background, and I know how to speak fluent Chinese. I'm proud to learn how to chant these soothing lullabies like Ma-Má did. She really reminds me of Quan Yin; she knew the meaning of mercy, too. Another benefit to being Asian in America is that I can read and write, get a good education, and I have a lot more opportunities than Ma-Má had.

. . . Now the sweet aroma of incense is fading away, and Ma-Má has gone with it. But I'll always remember her and treasure her in my heart . . . Quan Yin smiles on me with Ma-Má's face.

INHERITING MY MOTHER'S GARDEN

Ka Vang

*O*n the south side of Providence, where crime is high and run-down houses are prevalent, a garden is growing—a once emptied lot turned into a bountiful garden. The lot had been cleared and parceled off into plots which can be rented for a fee. This lot is fenced with Wednesday's trash treasures. The sidewalk of the lot is littered with papers, plastic, tires, and broken glass. Inside the fence, vegetation is sprouting profusely. Birds flock about and feed in the garden. Each plot is carefully tended and the greens are coaxed to fruition.

The plots are rented by women who, like my mother, are struggling to survive in this country. With each seed that these women sow, they hope to put down their roots. They have journeyed over land and sea to seek a new life for their family. They arrive in this country traumatized by the ravages of war. They have nothing tangible to claim as their own. The land they tend is not theirs to pass on to their children. The seeds of their native country cannot be passed on. Our mothers, these women, can only pass on their gift of gardening.

My earliest recollection of my mother's garden is the daily trips we made before and after school. A bucket filled with seeds and plant food in one hand, my mother would hold my hand with the other. On her back, she would carry my little brother. My elder siblings and I would each carry a gardening tool or an empty milk carton in one hand and a notebook in the other. Quickly filling our buckets and milk cartons with water from the nearby lake, we watered the garden. Afterwards, we would pluck out all the weeds and all other things that we felt would threaten the health of our vegetation. Once we knew the garden was well taken care of for the day, we would rinse our hands and be on our way.

As a child I did not understand the significance of my mother's garden. I saw it as a place of hardship: carrying heavy buckets of water from the lake to water the garden and plowing the hard earth under the burning sun and in the burning whips of cold winds. My mother was very strict regarding how well we, the children, should till the land. We had to make sure that we left no traces of any weeds laying about and that the new earth was turned over until it completely covered the old, enabling the sun to touch the earth which it never reached.

In my mother's garden, nothing lacks attention. Each stalk is carefully tended. Each lovingly nurtured. The stalks of the cabbages are always green, thick, and healthy. Their branches sprout out fully, not thinly and sickly. She always made sure that all the weeds are plucked, that her babies are well nourished, and that the hard earth is softened. The soil of her garden, like her babies, glows with life and acknowledges her love. It was there that I saw the powerful life-giving touch of my mother's hands.

I understand, now, that my mother's garden is more than a plot of land with growing vegetation. Her garden is about the power of love, faith, endurance, and vision. There, in her garden, I am showered with love and the history of our people—Hmong. Her view on gardening is rooted in our people's history. From our journeys from land to land, fighting for survival, Hmong had to envision the future existence of our roots. In order to make that vision a reality, our foremothers had to nourish and care for their garden the same way my mother has tended hers. They fought for the right to sow their garden—their roots and seeds. Their dreams and hopes for the future were all placed and mapped in their gardens. Without our mothers and foremothers, the history and existence of my people would have been lost in the shuffle of life's tragedies. They are the life-givers. Their garden is a symbol of their independence, vision, beauty, strength, perseverance, and courage. It is there in this garden that I am rooted and encouraged to spread—to multiply by leaps and bounds like dandelions.

My mother propagated from my foremothers' gardens. She is one of their seedlings. Like my foremothers, my mother had to flee from one country to another to keep her roots alive. Arriving in America from Laos, my mother had to re-root her seedlings. However, unlike my foremothers, who had no political power, in a country where more opportunity and rights have been given to women, my mother has gained her right to voice her opinions within the family and community.

For years now, the city has talked about discontinuing the garden site. My mother and the other gardeners formed a protest group. In the short time that they have been here, my mother and the other gardeners are not willing to let others force them to leave this new home. So far they have been successful in detaining the city from implementing their plan. For now, my mother and the other women will continue their cultivation of the garden until the next year when the city talks again.

This garden site is not only a means my mother and the other gardeners can use to grow vegetation, but it is also a place where they can bond and form a sense of communal identity and belonging. All the gardeners watch out for each other's garden. They share their different farming skills and seeds. Gardening is life-sustaining because it preserves the roots and seedlings of the past, yet it symbolizes growth and expansion of one's ability to adapt to new surroundings and create new relationships.

My mother's every action speaks of importance and purpose. From this, I have learned about the importance of standing up for my beliefs and founding a life on communal growth and love, which is crucial to the health of family, culture, and society. Unlike my mother and foremothers, I have not had to face the hardship of war. Instead, my struggle lies in the realm of academics. Growing up in the United States, I am fortunate to have an education. My mother and foremothers had no such right or opportunity. Therefore, academic achievement reflects not only my own accomplishments but the success of my mother and foremothers. Without the inspiration, love, and support given to me from them, I would not be so fortunate to have this life.

My garden, therefore, may not revolve around the actual physical labor that my mother and foremothers had, but the struggle of the mind and that of the pen and paper. My garden is my vision for the future of my roots, my seedlings, and our place in this new country. It is this insight that has deepened my relationship with my mother. We understand that we both have the same passion lingering in our hearts and minds. We share the same vision— to give voice to all the women of our past and to sustain the life of our future, present, and past.

SO TSI-FAI

Sophronia Liu

$\mathcal{V}$oices, images, scenes from the past—twenty-three years ago, when I was in sixth grade.

"Let us bow our heads in silent prayer for the soul of So Tsi-fai. Let us pray for God's forgiveness for this boy's rash taking of his own life. . . ." Sister Marie (Mung Gu-liang). My sixth-grade English teacher. Missionary nun from Paris. Principal of the Little Flower's School. Disciplinarian, perfectionist, authority figure: awesome and awful in my ten-year-old eyes.

"I don't need any supper. I have drunk enough insecticide." So Tsi-fai. My fourteen-year-old classmate. Daredevil; good-for-nothing lazy-bones (according to Mung Gu-liang). Bright black eyes, disheveled hair, defiant sneer, creased and greasy uniform, dirty hands, careless walk, shuffling feet. Standing in the corner for being late, for forgetting his homework, for talking in class, for using foul language. ("Shame on you! Go wash your mouth with soap!" Mung Gu-liang's sharp command. He did, and came back with a grin.) So Tsi-fai: Sticking his tongue out behind Mung Gu-liang's back, passing secret notes to his friends, kept behind after school, sent to the principal's office for repeated offenses. So Tsi-fai: incorrigible, hopeless, and without hope.

It was a Monday in late November when we heard of his death, returning to school after the weekend with our parents' signatures on our midterm reports. So Tsi-fai also showed his report to his father, we were told later. He flunked three out of the fourteen subjects: English Grammar, Arithmetic, and Chinese Dictation. He missed each one by one to three marks. That wasn't so bad. But he was a hopeless case. Overaged, stubborn, and uncooperative; a repeated offender of school rules, scourge of all teachers; who was going to give him a lenient passing grade? Besides, being a few months over the maximum age—fourteen—for sixth graders, he wasn't even allowed to sit for the Secondary School Entrance Exam.

All sixth-graders in Hong Kong had to pass the SSE before they could obtain a seat in secondary school. In 1964, when I took the exam, there were more than twenty thousand candidates. About seven thousand of us passed: four thousand were sent to government and subsidized schools, the other three thousand to private and grant-in-aid schools. I came in around number two thousand; I was lucky. Without the public exam, there would be no secondary school for So Tsi-fai. His future was sealed.

Looking at the report card with three red marks on it, his father was furious. So Tsi-fai was the oldest son. There were three younger children. His father was a vegetable farmer with a few plots of land in Wong Juk-hang, by the sea. His mother worked in a local factory. So Tsi-fai helped in the fields, cooked for the family, and washed his own clothes. ("Filthy, dirty boy!" gasped Mung Gu-liang. "Grime behind the ears, black rims on the fingernails, dirty collar, crumpled shirt. Why doesn't your mother iron your shirt?") Both his parents were illiterate. So Tsi-fai was their biggest hope: He made it to the sixth grade.

Who woke him up for school every morning and had breakfast waiting for him? Nobody. ("Time for school! Get up! Eat your rice!" Ma nagged and screamed. The aroma of steamed rice and Chinese sausages spread all over the house. "Drink your tea! Eat your oranges! Wash your face! And remember to wash behind your ears!") And who helped So Tsi-fai do his homework? Nobody. Did he have older brothers like mine who knew all about the arithmetic of rowing a boat against the currents or with the currents, how to count the feet of chickens and rabbits in the same cage, the present perfect continuous tense of "to live" and the future perfect tense of "to succeed"? None. Nil. So Tsi-fai was a lost cause.

I came first in both terms that year, the star pupil. So Tsi-fai was one of the last in the class: He was lazy; he didn't care. Or did he?

~~~~

When his father scolded him, So Tsi-fai left the house. When he showed up again, late for supper, he announced, "I don't need any supper. I have drunk enough insecticide." Just like another of his practical jokes. The insecticide was stored in the field for his father's vegetables. He was rushed to the hospital, dead upon arrival.

"He gulped for a last breath and was gone," an uncle told us at the funeral. "But his eyes wouldn't shut. So I said in his ear, 'You go now and rest in peace.' And I smoothed my hand over his eyelids. His face was all purple."

His face was still purple when we saw him in his coffin. Eyes shut tight, nostrils dilated and white as if fire and anger might shoot out, any minute.

In class that Monday morning, Sister Marie led us in prayer. "Let us pray that God will forgive him for his sins." We said the Lord's Prayer and the Hail Mary. We bowed our heads. I sat in my chair, frozen and dazed, thinking of the deadly chill in the morgue, the smell of disinfectant, ether, and dead flesh.

"Bang!" went a gust of wind, forcing open a leaf of the double door leading to the back balcony. "Flap, flap, flap." The door swung in the wind. We could see the treetops by the hillside rustling to and fro against a pale blue sky. An imperceptible presence had drifted in with the wind. The same careless walk and shuffling feet, the same daredevil air—except that the eyes were lusterless, dripping blood; the tongue hanging out, gasping for air. As usual, he was late. But he had come back to claim his place.

"I died a tragic death," his voice said. "I have as much right as you to be here. This is my seat." We heard him; we knew he was back.

. . . So Tsi-fai: Standing in the corner for being late, for forgetting his homework, for talking in class, for using foul language. So Tsi-fai: Palm outstretched, chest sticking out, holding his breath: "Tat. Tat. Tat." Down came the teacher's wooden ruler, twenty times on each hand. Never batting an eyelash: then back to facing the wall in the corner by the door. So Tsi-fai: grimy shirt, disheveled hair, defiant sneer. So Tsi-fai. Incorrigible, hopeless, and without hope.

The girls in front gasped and shrank back in their chairs. Mung Guliang went to the door, held the doorknob in one hand, poked her head out, and peered into the empty balcony. Then, with a determined jerk, she pulled the door shut. Quickly crossing herself, she returned to the teacher's desk. Her black cross swung upon the front of her gray habit as she hurried across the room. "Don't be silly!" she scolded the frightened girls in the front row.

~~~

What really happened? After all these years, my mind is still haunted by this scene. What happened to So Tsi-fai? What happened to me? What happened to all of us that year in sixth grade, when we were green and young and ready to fling our arms out for the world? All of a sudden, death claimed one of us and he was gone.

Who arbitrates between life and death? Who decides which life is worth preserving and prospering, and which to nip in its bud? How did it happen that I, at ten, turned out to be the star pupil, the lucky one, while my friend, a peasant's son, was shoveled under the heap and lost forever? How could it happen that this world would close off a young boy's life at fourteen just because he was poor, undisciplined, and lacked the training and support to pass his exams? What really happened?

Today, many years later, So Tsi-fai's ghost still haunts me. "I died a tragic death. I have as much right as you to be here. This is my seat." The voice I heard twenty-three years ago in my sixth-grade classroom follows me in my dreams. Is there anything I can do to lay it to rest?

MY FAMILY / MY GANG

Lilia V. Villanueva

Asian youth gangs have grown in proportion to the increase of new Asian communities immigrating to the United States. A survey taken in Alameda County, California, in the early 1990s revealed 125 active youth gangs, of which twenty are girl gangs and a third are exclusively Asian/Pacific Islander (API) membership. According to Alameda County police records, API gangs have been responsible for crimes from residential robberies to extortion and gambling, and drug and violent crimes. Between 1987 and 1990, Asian youths who were processed through the Alameda County juvenile system increased by 400 percent, according to county records. Nearly all were Vietnamese, Chinese-Vietnamese, Laotian, Mien, and Cambodian.

Unlike most Southeast Asian gangs, Filipino gangs have been around since the 1960s, most prominently in San Francisco and Los Angeles (Mark Pulido, UCLA, 1991). Several new gangs have emerged in the last decade, mostly in northern California's Alameda County.

While information and profiles of Asian male gangs are available through regional crime task force or police records, this is not true for their female counterparts. Most information about Asian girl gangs is gathered through observations by community youth service providers, local police and probation officers, limited media coverage, and a growing youth informant network.

Asian girl gangs are mostly an outgrowth of Asian male gangs. While gangs are a fairly new phenomenon among Filipino girls, two predominantly Filipino girl gangs actively exist in Alameda County alone. According to Pulido, "most are part of larger Filipino male gangs" and the girls are "rebellious and from very strict families." A study by Filipino for Affirmative Action youth service found that the reasons members cited most often for joining female gangs are (1) that they provide structure and support, and (2) that they satisfy needs for identity and independence (1993).

The story you are about to read is based on information gathered by the author from research and interviews. All the characters in this story are fictitious, and any resemblance to real characters is purely coincidental.

*I*t began with my name. *Onofria*. Who gives a child that name in 1980? Well, *they* did. My Ma, she says, "What you ashamed of, ha? Your gramma's name not good enough for you, ha?" I don't say nothing when she gets in that mood. We just end up fighting. We've been fighting for five years, since I was eleven. It's a little better with Papa. But not much. They just don't understand. They *look* young but they don't understand what it's *like* to be young—in America.

They bring us all the way here to America *So you kids can have a future like we never had*. That's what they told us every day we're growing up—I mean *every day*. My sister and I, we're the ones who hear the chant. My brothers pick up and leave when they start up. But we can't, because we're girls, you see, until I joined my other family. Then I left the house with my brothers when the folks started up with their *You're so ungrateful after all we've done for you* shit. *We should have left you in the Philippines and you'd grow up right*. Yeah, right. They're not home all day so no way they knew how we're growing up.

HOW IT STARTED

Like I said, it started with my name. I move to this new school when I'm in the sixth grade. My parents, they worked so hard, both of them, that finally they could afford a house in the suburbs and they're so proud of this. More Pinoys in this 'burb, including auntie this and uncle that. Yeah, more Pinoy kids, too, and gangs.

One day, this black girl in my class came up to me at recess and started yelling, "Give me that, give me that comb. Give it to me right now." I stood there frozen. I was scared 'cause she was so big. And she was yelling. I've never heard anyone yell that loud to me before. Even when Mama gets angry she didn't yell as loud as that girl. Spit was coming out of her mouth. I was scared shit but I had nowhere to go so I stood there and got rained on by her spit. Then she says "O-no-rea, O-no-rea. Rhyme with go-no-rrhea, go-no-rrhea." I didn't know what it meant but I knew she was making fun of my name, and she was making fun of Lola, my grandmother. So I stuck my hand in her open mouth and pulled her tongue out. That was my first fight. And that's how my sisters met me. My gang sisters.

When the girls jumped on me to rescue their friend's tongue from my gripping fingers, I didn't feel anything—the blows, the ripping of my clothes. All I heard was a crowd crying out *Go-no-rrhea, shit, go-no-rrhea, let 'er go, let 'er go, shit*. Next thing I know there were other Pinays on the ground, yelling and kicking at the black girls. Somebody squeezed my wrist so hard, that's when I let go of the girl's tongue. They dragged me out of the yard and into the alley before the teacher came.

THE SISTERS

All of them Pinay, like me. The tallest one, Nina, says, *Not bad, girl, for someone so skinny*. They were laughing at how I had the girl's tongue pulled out so hard her hands were flailing at her sides like a chicken. *You still have an ugly name*, Nina says and I lunge for her collar. Pura—she's the one who rescued the girl's tongue—caught my hand and told everyone to shut up.

Pura's quick with her hands. *Who give you that name, anyway? It's a funny name*, someone else says. I screamed back at all of them: *It's my Lola's name and I didn't ask for it!* I didn't say I hated the name, too, even though I love Lola a lot. That day they started calling me Beauty.

~~~~

Chrysta is the prettiest and the baddest. She's got a boyfriend since she was thirteen and she's always cheating on him. She says he cheats on her too, so it's o.k. She's always beating up on the girl she thinks her man's cheating her on. And the others have warned her to stop because she's not always right about the girls.

Jewellyn has gone in and out of the group for four years. She's never out more than two months so no one cares. The only time it mattered was when she started hitching up with a boy from a gang in the next suburb. We warned her she was gonna have her ass kicked if she didn't quit seeing him. It was enough trouble keeping our noses clean with the Brotherhood.

Pinky is one of the originals. She was the girlfriend of a Brotherhood and it was her idea to call the group Truly Yours, meaning, truly yours for the Brotherhood. Pinky's people are from Batangas and she's not scared of anyone. She showed us how to work the switchblades and butterfly knives that her brothers collect.

Blue's our color. Every year the shade gets lighter. Don't know why but we like it that way. You know, playing with the different shades of blue.

INITIATION

At first there was no initiation. Getting a boyfriend who's with the Brotherhood was kind of it, really. But as the Brotherhood got bigger in numbers, all of a sudden a lot of girls, Pinays and Latinas, started to hang out with us. We felt protective. So Pinky and Pura suggest we gotta test who's a real TY, you know.

We do real mild initiations, not like the other gangs. Just enough to prove that you're one of us, that's all we're looking for. You gotta be willing to fence for the guys, like carry and hide weapons, drugs or stolen goods. Me, they asked me to dog this girl in the mall. They knew she belonged to a gang but I didn't know. I went up to her and stared in her face. We got into a screaming match, then we were punching away. I drew blood from her chest before we were chased out of the mall by a couple of security guards. Yeah, it felt good to draw blood. I admit that. That same girl spotted me a few months later at the Filipino fiesta weekend celebration in the city and she had her entire gang come down on me. I was browsing in this bookstall and before I know it all hell broke loose. Luckily the TY girls were nearby and I wasn't hurt too bad. The security kicked us all out and chased us out of the parking lot. It was kinda messy.

Pinky did her own initiation. She gave herself to several guys in the Brotherhood. I wouldn't do that but several guys thought it was a good idea. No way. I told them I'm out of there if they tried to rape me. I wouldn't let them and they wouldn't dare either. They know I'm good with a knife. I can't come down on Pinky for doing it though. She's such a needy bitch she's always looking for sex. She says she's watching out for disease and stuff like that but I don't believe her.

OUR LIFE—THEN

I just turned twelve when I joined TY. That day I yanked the girl's tongue out was a happy one for me. I felt powerful and the sisters made me feel even more powerful. Going to the mall with them after school was fun. We'd chill at the bus stop right outside of Macy's and drink Coke. We'd hang out there until the Brotherhood showed up. First it was only Pinky's boyfriend. Then he started to bring a friend who hooked up with Chrysta. He was so good-looking we were all jealous of Chrysta. Before long, the Brotherhood gang was protecting us. They were also taking us all over the place—the mall, movies, fast food places.

I didn't want to have sex in the beginning. I was too scared my Mom would find out and I'd get kicked out of the house. My brothers threatened me, too. They saw me with Brotherhood guys so they didn't want to mess with me. But I knew they'd do something if they found out I was having sex. I held off for almost two years.

It wasn't a good experience, I don't think. I liked him a lot but I don't think he felt the same way about me. We were at his friend's house and he jumped me when we were alone. I let him because I liked him, you know. But he wasn't very gentle and when I told him that he got on my case—yeah, like I'm not supposed to notice. *Putang ina*. I didn't let on how much I cared for him, though. When I found out he was making it with other girls I pretended not to care. But it hurt. Sure, I wanted to talk to somebody about it. But not anyone in my family. They'd kill me. I was still going to church with Mom and Dad every Sunday. Most of us did, except for Jewellyn, whose folks were Protestants or something.

School was a place to meet, that's all. My heart was not into studying or anything like that. The teachers were o.k. but they couldn't control the kids and they didn't know how anyway. The gang was everything to me. It was a reason to live. At home everyone was either fighting or lecturing or yelling. My mom was getting down on me for everything. She didn't want me to wear dangling earrings because I looked like a prostitute and not like a good decent girl. I wasn't setting a good example for my kid sis, she said. My kid sister was throwing up every meal and no one wanted to talk about it. She was too nervous to join TY so she turned bulimic instead. She said she was used to Mom yelling at everybody—my brothers, even my aunt, her younger sister who lived with us. She yelled at Dad, too, but she'd stop when he raised his fist at her. Then she'd cry in the bathroom for hours. She'd pray in there too, loudly. Nobody could figure out what was wrong with her—like she was going crazy or something. So I started staying out of the house and spending more time with TY.

The only time I had a run-in with cops was the time I agreed to drive with the Brotherhood when they did this job on a small mom-and-pop store in the east part of town. They said they wouldn't use a piece, but Pinky's boyfriend pulls a big one out of his pocket when they got out of the car. I was scared shit when I saw that piece. When they ran back to the car he gives the piece to me and says, *Hide it. I'll take it later.* It was very warm. I didn't ask questions. Later when we were parked at the drive-in, this cop car pulls up next to us and two big cops get out. They start asking questions and the guys tell us girls not to talk. The cops quickly throw three of them against the car and tell them to spread their legs as they searched them roughly. I was pissing in my pants I was so scared. But then I saw how brave the guys were—no one showed any fright. So I stopped being scared. When Pura put up a stink with the cops they slapped her around and told her to stay out of it. Then this cop comes around the car and starts asking me questions. I said I knew nothing, just acted dumb and then he went back to rough up the guys again. I kept seeing the piece in my mind and hoped it wouldn't start beeping or something like that.

OUR LIFE—NOW

Jewellyn got pregnant last year and she dropped out of sight. Her family sent her back to the islands, to another city other than where her folks are from, until she had her baby. Last week she showed up in the mall with her mother and she was pushing a stroller. She looked uncomfortable with us and her mom wasn't excited about seeing us either. Jewellyn looked fat and she said she'd talk to us real soon. She wouldn't let us call her at home though and we said o.k. It's usual. When a girl gets pregnant, she quits the gang and goes home to mama. I know the father of her kid. He's cute and speaks with a thick accent like everyone in his family. He got in trouble with a gang member and the Brotherhood rescued him. So he joined. He's cute but real short.

Nina graduated from high school but Pura didn't—she quit after tenth grade. Nina's talking a lot about working someplace that serves Pinoy youths. She must be seeing that counselor in the youth clinic. He's kinda cute but too goody-two-shoes for me. I saw him once to talk about college. He was interested; I wasn't. But I went because we got an extra free period if we signed up to have a session with him. Nina saw him many times after his first visit at school.

I suggest that TY should be free from the Brotherhood. Pura's not interested. But Chrysta and the new member, Isa, are. I'm getting tired of being treated like their personal slave. We go to movies they wanna see; to malls they wanna hang out; and dress baggy like they do. I remember the guys came down real heavy on Isa for wearing a tight skirt. Pura's still not listening. Lori and Devonne, who joined two years ago, they're listening. They're sisters, both *mestiza itim*, whose father was a black G.I. Lori and Devonne call him Army, short for Armstrong, just the way their mothers call him. Not Dad or anything like that. Lori and Devonne are both the same age, almost like twins. They had different moms, one from each bar on the main street off Clark Air Force Base. Army stayed on in the islands after the Vietnam War. When the girls were little, their grandma in Oakland took them both back with her after she buried her son in a remote barrio in Pangasinan. Yeah, Army died there and the girls' moms wanted the grandma to take them with her to America. When the grandma died a couple of years later, Lori and Devonne were taken in by some Filipino aunt and uncle. Now Devonne is seeing this guy from another gang and she wants the Brotherhood off her back. It's not a rival gang but like they own us so we're not supposed to be with anyone except them. *Fuck that*, I say. I've had two boyfriends with them and they were nothing to brag about. And I say we've saved their ass as many times as they've saved ours in fights. Everyone agrees except Pura.

OUR LIFE—AHEAD

Everything's changing fast. Papa says he won't support me after high school unless I go to college. Shit, I don't wanna go to college. Last summer I tried working at McDonald's and that sucked. So I don't know. Maybe I'll think about college next year when I'm a senior. All I know now is I don't want to be a mama yet. I've been taking precautions but I feel guilty. Like I don't care about children or something but I do. I keep thinking, *What if I can't get pregnant in the future when I'm married and settled down?* You know, like a punishment from God for taking birth control pills now. I don't know. Sometimes it doesn't make sense and sometimes it makes a lot of sense. Nobody in the family knows this. Oh God, Mama would die if she knew I was on the pill. I pray for God's forgiveness all the time. I know He understands why I don't want to be a mama yet. I hope so.

TY still means a lot to me. I love my sisters a lot. More than my own sister, you know. I know they can protect me and they do. We all protect each other. And we don't stab each other in the back. At least not anymore since Jewellyn left. There are more girl gangs in the neighborhood nowadays but we're one of the oldest so we get a lot of respect. And that's real important. I wonder if Jewellyn will tell her kid about us someday.

Who knows what's going to happen in a year or two? I've been with TY six years and I have lots of photos to prove the good times. And the bad times? No one remembers to take pictures during those times. So we don't remember them.

PART 2

IMPLOSION

*where
dreams
are
necessary*

MANGO

Passion Cummings

*O*n Kaua'i where I was born
mango season starts in May
and ends in August. Mangoes
grow on full lush trees, in mountains
and ravines, on the side of the road
and in backyards. The locals picked
and filled plastic and paper bags, boxes
and buckets and gave mangoes away.

Green ones, Aunty Sally sliced and pickled
in sweet red vinegar until they turned pink
and soft. She gave a couple
jars to Mr. Watanabe, who for a nickel sold
fresh blocks of ivory tofu stored in large
wooden barrels from his green 1950 Chevy
pickup. Mom poured shoyu on large pieces
she served to my brother and me for lunch.
I remember the awful taste of soft mushy
curd that she said was full of good things
that made me big and strong, so I could play
and climb the mango tree in our backyard,
where I picked half-ripe fruit and dipped
them in salt and pepper on rolled waxed
paper. I sat cradled in the V of the huge
sprawling tree, eating and daydreaming
about a future I couldn't see until my
stomach ached.

The overripe mangoes Dad gave to Isamu,
for his pigs. I remember how Dad and Isamu
sat in the backyard and talked-story for hours
over a six-pack of Primo. A cool afternoon
breeze wafted their laughter up through
the branches and leaves, where I sat hidden
from the men below. I listened to their
fish stories, their gripe about work at the
sugar mill, and the dreams of returning to
their homeland. . . . They never did.

Now where I live there are no mango trees.
Mangoes appear as exotic produce at the
grocery store and I can't afford more than
one or two. The ripe mangoes are a messy
treat: and when I sink my teeth in golden
juicy flesh, sweet and sticky liquid smears
over my mouth and lips, and slides down my
arms, sticking to my fingers and hands like
memorabilia and I savor the fragrance that
takes me back to Kaua'i, where everyone gives
mangoes away.

HOMECOMING

Ching-Fei Chang

*t*he sizzle of vegetables as they hit the red-hot wok caught my attention. I looked up from where I had been sitting reading the newspaper and watched the steam balloon up into the face of my mother. Even now, after three years of college and months of telephone silence, I am amazed at her complete and utter calm. Despite the fact that I had stormed out of the house without even a backward glance, chosen to move to another state and erase their phone number from my mind, she still maintained the same stoic expression, the same air of professional distance, as the day she abandoned me in Taiwan, twenty years ago, to follow the dreams of my father. It seemed as if my cries of "ah-ma" instead of "ma-ma" meant nothing to her—as if the fading of her memory in my eighteen-month-old mind was just another inevitability to accept and endure. Only now am I beginning to realize how much it must have slashed her heart to lose mine.

"It's three-thirty," Mother mused aloud. "Your brother and sister will be home soon." She smiled fondly at the thought as she shielded herself with the wok lid and stir-fried vigorously. "David, Jennifer—they very excited to see you. Ever since I call you in Berkeley, they count down the days like Christmas. 'Mama,' they nag me, over and over again, 'when will jie-jie come home?'"

Something in the simplicity of their question touched me. If Father had not had a heart attack, I silently wondered, would jie-jie have come home at all?

"How are they doing?" I asked softly.

"Aiieeya!" she exclaimed, "They not like you, Su-Lin. They not have your will to study. David, his teacher says his handwriting is so sloppy! I tell him, you learn to write better, I give you star. When you have ten stars, we go to Dairy Queen. Now he show me all his homework—show me how good he writes! I smart—learn to play your father's game. Use point system. Better than spanking."

Spanking.

Memories flooded back . . . memories of my childhood when Mother beat me with a stick. Told me to extend my hands, palm upward, to receive the blows bravely. Unflinchingly. Told me it hurt her more than it hurt me . . . that it made her cry to have to hit her own baby. *But is necessary*, she always insisted. *You like young tree—grow crooked if I don't tie you to straight stick.* Back then, Mother was like a god in my eyes; back then, I was willing to believe anything she said—anything at all—to the point where I would go to school and spread the gospel. *When your mama spanks you*, I'd confide to all my five-year-old friends, *that means she loves you.*

"Your father want to clear more space for the garden," Mother chattered above the noise of her cooking. "I tell him, aieeya—Daddy! You already dig up half the backyard for your vegetables and now it look like mess!" She flipped open the funnel of Morton's Iodized Salt and poured an experienced tablespoonful into the cup of her hand.

"You know your father, Su-Lin. He never change. He never organize his planting, never label anything—he just throw his seeds up into the air and let them fall wherever. Now, they all grow up scattered and mixed-up among weeds; now I always have to wonder if what I pick up is Chinese lettuce or dandelion!"

Defiantly, she tossed the salt into the wok.

"Aieeya—why your father make my life so difficult?"

The ad at the right-hand corner of the paper caught my eye: *Tired of hearing your mate whine? Fed up with listening to their problems and not yours? Call now for psychic counseling: 1-900-549-4491.*

"Your father can be so two-faced, Su-Lin. He say I spend too much money, waste his hard-earn cash on silly things like nice clothes and birthday parties and violin lessons for your brother and sister. He say I don't know what important in life, what not." Viciously, she poked at the bits of beef simmering in a bed of orange and green. "But then he turn around and buy rental property without asking me, spend $80,000 that we don't have, on a house we aren't even going to live in! Tell me Su-Lin—now who is more wasteful?"

The pages of newsprint crackled beneath my hands.

"Su-Lin, why your father never listen to me?"

Maybe it's because you never say anything, I shot back in my head.

Three years could have been yesterday for all that had changed.

~~~

"Hello," I waved to the nurse on duty, "I've come to visit my father."

Looking up from her charting work, she smiled at the huge bouquet of flowers that I cradled in my arms and said, "My, but aren't you the filial daughter! Mr. Wong is one lucky man."

I blushed.

"These are from his co-workers in the city," I quickly explained, "not from me. I'm just the messenger."

"Well, I'm sure he'll be delighted to receive them anyways," she amended. "Go right on in."

I knocked softly and then opened the door.

"Father?" I whispered, peeking over the edge, "I have a surprise for you."

He grunted from his bed.

I stepped in and turned on the lights so that he could see the flowers.

"Ta-da!" I exclaimed with a flourish.

Silence.

"They're from the city," I prompted him helpfully. "Your secretary bought the flowers and everyone chipped in."

More silence.

"Here's the card," I said, hastily pulling it out and extending it toward him, "See—all your friends signed it."

He made no move to take it.

"Father—what's wrong? Don't you like the flowers?" I finally burst out, exasperated.

"Take them back," he snapped.

I just looked at him, stunned.

"TAKE THEM BACK, I SAID!"

"Father, why—"

"I DON'T WANT THEM! I DON'T WANT THEIR SYMPATHY!"

"But—".

"GO! NOW! GET OUT!"

I stumbled out of the room, trying to hold back burning tears of anger. As the door slammed closed behind me, I could hear him muttering to himself. "What a waste of money . . ."

～～～

Father hadn't changed one bit. Even now, when his income placed him among the top ten percent of the nation, he still insisted on being a miser. I have a feeling, though, that Father's obsession with saving money went far beyond bad childhood memories—far beyond any physical need for financial security. I have a feeling that Father saved money for the sake of saving money alone. To him, the process was more exciting than the profit. One could almost say that he was addicted to the sound of coins clinking in his pocket . . . to the feel of green bills between his fingertips . . . to the satisfying string of numbers next to his name on his monthly banking statement.

Father has always loved to play with numbers. Like his favorite game of Monopoly, he bought houses around his alma mater and rented them out to students. Yet though he'd often boast of his "rental property empire," I knew that the houses were his on paper only—the product of clever stacking of mortgages on mortgages. I often worried that this rickety card-house of debts would one day come crashing down on top of us, but whenever I voiced my fears, he would merely grow impatient and growl for me to keep quiet. His schemes were too perfect—*he* was too perfect—to fail. After all, didn't he win his way to the best university in Taiwan and then to America without any financial support from his father? How dare I question the solidity of his plans with the foolish, shortsighted blatherings of my female mind!

Yet, despite his bravado, his grand tapestry sometimes wore a little thin. Once in a while, his renters would be behind in their payments, and he'd find himself with no money to meet the monthly mortgage bills. *All right*, Father would say to us then, *no more purchases until the end of the month. No more meat. No more new groceries. Make do with whatever is left in the pantry.* I would fume at his orders—fume that the comfort of our lives hinged upon the capriciousness of his current poker hand. *Ma-ma*, I would wail, *talk to him! Make him stop this silly charade!* Yet her reluctance to challenge him was all too apparent, and, usually, nothing happened. Even when she did try, the attempt was half-hearted, for Father was able to silence her weak protest with one simple promise. *Once I have ten houses to my name*—he reassured her, *ten American houses to show my father that, despite his efforts to retard me, I have succeeded far beyond his wildest dreams*—then *I will stop.*" Mother would soften and give in. His need to prove himself to his father always touched some old refrain in her heart and drained away her anger.

But not mine.

～～～

"Ready, Su-Lin?" Father asked. Across the black-and-red checked board, his dark eyes glittered with anticipation.

"Ready," I said, returning his gaze with a tight smile. For as long as I can remember, I have been on the other side of the chessboard—never the ally, always the enemy. Father raised me to face the world with a cautious knight in one hand and a ruthless queen in the other. There was no time to daydream, he chastized, no time to rest on past-earned laurels. The future was upon us, already too old to shape.

～～～

"Su-Lin! What you doing?"

I jumped at the sound of his voice behind me and quickly turned off the TV.

"I was just . . . uh . . . just taking a break, Ba-ba."

"You know rule, Su-Lin," he glared at me, "No TV except news program. TV waste of time! And why you not ask my permission to turn it on?"

"I forgot, Ba-ba," I said, grasping for excuses. "I'm sorry . . . I won't do it again—"

"Sorry? You think saying sorry solve all problem?"

"No, Ba-ba, I just—"

"You think you steal something, say sorry, and ok again?"

"Watching TV is not the same as stealing—" I began.

"What? You using my electricity, my TV, my couch without my permission! That not stealing? You think I allow strange man come in here and sit in my house, with my air-conditioning, and watch my TV without charging him?"

"I'm your daughter!" I screamed at him, "I have a right to be here!"

"My daughter does not raise her voice at me," he whispered hoarsely. "My daughter obeys without question. Hold out your hand!"

"We're in America, Ba-ba!" I spat. "You can't spank me—if you do, I'll report you to the police for child abuse!"

His face grew mottled and dark.

"You want to be American? Fine! I treat you just like American. When you turn eighteen year old, you out of my house!"

He grabbed a piece of paper from the coffee table and thrust a pen into my hand.

"Write," he commanded. "Write down everything you said. Write down when you eighteen year old, I no longer support you. Write it down and sign it. No more food, no more clothing, nothing. Just like American."

"But—" I blustered, close to tears, "But what about college?"

"Find your own money," he snapped. "And if you don't go, you can always wash dishes for a living. That's why I give you so much practice."

~~~~~

I remember how Father once said that the best way to build a person's character was to constantly tear it down. Relentless competition forged strength within the individual, he said; endless obstacles nurtured a tenacity to survive. As the wood-chipped pieces moved before me on the black-and-red board, I pondered the meaning of his words and my four-year reprieve from hearing them.

It's been a long time, Father, my mind echoed. *I have changed . . . have you?*

"Checkmate."

"You played very poorly today, Su-Lin," Father said as I gathered up the chess pieces from his hospital bed blanket. "What's wrong with you? Why you so careless?"

"I don't know," I mumbled. Though it was just a game, I still felt sore that I had lost to him in less than fifteen minutes. Lost to the man who'd never let me live it down.

"Long time ago," he continued, lecturing me from his propped-up position, "you always think before you jump. Long time ago, you gave good fight. Now, your head in clouds—concentration scattered in four different directions. I win in nine moves. College make you stupid or something?"

Biting my lip, I glanced across the room at Mother. *Say something,* my blurred vision begged, *say something in my defense!* But, like so many times before, she had averted her eyes, numbed her tongue, and melted into the shadows of the corner. Like so many times before, she had fixed her gaze on the dust of the window sill behind me and ignored my silent pleas, playing deaf and dumb in the presence of my father's tyranny.

Slowly, I closed the lid to the game piece box, fighting back the tears . . .

~~~

"And the first place winner of the Cartwright District writing contest is—"

The Chair of the School Board fumbled with the envelope and withdrew a slip of paper.

"—Su-Lin Wong, from Desert Sands Junior High!"

Applause rippled across the audience as she stood up from her seat and stepped across the stage in a daze. Lips trembling—half-smiling, half-crying with joy—she accepted the trophy and shook his hand.

"Congratulations, Su-Lin!" he boomed into the microphone. "You wrote a fine essay. Tell me, who inspired you?"

She paused, as if tongue-tied.

"Your parents maybe?" he prompted helpfully.

She slowly nodded.

"And are they in the audience today? Oh, but they must be!"

He turned to address the auditorium without waiting for her response. "Mr. and Mrs. Wong!" he called out. "Will you two very proud parents please come up to the stage?"

Two figures hesitantly detached themselves from the seated masses and slowly made their way up the aisle. The mother clung to the father's arm and looked overwhelmed, embarrassed by all the attention. In contrast to her darting, timid eyes, however, the latter sauntered up to the stage.

"Mr. Wong," the stout, ruddy-cheeked Chairman asked into the microphone, "How do you feel about your daughter winning such an honor?"

He was silent for a moment, as if pondering the question, and then said, almost apologetically, "You too generous."

"What do you mean by that, Mr. Wong?"

"Su-Lin not very bright," he stated matter-of-factly. "She always a daydreamer. Always head in the clouds. Not good for math."

"But, Mr. Wong," the Chairman laughed nervously, "this award isn't for math."

"Too bad," he replied shortly.

~~~

"Su-Lin," Father said, breaking into my reverie. He slurped at the rice porridge Mother had brought for him and then asked, "What classes you take at university?"

"Well," I replied, counting off my fingers, "right now I'm taking a Shakespeare class, a psychology class—"

"You taking advance math?" he interrupted brusquely.

"Uh, no—" I began, but then hastily added, "My physics class involves a lot of math, though."

He didn't seem to hear.

"How many times I have to tell you, Su-Lin?" Father growled, "Math very important."

"Yes, I know, but—"

"Math make money. Lot of money. I very rich man because of math."

I sighed. I could already hear the oncoming lecture.

"Ba-ba," I cut in, hoping to skirt the inevitable, "I don't need math for my major."

"What you say?" he barked. "Not need math? You stupid girl!"

I flinched, but held my tongue.

"You know what your problem? You always foolish dreaming! I tell you, study hard in math. Math key to success. But you not listen! You continue to dream, continue to say you want to be artist! Writing, drawing . . . Bah! What they earn you, huh? You still poor student!"

"But all my scholarships were won in essay contests!" I shot back hotly, then swallowed the rest of my retort. I didn't trust my voice to say more.

"Essay contest?" he scoffed, "Stupid girl. You think they still give you money when you thirty-four years old? No! They will laugh at you!"

"Not as much as they laugh at *you*!" I burst out, "You, with your Ph.D. in engineering—you, working in a blue-collar job any high school graduate can fill!"

"Su-Lin!" Mother snapped at me angrily, "Your father sick! How can you shout at him like that?"

For a moment, our eyes locked. Try as I might, I saw no glimmer of sympathy, no hint of understanding within the depths of her pupils. Bitterly, I shut my mouth and turned to stare at the wall. It didn't matter if Father was sick or not. She would always take his side, always defend him, always follow him and abandon me. Just like she did twenty years ago in Taiwan.

~~~~

Mother has a habit of pretending certain events never happened. At dinner that night, she was all smiles again.

"Su-Lin," Mother said brightly as she scooped some broccoli beef onto her rice. "Tell me about school. Is it hard there? Do you have many friends?"

"Mmm-hmm." I mumbled, mouth full.

"I tell all my friends— 'Su-Lin going to Berkeley.' And you know what they say? They say, 'Wowww. Berkeley number one public school. She must be very smart.' And then I say, 'Yes, she very good. Very independent. She

win everything all the time in high school. Writing contest . . . speech contest—'"

I felt edgy.

"Mom," I interrupted her brusquely, "that was a long time ago."

She didn't seem to hear me.

"Yes," she went on, eyes soft with nostalgia, "you win so many things! So
many scholarships! I tell your father now—See, Ba-Ba? Su-Lin not useless
dreamer. She go to very best college without your help, without your
money!"

The grip on my chopsticks tightened.

"I tell him, you wrong to kick her out of the house. You wrong to say that,
when she eighteen year old, she no longer your daughter!"

I choked on a piece of rice. Why was Mama telling me all this? Why was
she dredging up the past, dredging up ugly memories that could only serve
to open old wounds?

"Aiieeya," Mama sighed. "He stubborn old man. Never listen. Never
change."

She chewed on her food for a while, lost in thought.

I silently sent up a prayer of thanks. There. The dreaded words had
been spoken, the past retreaded. Now we could both put it behind us.

But Mother wasn't through yet.

"You father has big mouth, Su-Lin," she continued after swallowing.
"Do you know what he did? He tell all his friends at the Chinese School
about how successful you are at taking care of yourself—boast to all the
other fathers about how he never has to send you money."

My jaw tightened. Father made it sound like it had been a voluntary decision on my part—like he had offered to pay for me, but that I had declined.
A knob of anger began to form at the pit of my stomach.

"Now they want him to write essay for school magazine. Tell them how
come he never has to worry about you, how come he never has to send you
money. They want him to tell them his secret to raising such a successful
daughter."

Inside, I laughed bitterly. Yeah, his secret strategy. Make them wash
dishes every night, clean house every weekend, weed gardens all day so that
they will appreciate the vegetables they have for dinner. Forbid them from
watching TV, talking on the telephone, going out at night with friends. Forbid them from wasting their free time reading and drawing instead of practicing math. Punish them for wanting privacy.

"You father so puffed up with importance now. He write essay called
"How I Raised My Kid," and fill it full of ridiculous lies like how he taught
you to feed yourself when you were two weeks old. Aieeya! Everyone know
two-week-old baby can't hold bottle by themselves!"

Mother was in her element, caught up in her storytelling, seething with righteousness. Years of pent-up frustration and disillusionment with my father came spilling out on one subject.

"At first, he write my name down too as coauthor. I yell at him, "No! I want no part in this! You make fool of yourself if you want to, but I am too ashamed of what has happened, of what you have done to destroy our family. How can you do this now—expose our terrible secret to the world, flaunt your shameful act as if it is something to be proud of?"

Mother began to wave her arms violently in the air, infusing her shouts with substance, underscoring each word with a whip. I stopped eating and stared at her tempest of rage.

"He get angry and says he will write, 'My wife won't say anything. I don't know why. Perhaps she is not proud of Su-Lin. Go ask her yourself.' I shout back to him, 'Fine! Let them ask! Let them call me up personally so that I can tell them the TRUTH! The truth of how you disowned Su-Lin and forced her to struggle by herself! The truth of how you now try to take credit for her success after refusing to fund her college education!'"

I stared at Mother. She stared back wordlessly, face flushed, lips trembling, drained of all power to say more. For so many years, I had thought of her as a cold, unfeeling, dictatorial matriarch in league with my father. I never knew how much my leaving had tormented her. I never knew how much she really loved me.

I began to cry.

~~~

For better, for worse,
For richer, for poorer,
In sickness or health
Till death do us part.

Mama was a great believer in promises. The day she gave herself to my father, all other ties fluttered to the side, cut from her chemise like a body that had outgrown its childhood dreams of romantic love.

He is a good man. A smart man. One who can take care of you.

But Ba-ba—she protested, He is penniless! Rumors say he funded his own education through selling acorns in the market . . . hen bu how yi shi! Would you have me marry beneath my class?

Wealth is not always measured in established cash, Mei-Ling, Grandpa had answered, but rather the potential for earning cash. In only seven years, he has scaled his way out of poverty, put himself through normal school, and earned a teaching position in our village. Now, with a full scholarship to an American university, he is about to embark upon an even greater journey—beyond the mists of our mountains, across the great waters, to the land of golden opportunity. Can any of your other suitors lay claim to such achievement?

Still, Mama hesitated. He is seven years older than me . . .

Mei-Ling, Grandpa said, age holds no meaning to survival.

Survival. The world seemed to pivot upon that single fulcrum of a word. Despite the fact that he was an aged pauper, bordering on the edge of permanent bachelorhood, Mama believed in his uncanny ability to survive. She did not bother searching for affection in him; she did not care if their thoughts, feelings, dreams coincided. To her, Father was merely a route to future success—her one-way ticket to America. But, in the end, the America of her dreams turned out to be just a sugar-coated prune.

She jumped at the sound of the front door slamming.

Tang yuen? she called out tentatively. Is that you?

Shoulders slumped, face shadowed by pent-up frustration, he entered the kitchen and tossed a manila folder onto the countertop. Papers flew everywhere.

I give up, he muttered. No use trying anymore.

Tang yuen—what has happen?

My supervisors at the City—they are all fools! I tell them, this is the way to fix the problem in the water system. I try to explain to them, this is the way to cut down costs while increasing efficiency. But will they listen? No . . . not to the ideas of a Ph.D. in civil engineering.

Perhaps you did not speak loudly enough . . . Mama ventured.

Father snorted in disgust. More likely, it is because I am Chinese. The high school diplomas that secured them these jobs tell them that broken English equals broken mind. It does not matter how loudly I speak—they will still only hear static.

Tang yuen, she soothed, you must learn to speak the language better. How can you complain? This is their country after all; it is not their responsibility to learn your language, it is your duty to learn theirs—

Stop your female blathering! he snapped. You know nothing of what I face each day at the City.

That's not exactly fair—

Fair? What do you know of fairness? All day, you linger in the comfort of your housework, in the familiarity of your cooking, in the joys of spending the money I sell my own face to earn. How can you even begin to comprehend what it feels like to be stepped on, spit upon, treated like dog-shit because you say Toyota instead of Chevrolet? How can you, a pampered woman, possibly understand the meaning of suffering?

Mama, lips pressed tightly in a thin line, turned away from him and silently began to prepare dinner.

~~~

That night, when the whole house was dark except for one soft bulb that hung above the kitchen table, Mama told me how, through the course of their marriage, my father had changed from a determined, idealistic young scholar into a disillusioned, embittered old man. Language barriers and racial tensions barred him from well-deserved promotions and forced him to serve under the direction of those less educated. Disillusionment led to eternal cynicism—a negative attitude toward life that cast a shadow across her domestic happiness. Yet, despite the tempo of the times, Mama was still unwilling to divorce him. For the sake of her children, she tried to preserve her marriage by playing the subservient wife—smothering her protests, pacifying his volatile temper, swallowing her own pride to bolster his.

For the sake of the children, she learned to abandon them in his presence.

I looked across the table at my mama when she finished talking—at the dark hollows under her eyes, at the greying of her hair, at the fine lines which now marred her once-prized skin. In shock, I realized that she was no longer the beautiful matriarch I had once envied and resented in my youth; she was no longer the silent monarch that condoned my father's deeds. For the first time, I saw Mama for what she really was . . . and the very humanness of it all smote down the final wall which separated us.

The legacy of leaving no longer delineated our lives.

For both of us, it was time to come home.

NO STONE

Catalina Cariaga

*t*he stone

     "di angel rolled away"

has landed
    on the bathtub ledge,
        near shiny porcelain tile

    "waiting,"

my mother told me,
          "for the river to rise on the shore of the island;

    we had no soap in those days—

    only the smooth stones and the pure water."

We cooked,
    we washed,
        we cried,
            we drank.

SUMMER OF MY KOREAN SOLDIER

Marie G. Lee

*b*eing back in Korea, the land where I was born, was, in a word, sucky.

I had come here with this idea to learn Korean and, in my off hours, search for my birth parents, who were waiting for me somewhere in Seoul.

So far, though, all I'd met were a bunch of spoiled Korean Americans, *chae-mi kyopo*, who were spending their parents' money like it was water.

Korean classes weren't all that bad. But it was hard to be in a room full of kids who looked just like you, and have the teacher ask, "What's wrong with *you*? Why can't you learn this? You never heard it before?"

"Actually, no," I said, and then the teacher, a well-meaning lady who sometimes got a little too excitable, looked really confused.

"Don't your parents speak Korean at home?"

"No," I said. "My parents are white. I am adopted."

And then she looked shocked and speechless. It was like all of a sudden she'd forgotten that she was in the classroom to teach, to pound Korean into our brains.

"Do you consider these Americans to be your *parents*?" she asked in amazement.

"Hey, I didn't know you're adopted," said Lee Jae-Kwan, otherwise known as Bernie Lee. "No wonder your accent is so fucked up. That must be so weird coming back here."

"Yeah, it is," I said, and then I gave him a look that meant that I was through talking about this subject.

Even in the beginners' class, Korean rolled off the tongues of the students so easily. There was only one other person who sounded like me; she was a nun. And from France. And had blue eyes. She had a visible excuse. Our teacher would often sigh impatiently, make that woeful "haa" sound at both of us; but at me I saw her snatching secret looks, like you do through your fingers at gory scenes in *Texas Chainsaw Massacre IV* or something like that.

It bothered me that people like Bernie Lee—who never did his homework, couldn't read or write Korean for beans, who thought that the most important part of college was "the opportunity to party"—would always speak Korean better than me, and would always, while we were here in Korea, feel superior because he was more Korean than me, whatever that meant.

The only Korean word I remembered from my childhood was *ddong*, the word for crap, *merde*, excrement. When I heard myself say it, it was the one word for which I had the perfect, clear, ringing pronunciation. Needless to say, I never had a chance to use it.

There was a time when I spoke better than everyone in the whole class. But those days are gone, and here I am marooned into this life, trying to make the best of it.

~~~~~

I can't blame Mom and Dad for adopting me—they wanted a kid. And wouldn't it be nice if Mr. and Mrs. Jaspers took a kid out of some poor Third World country? "We'll name her Sarah, which means God's precious treasure," they said.

Ever since I came over here, I've had what's been labeled a "bonding problem." It makes it sound like there's something wrong with my dental work. But what it really means is that I didn't bond with my parents the way I was "supposed" to. I found this out when I turned eighteen and could finally access my file in the social worker's office.

Frankly, I wasn't surprised. My earliest memories are of my mom and dad asking me if I loved them, and of me wondering what I should answer. And then they became panicky and, eventually, sent me to therapists and counselors all over town.

Why do they call this a bonding *problem*? Maybe I'd already bonded with my folks in Korea, and once was enough.

I like my adoptive parents, though. I called them Mom and Dad, but I'm sorry, that's the best I could do for them. The best they could do for me was to live in an Edina neighborhood with only white people and their children, who would later go to school with me and call me things like chink and gook and not include me in their games, their parties, their groups, their proms. Could anybody really blame me when I started staying in my room a lot, wearing black, getting my nose pierced at a head shop on Hennepin Avenue just because the spirit moved me?

I'm a virgin, though. Ha, gotcha.

God, I've got to find my real parents. They're waiting for me, and I know they feel as gut-wrenched about this as I do.

~~~~~

"You know what you need," my teacher said to me, "is to do a language exchange with someone—an hour of English, an hour of Korean a few times a week. It would improve your conversation."

I looked at her and felt very sore. Every night, from the dorm's study room, I could see Bernie and the other kids going out, dressed to the teeth and jolly. Sometimes when I woke at five to start studying, from my window I could see them getting out of elegant black taxis, stumbling to the door, then yelling in guttural Korean for the old *ajushee* to let them in, even though they'd broken curfew by a good six hours.

I wanted to be able to answer her in Korean, to say, "I'll think about it," in polite, precise Korean. But of course, I couldn't.

"I know a person named Kim Jun Ho, a friend of my younger brother's. He's at the university, although right now he's completing his time in the army. He wants to practice his English, and he would probably be a good teacher."

"Fine, fine, *gwenchana*," I said, more to get her off my back than anything. My eyelids felt sandy from staying up so late studying, and for the first time, I thought of quitting. Maybe after I found my parents I would.

~~~

"You don't need a language exchange," I said to Jun Ho Kim, who sat across from me and drank celery juice while I sipped at a ginseng tea that I'd tried in vain to sweeten with three packets of sugar.

We were at the Balzac Café. The neighborhood near school was full of those trendy coffee/juice bars that had the names of dead French authors: Flaubert, Rousseau, and, around the corner, Proust.

Jun Ho seemed nice enough. He was tall, had short hair (because of the army, he said).

His English was perfect. He spoke with better grammar than half the kids I went to junior college with.

"No, no," he said modestly, "I want to improve my conversation. I want to speak like an American."

So in English, we talked about nuclear plants in North Korea, dead French writers, and stories he'd read in some old American *Newsweek*s (for instance, he wanted to know how to pronounce *Hillary* and *Chelsea*).

When it came time to switch to Korean, we talked about the weather and studying. I ran out of words in about twelve minutes. He then asked me about my family, did I have brothers and sisters? What were my parents like? Even though he spoke wholly in Korean, I somehow recognized—but did not know—the words connected to family.

I answered, substituting the English word for every Korean word I did not know and basically ended up speaking in English. I told him how I was born in Korea but hadn't ever been back—until now.

"Are you sad?" he asked.

I shook my head. "No, because my family is somewhere in Seoul and I'm going to find them."

He nodded thoughtfully. "I will help you if you want."

"Thank you," I said. "I'll keep it in mind."

Jun Ho's face then folded in on itself, like origami.

"It isn't, 'I'll keep it in *my* mind'?" he asked.

"No, it's not," I said. "I don't know why, but the expression is 'I'll keep it in mind.'"

He laughed good-naturedly. "I'll never learn English, it's too hard." He got up and paid the bill.

The first time I called the orphanage, the person who answered the phone hung up on me. The second time, too. It wasn't necessarily that they were being rude, but they spoke in Korean to me, I spoke in English to them, and this went on for a number of minutes until the person at the orphanage hung up. It seemed to be a gentle, almost apologetic hanging up, though, as far as I could hear.

When I saw Jun Ho again, we went to the other side of the neighborhood to the Kafka Coffee House. He asked me, in English, about our secretary of state, Warren Christopher (it was lucky that I even recognized his name, much less knew anything about him). In the Korean hour, he talked about food (I had learned to order at restaurants) and studying. Then he asked me how my search had been going. I asked him if he'd help me, and he said he would.

We went to the closest pay phone, and he dialed the number. Soon he was talking in a continuous Korean from which I couldn't pick out any words. He looked at the piece of paper on which I'd scribbled my full name, as well as the Korean one that had been given to me at the orphanage: Lee Soon-Min.

He talked and talked. The longer he talked, the more hopeful I became—obviously the key to everything must be at the orphanage. Finally, he hung up.

"What happened?" Excitement was flowing out of every pore.

"They cannot tell me anything over the phone."

"Huh?" I said. "What'd you talk about?"

"How to get to the orphanage, that kind of thing," he said.

"Can we go now?"

"I made an appointment for two weeks. That is the soonest someone can see you."

I sighed. My family was going to have to wait, again. It seemed unfair, but after waiting for so long, I guess I'd have to do it. I'd also have to tough out at least another two weeks of this stupid Korean language school when what I really wanted to do was just take off, live with them, eat Korean food, and sleep in a Korean bed. I was sure my Korean would come back to me naturally. I admit I was starting to feel impatient.

The next time I met Jun Ho, he had his army uniform on, and he was also driving a car.

"How about if we do something different?" he asked, opening the door. I slid in. He grinned at me. Unlike the poker-faced seriousness of a lot of Korean men I'd seen, Jun had a dash of mischievousness, a kind of sparkle that flashed at you like summer lightning, when you can't quite tell if you've actually seen it, or if you've just blinked or something.

He pulled into the vortex of Seoul traffic as he explained that he'd borrowed a car from his friend so he could show me around a little bit. I was suddenly aware that I'd seen very little of Seoul besides the immediate neighborhood of the school, so I sat back, pleased.

"Next week is the orphanage," I said. "You'll come with me, right?"

He cracked another grin at me. "Right now we will have fun," he said. "We will talk only about fun things."

"Okay, later," I said agreeably. I wondered if things would be different when I could speak Korean. Would there be things I could say that I couldn't before?

We went to the Sixty-three Building. It's called that because it has sixty-three floors, or it's supposed to—I didn't count. The top floor has an observation tower. We got lucky, because during the humid summer the city is pretty much always obscured by industrial smog; it had been raining the last few days, and today the air was mountain clear.

The observatory was a whole floor, and you could walk all around it. Having been mostly on the ground between tall buildings, I'd forgotten about the mountains rising along the sides of the city. Now they loomed in all their majesty, forming a ring around the city. When I'd flown in and seen those mountains—so familiar, somehow, so much like home—I'd started crying.

I leaned and looked out for a long time. Somewhere out there was my family. On what side of the Han River would they live? Would they be rich? Poor? I thought of how each ticking of the clock brought me closer to them, and I felt happy.

At the souvenir shop there, Jun Ho bought me a pair of figures that looked like warped, demented totem poles. At the top, each one had a monster head. It was not pretty to look at. Jun Ho said that these were miniature versions of ones people used to erect outside their villages to scare the demons away.

"Will it scare my demons away?" I asked.

"It might," he said.

We stepped into the elevator, where a young woman bowed mechanically to us before pressing a white-gloved hand to the button for the lobby. You couldn't feel any motion in the elevator as it descended. When the doors opened and the familiar lobby scene appeared, I felt like I'd been beamed in from another planet.

The day for my appointment came, but before we went, Jun Ho sat us down at the Kafka.

The orphanage had very little information, he warned me. They wouldn't be able to help me find my family.

I jumped up, wanting to hit him. What nonsense was he talking about? He'd talked so long on the phone, made an appointment for me.

"Sarah," he said. There was no news. He'd made the appointment for two weeks hence in hopes that perhaps I'd give up on my own.

"It's better this way," he said. "Perhaps better for your family."

"How could that be?" I yelled. "My family is waiting for me. You're like all the rest—keeping me from them."

I think that's when I collapsed back into my chair, sobbing. I think I might have knocked over the sugar bowl, too. Koreans don't show their emotions, especially not in public. *What a crazy foreigner*, they were probably thinking.

"We'll go," Jun Ho said. He took my hand, and we caught a taxi.

The orphanage was filled with babies. There were loud, shrill cries, the smell of unwashed baby bottoms. The heat pressed down on my shoulders almost unbearably.

But this was my last hope; I had to push on.

A woman in a severely tailored Western-style suit met us. Jun Ho told her who I was and handed her my letter of introduction from the social services agency in the States. She stared at me hard, as if trying to make the connection between me and those squalling babies.

"I told her you want to see your file," Jun Ho explained. I leaned into him gratefully. There was always that hope, I was thinking. Something undiscovered in that file.

She brought out a file folder that had a few sheets of paper filled with single-spaced Korean writing. My heart jumped. There had to be something in there . . .

"Please read it to me, Jun Ho," I said. "Read every word."

Jun Ho scanned the page, then looked up.

"Sarah," he said. "It doesn't say much. It just says about your eating habits and so forth."

"Read it to me," I said, desperation beginning to crawl up my back. "Promise me you won't leave anything out." My whole Korean life lay among those spidery interlocking symbols.

Jun Ho looked at me again. His eyes were so black, they were liquid. He lowered his head and began to read.

"'A newborn baby girl was found on the steps of the Hoei Dong fire station on July 12, 1974. There was no note attached or any other kind of correspondence indicating any relatives.'"

Jun Ho paused, but I urged him on.

"'The baby was found covered with feces.'"

Ddong, I was thinking. I know that word. The baby. I was that baby.

"'The baby appears to have been born in a toilet or some kind of commode . . .

"'. . . cleaned her up. A name of Lee Soon-Min was given . . .

"'. . . was placed in foster care . . .

"'. . . was adopted by an American couple, Sue and Ken Jaspers.'"

I couldn't see anymore. It was like the day I stood behind a waterfall and tried to look out at the lake. Minnesota has more than ten thousand lakes.

Today was July 12. "It's, like, my birthday," I mumbled.

Jun Ho took my hand. He was leading me back to a cab. He barked directions to the driver, a large oily man who looked back at me, my tears and some stray hairs clogging my mouth. Jun Ho barked something else, and he started the car.

"Where are we going?" I surprised myself by speaking in Korean.

Jun Ho only smiled and gave my hand a squeeze.

"Home," he said.

Out the window, the rows of tiny stores were pressed together so tightly that they looked like one continuous, rickety storefront, save for the different signs in Korean writing each had in front of it. As the taxi picked up speed, the signs began to blur.

THE BABIES: I

Chitra Divakaruni

*a*gain last night as we slept
the babies
were falling from the sky.
So many of them—
eyes wide as darkness,
glowing lineless palms.

The dogs crooned their coming.
The owls
flew up to them on great dusty wings.

And all over the world
from beds hollow as boats
children
held up their silent scarred hands.

THE BABIES: II

Chitra Divakaruni

*a*s in the old tales, they are found at dawn. Before the buses start running. Before the smoky yellow gaslights in front of the Safdarjung hospital are put out.

It is usually the sweeper who finds them. On the hospital steps, among Charminar butts. By the door, beside crumpled paper bags and banana peels. He lifts them up, his calloused palm cupped behind a head that has not yet learned how to hold itself on the brittle stalk of the neck.

Sometimes the sky is tinged pink. Sometimes it is raining. Sometimes the *gul-mohur* by the gate is just beginning to bloom.

I am about to leave, the night shift over, when he brings them in. Wrapped in a red shawl the color of birth-blood. Or a green sari like a torn banana leaf. Jute sacks. Sometimes their eyes are blue as pebbles in their brown face. Sometimes they have notes pinned to their clothes. *Her mother died. Her name is Lalita. Please bring her up as a Hindu.*

The babies hardly ever cry. They open that grave unfocused newborn gaze on me, as if they knew. I do not cry either. Not anymore.

I find them bottles, milk, hold them as their mouth clamps around the nipple, their whole body one urgent sucking till it slackens into sleep. Their head falls back against my breast and I smell their warm moist breath.

I take them to the Children's Ward and lay them in cribs, their small fists dark against the white sheets, their eyeballs darting under closed lids. Sometimes they smile without waking up.

I do not kiss them. I do not look back when I leave. By the time I return at night they will have been sent to the orphanage.

At first I wanted to take them home. At first I wanted to find out what happened to them.

Now I know the stories. The stories stick in me like shards of glass. *The nuns taught her she was a child of sin. She was taken to be a maid. She ran away and was brought back. She ran away and was never found. No one would marry her. When she grew up, she left her child on the steps of the hospital.*

At home I take a long shower. I scrub myself all over with the harsh black carbolic soap that stings the skin. Arms, legs, belly, breasts. But when I lie down in my narrow bed with its taut sheets, I smell them on me again, their clean milky smell. Their weight in the oval of my arm, their fuzzed hair tickling my cheek. They suck and suck all through my sleep so that when I wake up I will carry inside my buttoned-up body the feel of their tugging mouths.

A LETTER TO MY SISTER

Lisa Park

*i*t's been almost six years since your suicide. Now when I think about you (and I think about you often), I feel you are somehow with me. My dreams of us together are as vivid and life-composing as any conscious, waking moment. Some like to think that our waking lives are more real, because we believe we can determine them through the choices we make, and that our dreams are merely their epiphenomenal reflections or, worse, expressions of unfulfilled desires. Your presence is more than a memory or a wish. My dreams are ghostly impressions of our collective past, as well as a *spontaneous living* of experiences I know we never shared before you died, like the dream I had of you and me walking arm in arm. I remembered it as if it was a lost memory, even though I know it never "really happened." I am sometimes grateful for this, because your phantom presence helps me to continue remembering, which I know is important even though it almost rips me apart. No matter how hard I try to subdue, through forgetting, the pain that came with the destruction of our lives, I must bear witness to the crimes committed against you (and against us) that led to your suicide. Conscious memories require constant attention, or else history will erase what happened, and you will disappear as if you had never existed at all. Isn't this why you haunt me to this day, to inscribe what you had learned from living under siege?

I remember the first time, when I found you after you had cut your wrists with a kitchen knife, and later when our father, using his deft surgical skills, sewed you back up in his office. For a while after you had cut your wrists, you undertook to "better" your life and attitude, even though it inevitably meant reinserting yourself into the old vise of conformity. One of the ways you tried to affirm your "new" resolve was to change your physical appearance through plastic surgery, for which our parents willingly put up the money in an effort to keep you happy. They were at their wits' end trying to appease you, but their efforts to pacify you pushed you further into self-hatred. (The annihilation of uniqueness and self-worth is indeed the pacifying aim.) Your obsession with plastic surgery exposed the myth of the whole beauty industry, which portrays plastic surgery as a beautifying, renewing experience, "something special you do just for you." It began with your eyes and nose, and you continued to go back for more. You tried to box yourself into a preconditioned, Euroamerican ideal and literally excised the parts that would not fit. But plastic surgery is irreversible, and so were the twenty-one years of assimilation. You told the doctors in the psychiatric ward, where they placed you just after your second suicide attempt, the reason you took all those pills (which your psychiatrist had given you) was because the plastic surgeons had "ruined" your face. Did you come to a realization (under the advice of your doctors) that you were obsessed with changing your looks, which could only dishearten you further because it medically legitimated your neurosis? Or did you think that the surgery botched up your corporeal plan, which you realized you would have had to live with for the rest of your life? The plastic surgeon referred you to a psychiatrist to help you "work out" your obsession. Help is a four-letter word. You decided death was your only alternative to being stuck with an inescapable body. As soon as you were released from the hospital, you committed yourself to finding a way to kill yourself. Now, on top of what you considered a mistake of a body, you wanted to avoid being thrown into a mental institution, where you were sure you were headed as a consequence of being found out by the psychiatrists.

The first time was different in many ways. First of all, no professional psychologists or mental health experts knew about it. Everyone in our family kept your suicide attempt secret and normalized it as if it had never happened. Secondly, I know you did not want to die, but to get our attention. I remember coming home and discovering you in bed with your wrists bandaged and the bathtub full of blood and water. You thrust your limp arms into the air and cried, pleading for my help. I was devastated, broken-hearted, sickened, and bizarrely nervous all the while about what our parents would do if they had to be interrupted at work! I looked to our brothers for direction, but they acted as if there was no big emergency. I convinced myself that you were not dying, that your slashed wrists were not much worse than a cut finger. When our parents finally discovered you, they became hysterical and burst into wails of anguish—I was so taken aback by their rare show of sympathy that I began crying myself, throwing my body onto yours, because only then did I feel safe enough to reach out to you. Once our mother wondered aloud why I had not told them right away about your suicide attempt. I did not explain myself to her, but it was because all the violence in our lives, both physical and emotional, made your suicide attempt seem normal, everyday. It was not that I was unaware of what a crisis looked like, but that I was used to having to assimilate them into quotidian experience. I was more worried about controlling the "disruption" than about what was actually happening to you. That was the extent of our spiritual and emotional isolation. Do you see how our culture of pain worked? I knew there was an emergency, I was ready to do something! But then I felt I was supposed to walk away, like all the other times when one of us was in distress. Silence was disciplined into us. How did we get to be so utterly ruined? How did we get to the point where we turned our backs on one another?

I feel comfortable placing blame on everyone, and some more than others. We have taken in the values that ultimately hurt and divide us, while some benefit from the suffering of "others." We were too stupid (not innocently, but the result of engineered ignorance) to see it happening to us. Even when it was clear, oftentimes all I could bear was to take care of myself, for my own survival. Most of all, I blame dominant institutions and mainstream society, because of the impossible alternatives they set up for us. They set up what is "good," what is "normal"—everything else is secondary, the "other." And they are very clever about it—they fix it so that the suicide looks like an individual problem, not a social or political matter. Labels of "mental illness" and "madness" are ways of silencing difference and shifting blame from the social to the individual. The social stigma of "dysfunctionality" kept our family secret and prevented us from seeking assistance from those who could offer it. For a long time, I felt we were atypically and inherently flawed, as individuals and as a family, but later learned from other Asian women that our experiences were neither unusual nor indicative of an intrinsic, Asian cultural pathology. However, regardless of any real possibility for collectivity, we had few means for support outside the family. We distrusted social workers and counselors, who had little insight into what we were experiencing.

The Asian "model minority" is *not* doing well. Do you see what a lie it is and how it is used to reinforce the American Dream and punish those of us who don't "succeed," or who succeed "too much"? It is making me mad knowing the truth of this culture, which is so obvious and yet so strategically dissimulated in the everyday that it becomes invisible, and nothing is left but the violence that results from its disappearance. How do you point out the horror of something that is so fundamentally banal and routine that it ceases to appear traumatic? And when you do point out the lie that is the truth, you feel (and usually are) alone in seeing this and wanting to root it out. It's enough to make you paranoid, because it is such a thorough conspiracy—how can you reform something that is so structural, so absolutely essential to the constitution of this society? Therapy and social work are out of the question, because the point is not to heal or to cope—no token of change can rectify our injury. Why would you want to place yourself into the hands of an institution that seeks to resocialize you into the environment that made a mess of you in the first place? Our inclusion into the American process turned out to be our worst form of oppression. Most people are proud to call themselves Americans, but why would you want to become a productive, well-adjusted citizen when the primary requisite of American-ness is racism? Isn't our madness often the only evidence we have at all to show for this civilizing terror?

I remember when you got arrested for stealing a car in order to escape the nearly all-white university you were attending. A white woman social worker ordered by the courts came to check up on you at home, where you were remanded for probation. Even though you had locked yourself in your bedroom, the social worker tried to break down the door when you refused to see her, despite all of our protests. I was desperate for you to break out of our circle of torment, but I knew my familial and social duty was to defuse the awkwardness and shame of divulging our "personal" problems. As far as our family was concerned, the state was the last place we would look for help, and, according to standards of social acceptability, there was no such thing as a family problem that could not be solved within the family. So I put on a calm, diplomatic facade for the social worker, who had finally given up on making you understand that she was only there to help and decided to interview me instead about our family situation, which her limited thinking deduced to be the problem. I assured her she was wasting her time and that everything was fine. That was enough to satisfy the social worker, and she never came back.

It is a very insidious process that starts when we are young. One of my first memories of the "weeding out" was when we visited our father's place of work. When we were introduced to his co-workers, one of them looked at me and said to our father, "Oh, this one has big eyes." Pretty/normal = big eyes, white. And I at least had relatively "big" eyes. So, did I pass? Can my brothers and sister come, too? Racial passing was impossible for us, even though we were continually pitted against each other according to their racial fantasies.

Another memory: we were on a school bus; our brother broke an implicit rule and occupied one of the rear seats, which one white boy decided he wanted. I burned with rage and humiliation, not knowing what to do, as I watched the white boy repeatedly bang our brother's head against the bus window. (Our brother remembers it a different way, but for a long time I could only recall the young thug's taunting laughter.) Although I pleaded with the bus driver to intervene, which he did only too slowly, I felt helpless. I was afraid to call attention to myself and my already awkward difference. This was only the beginning of our conditioning by their divide-and-conquer strategy.

We became pathetic victims of whiteness. We permed our hair and could afford to buy trendy clothes. Money, at least, gave us some material status. But we knew we could never become "popular," in other words, accepted. It had something to do with our "almond-shaped" eyes, but we never called it racism. You once asked, "What's wrong with trying to be white?" You said your way of dealing with racism was not to let them know it bothered you. But they don't *want* it to bother us. If it did, they would have a revolution on their hands. The "just-convince-them-they-should-be-like-us" tactic. It is so important for the American racial hierarchy to keep us consuming its ideals so that we attack ourselves instead of the racial neuroses it manufactures.

I feel disgusted and angry and so, so sorry when I think of how I participated in the self-hatred that helped to kill you. I did not like to be reminded of my own "Orientalness," and I could not be satisfied with our failure to fit into the white American mold. Our parents were accomplices and victims, too. I remember when our mother once criticized you for cutting off your long, straight, black hair (in your effort to appear less "exotic"). Insulting you, she said, "You have such a round, flat face." She always told us, "You not American. Why you try to be American?" Our father could not understand our dilemma, either: "Your only job is study—Be number one—Do what your father tell you and you never go wrong." When he was challenged, which was usually by you, the one-who-paved-the-way-for-the-rest-of-us, he became a frustrated madman and abuser. We interpreted this as a failure in communication, a clash of cultural values, but the conflict ran deeper than a matter of individual understanding or cultural sensitivity. We did not believe in the possibility of surviving as an Oriental in an American society. Oriental/American. Our only choices. This is what we call a serious identity crisis.

I know people thought they could pick on you because you wore pink Laura Ashley dresses and glasses. Racists think "Oriental" girls never fight back. You told me some white girl, backed by her white thug friends, was threatening to beat the shit out of you. But you were more than this Laura Ashley reflection. The white girl was in for a big shock the day you put on your fighting gear and confronted her in the girls' restroom. You had to "toughen up" just to survive. (What does that entail, what price did you pay?) Our schizophrenia was a conditioned disease. You always and never had a grip on who you were.

You could draw a picture of a tiger springing to attack, frontal view, at the age of nine, and it would be good enough to pass for a *National Geographic* illustration. You were the fastest runner in elementary school and broke the school record for the fifty-yard dash. You made the junior high school track team, but our mother forbade you to run because she thought it would make your legs big and ugly. When our mother told your track coach, you were so embarrassed and humiliated that you never tried to run again. You stopped drawing, too, because you were being groomed by our father to become a doctor. You used to sell your drawings for twenty-five cents each to other classmates in elementary school, but soon learned you had no time for art (or "fooling around," as our father would say) because you had to study hard. You broke down one day after having received a B on an exam, because you were afraid it would ruin your straight-A record. Our father told me you had asked your white, male professor to reconsider the grade, but he told you he never gave *foreign* students A's! The real irony was that you were always a capable student, and more important, an insightful, critical thinker.

I had a desperate feeling something very bad was going to happen. So I wrote a letter to you a week before your second suicide attempt, warning you about my premonition, but the letter never got to you. I wrote that I wanted you to take care of yourself and that, like you, I was barely getting by. (You once wrote a goodbye note to me before you ran away—or was it meant to be read after your death?—that read, "I still don't know how you do it.") I wrote that I would be there for you and to have FAITH, because no one else was going to do it for us. But mostly, I expressed a deep sense of urgency. I sensed that if you did not do something about the crisis you were living, you would explode.

We spoke on the phone two nights before you took the pills. I was worried and impatient with you, because I wanted you to reassure me that you would not do anything self-destructive, so you told me you were not feeling suicidal. You even said you thought you were "probably the most fucked-up person on this planet," but you felt "good" about how you were going to handle it. I got off the phone feeling relieved, for the moment. Handle it? Was it supposed to be a hint (but I couldn't get it)? Our mother told me you cried, "Mommy, I'm sorry," which she believed signaled your regret for the "mistakes" you had made. "If you can't do anything good for society, you might as well kill yourself." Still, she told me your death took an important part of her, a connection she felt most strongly with you because you had her face. The same face she insulted and helped you to "reconstruct." Our father laughed when you told him the reason you wanted the plastic surgery was because you did not want to look like our mother.

In some ways, your death has shocked this family out of denial. For the first time, our parents owned up to the abuse they inflicted, as well as the suffering they endured from their own social alienation. Imagine how hard it was to maintain their dignity, having to work three times as hard as their white colleagues, who turned up their noses at broken English, and their own kids thinking they were stupid. Our brothers began to rely on me for support they used to get from you. You once told me what our lives would be like if you died. I realize now all the things you told me are true. But without these traumatic changes, I never would have appreciated your wisdom. I wonder if your vision was part of a plan. Did you know what you had to do?

I think you left because you could not live in the world that you knew. It hurts (so much) to imagine your pain and loneliness, . . . but I also know of your courage. You told me you were not afraid to die. *How much you must have known to feel so comfortable with death*. You weren't just a victim. However compromised, your suicide was also a form of resistance, a refusal to carry on under such brutal conditions.

I still have some of your old belongings, including some postsurgery photos that were hidden in a box. I didn't recognize you in the pictures at first. *My* sister is the girl I joked around with, shared a bed with and respected, who cut my hair, let me tag along, took some beatings for me, tolerated my impatience, envied me (too much) and was sometimes proud of me, saved animals with me, spoke Korean more fluently than the rest of us, was the dependable one, the pride of our father, the closest to our mother, the one with the "good heart," the confidant of our grandmother, the toughest one, who could beat us up and occasionally did, our younger brother's favorite sister, the only one who could really talk to our older brother, the one to have my teachers first, and the smart one. My perceptions of you. You said later, "I always feel obligated." Mired in my own worldview, I refused to believe you had it so hard. Your suicide was finally something that belonged to *you*.

I pieced together the events of your suicide through stories told by our family. You pawned a TV set and bought a .38 Magnum. Put blank cartridges into where the bullets should be and sat in bed with the gun hidden underneath the covers. Our mother had spent the day tailing your car around the city, following you from one pawnshop to the next, begging the dealers not to sell you a gun. Eventually she found you at home safely in bed, and reassured you that everything was going to be fine. You asked her if you would have to go back there, to the psychiatric place. Our mother tried to comfort you and then left to get you a glass of orange juice, but she had walked no further than the bathroom down the hall when she heard an explosion. You were declared "dead" a few hours later.

So, why am I writing to you, dearest sister? It would be nice to extract an ultimate meaning from all this, to acquire some comfort from analysis, but I am still confronted with the abysmal magnitude of my soullessness. (That is what it feels like, the utter uprootedness of living in this lobotomizing culture.) I cannot hope to achieve a level of wholeness, because my soullessness refuses to be quiescent under this civilizing regime. I am writing to let you know that I still remember, and I will live to tell it regardless of my state of ruin, which means I think it is possible to militate against violence and loss without buying into civility and unity. I am not even calling for anarchy; I cannot allow myself that luxury because we already live in a (nation-)state of organized chaos. Your presence haunts and compels me to recount your death. Maybe my story will be useful in some way—to galvanize a historical or political consciousness—who knows? Maybe through remembering I will even find a patchwork place for myself to take root, just as we do in my dreams.

THREE WOMEN AND A MASTER

Isabelle Thuy Pelaud

*t*he brown Toyota drives down Bolsa Avenue, a street bordered by Vietnamese American shopping centers in Los Angeles called "Little Saigon." Comfortable in the back seat, I inadvertently stare at the pendant dangling from the rearview mirror, a picture of a woman in a Santa Claus costume smiling, ticking from right to left to the rhythm of the engine. A soft and charismatic voice from an audiotape is bringing spiritual life into the space, talking, explaining, "saving" my aunt number nine from her eternal recycling of lifetimes. My aunt calls the dweller in this voice "Supreme Master Ching Hai." Like Jesus Christ or Buddha, my aunt believes Master Ching Hai has come on earth to help and save sentient beings from their deeds.

After six years of intensive teaching in Taiwan, Latin America, and the United States, Master Ching Hai draws her largest group of followers from among Taiwanese, Korean, and Vietnamese Americans. "I don't do anything different from Jesus—we have the same mission," Master Ching Hai explains to her disciples who no longer feel they need to pray to Buddha or Jesus Christ. They say they now have the privilege to be in contact with a "Supreme Master" who is alive and can *directly* help them to be "instantly enlightened." This occurs through a period of initiation, a ritual performed in silence whereby disciples free themselves from their past lives' karma (or debt) caused by wrongdoing. Once they are enlightened they will never again have to reincarnate into this world, but instead they say that after they die, they will "go Home." Home for them is a wonderful and spiritual place where all enlightened human beings can stay forever without having to reincarnate into this world of suffering. As part of the process of being enlightened, all disciples have to meditate two and a half hours every day, be full vegetarians, and follow the five basic Buddhist moral precepts, which are to refrain from the following: taking the life of any sentient being, speaking what is not true, taking what is not offered, engaging in sexual misconduct, and using intoxicants. If their faith in their Master were to diminish, initiates could freely leave the group and return to their previous ways of life.

Master Ching Hai claims she is teaching the "Quan Yin Method" of meditation. By naming her method after Quan Yin, and sometimes by dressing in a way identical to the popular representation of Quan Yin herself, Master Ching Hai reenacts, and for some, reincarnates the figure of Quan Yin, the famous Buddhist Lady of Compassion. It is to her that many Vietnamese, ethnic Chinese, and ethnic minorities from Vietnam prayed when they escaped from their country by boat. This reenactment may have ample meaning for those who believe and feel that their coming to the United

States, as well as their physical survival, was made possible through their prayers. The transplantation of this Vietnamese religious symbol to the United States suggests the existence of a fluid cultural border that transgresses the notion of fixed and separate political nation-states.

The examples of my two aunts and mother may help to illustrate the impact Master Ching Hai's teaching has had on many of her followers. Their lives have indeed been profoundly transformed since their initiation with the Master. When I went to the United States for the first time from France in 1984, I lived with Di Chin, my aunt "number nine," the eighth child of the family. She used to tell me endless ghost stories and magic tales. As the years passed by these anecdotes began to fade. She never found in America the dreams she hardly had the time to formulate in her abrupt departure from Vietnam in April 1975. Shortly before leaving Vietnam she had married a man her mother had chosen for her. He was an ideal mate, an administrator who was unlikely to fight in the war. She was then working for an American company and was able to bring him with her to the United States after the fall of Saigon. Contrary to the life she expected in America, she ended up working two shifts, day and night, as a data entry key operator while her husband retrained at a computer school. Every night she returned home at one o'clock in the morning, falling asleep with her newborn baby in her arms. Six years later, her son was run over by a car and died in a hospital.

Her soul entirely broken, she started to increase her visits to the Buddhist temple, kneeling in front of the statue of a Buddha and staring avidly into His golden eyes. Emptiness was the only answer she received from the prayers she diligently repeated in a language she did not understand and whose meaning resonated only as an evasive echo. At home, fights with her husband had become intolerable, but the idea of a divorce was inconceivable. She was pregnant again and needed to protect her baby. Too many tears shed, she thought, would reach her unborn child's heart and cause unpredictable damage.

A few years later a nun lent her a videotape of Master Ching Hai. My aunt lay in bed that night after inserting the tape in her video machine. The image of a small woman in a white gown appeared to her on the screen saying, "When I am teaching, not the body is talking but Buddha's and my inner Master speaks."[1] My aunt observed: "The first time I watched the videotape, I felt something. It made me want to change, it made me want to see her and become initiated so we could have power from her." Di Chin's interest in religion, but also in life, was revived. "It's better than winning the lottery," she would tell me with a smile, trying to persuade me to watch one of the many videotapes she now watched daily. With delight in her eyes she narrated stories about the royal origins of the Master's past life or described with secrecy in her voice how the Master had awakened the "god of rain" who, she said, accidentally fell asleep and caused the five-year drought in southern

California. She also meditated and became a vegetarian. "She [Master Ching Hai] just showed us how to sit, and to relax. When we meditate, we see where and who we are. After that we feel love for everyone," she said.

The walls of her house soon became covered with colorful portraits of the Master. In the Buddhist altar, the image of Master Ching Hai gently and resolutely smiles on the side of a placid Buddha. "Master is right, each of us has Buddha inside us. Only a Buddha can endure the life we have," Di Chin once said. In her manicure shop, Di Chin has installed a television set with videos of Ching Hai playing constantly. To the customers unfamiliar with the Master, she patiently explains her new philosophy. From a meaningless job she has added the dimension of educator. At home, she no longer fights with her husband, who finally accepted her opening her own business, something he had fervently resisted in the past. He is a disciple of the Master himself and became initiated a few months after my aunt. The case of my aunt and uncle is not unique in this sense; Vietnamese American women often become initiated first, and are later followed by their husbands. Every night, my aunt sits meditating in a living room with her husband and two children.

Di Ut, my aunt number ten, the ninth child of the family, arrived in the United States seven years ago. The last time I visited her I found her sitting in her garage bent over a sewing machine, half hidden behind a huge pile of navy blue material. She ran a piece quickly through the machine, dropped it onto a bigger pile, and immediately seized an identical one from another pile. I remembered the day I picked her up at the airport with her son when she first came to the United States. When her husband came to America in 1975 she was pregnant but was not able to leave Vietnam. After ten years apart, they finally reunited in that concrete hall of the Los Angeles airport. They stood there, looking at each other with polite smiles, a skinny ten-year-old boy with wondering eyes at their side, all posing politely for the photograph I was demanding of them. My uncle had shown me her picture before. She looked so beautiful then! In the frame of the camera was now an older woman bundled up in a heavy old-fashioned coat, with abraded skin and her hair in disarray. Speaking hardly any English, Di Ut did not, however, stay home without working. She found one of the only jobs available to her that did not require English proficiency. Though she had taken a few business classes in Vietnam, she became a garment worker in America, making three cents a t-shirt.

What was she thinking while bending her neck over the machine? Maybe her husband had become somewhat of a stranger. What had he done in the past ten years? How could she trust him again? He was not the same as she remembered! And her son was learning English too fast and seemed distant from her. What would become of her family? Alone in her garage, Di Ut listens to the sound of the voice of the Master while passing the pieces of cloth, one at a time, under a restless needle. She has difficulty understanding the words because the motor is too loud. That's all right. Sunday, she will go to the temple where she will help with the administration and the organization, using the business skills she acquired in Vietnam. Her husband has also become a disciple of Master Ching Hai and will accompany her. She no longer worries about him and has found confidence in herself. Her son, now seventeen, refuses to become initiated. She does not press him and, though she remains protective of him, it is now easier for her to accept the changes he undertakes by growing up in America.

When I went to visit her and asked about her experience with Master Ching Hai's teaching, she called a friend, also a disciple of Master Ching Hai, to come to her house. She said these people were more educated and more articulate than she was, and therefore would be in a better position to explain the teachings of their beloved Master. I was surprised to see her new friends, a middle-class couple with their daughter, a USC student. They were sitting at the table, crowded in the tiny room with dim light, looking out of place with their beautiful clothes. Di Chin invited similar friends to educate me about Master Ching Hai's teaching the next day. These were the kinds of friends I had never seen in their house during the two years I had lived with her. Class differences in this case did not seem to be as much of an obstacle for communication, perhaps because they now had common experiences, visions, and stories to share.

My mother immigrated to France in 1965. Her dream was to study in France and marry the handsome and prestigious French teacher she had met in Vietnam. Perseverance and luck brought her to France where he had said he had bought her a beautiful home. Upon her arrival she found a big but rundown house situated in the cold north of France and a sick, old-looking man stripped of all his colonialist prestige living a secluded life as a gardener with his elderly parents. She was welcomed by his family with condescension, anger, and hatred. By the time she realized her mistake it was too late. She was pregnant. In an incredulous daze, she heard the voice of her old prince telling her he was married and recommending that she live by herself in a house reserved for single mothers until the end of his divorce. She had no choice but to listen to him. She thus lived on the margin of French society for a period of nine months, hiding both her shame from her family and her fear of bearing a child without a legitimate father. She felt lucky when, two years later, he obtained a divorce from his wife and asked her to marry him.

Though her life has improved considerably over the last twenty-eight years, she is still treated as a foreigner by her in-laws and all the neighbors. Since her initiation as a disciple of Master Ching Hai, her anger and bitterness have evaporated. "We have to be content with what we've got. We have to accept, accept all the conditions of life," she said. My mother has more time than my two aunts to practice the "Quan Yin method" because my father does not want her to work. Her free time used to be a burden filled with boredom. She now cherishes it. She meditates, practices Chinese exercises similar to Tai Chi, reads religious and health-related books, and paints. "I paint better because of meditation, everything is better. [Now] everything I learn I remember, before I would forget!" she said. My father has not been initiated and, I suspect, never will. He, however, likes to see my mother move graciously to the sound of Chinese music as she does her exercises. He also admires her paintings and, while he says he is suspicious of the Master, he enjoys aspects of what he sees as a somewhat "exotic" philosophy. Finally "respected" and "loved," my mother now engages in aspects of Asian culture that she had previously ignored. She no longer tries to replicate French ways in a manner that consistently leads to failures. She has—relatively speaking—become the head of the family.

It isn't surprising that my mother and two aunts became numb to their pain as it continuously rubbed against the back of their everyday lives. They took life a day at a time, trying their best to forget the past and fulfill their familial duties. Their existence had become little more than mere subsistence temporarily interrupted by periods of self-destructive crisis. They hardly dared to formulate dreams. For all three, Master Ching Hai ripped this pattern that desperately longed to be torn. Now, as followers of Master Ching Hai, the three women were able to rebel against traditional values without disturbing its outer structure. My aunt number nine could insist it was necessary for her to sleep separately from her husband so that she could meditate peacefully. She was able to convince him that, with the protection of Master Ching Hai, she was capable of taking care of a business of her own. Her sister, Di Ut, could use her business skills through her involvement in the temple's management. Not having a driving license, she asked her husband, also a disciple of the Master, to accompany her to the temple. She finally could be certain of his everyday actions and regain her trust in him. By meditating diligently, the two women gained an equal or even superior "enlightenment status" to their husbands. My mother, by including painting and Chinese exercises as part of her meditation practices, was able to reclaim her uniqueness and become respected by her relatively educated husband. Through Master Ching Hai, my two aunts and mother feel that they are now not solely judged by their level of education, physical beauty, social background, or ability to adapt to a foreign environment, but instead are valued based on their level of enlightenment and wisdom.

The family of my uncle number two, Diep, suffered extensively in Vietnam after April 1975. Sponsored by Di Chin, he and his family were not able to enter the United States until 1988. The conditions of my uncle's family's resettlement never reached, however, the degree of uncertainty and despair experienced by my aunts and mother. In Vietnam my uncle was the only son in a family of nine and the only one to receive a formal education beyond high school until graduation. As a result he became governor of a province in the South and married a beautiful woman who never worked outside the home. All his children attended French high schools and were raised as traditional Buddhists. Well educated, they had relatively little difficulty pursuing their education in the United States and acquired lucrative enough careers to support their parents. Their family remains strong and closely connected to the Vietnamese traditions. If my uncle's wife and children were to follow Master Ching Hai, his authority as patriarch would be threatened. In the United States he was able to replicate the basic family structure of his life in Vietnam, keeping a strong connection with traditional Buddhism. He has no need for internal changes as his sisters desperately did.

My uncle number two fervently condemns Master Ching Hai. He calls her disciples fanatics and gives examples of Vietnamese people who have given up their houses and savings to join the group. "What she teaches is not Buddhism," he says. "She uses Buddhism as a trick to attract followers." "How can she dare to wear a Buddhist nun's clothes when she has been married before?" he asked. (The question of whether Master Ching Hai has ever been formally ordained as a nun by the Buddhist church is a source of heated debate.) He denounces the number of families that have been broken because of Master Ching Hai. In the cases where a spouse or significant other has not become initiated, grave conflicts have indeed arisen within certain families. My uncle also cannot tolerate the fact that Master Ching Hai wore clothes that revealed her shoulders when swimming at a camping retreat in Taiwan. "When she washed herself in the river, people were waiting downstream to drink the water!" he said with disgust. From my uncle's point of view, Master Ching Hai is a heretic and a dangerous charlatan whose meditation techniques could eventually drive her followers crazy. Like him, many Vietnamese traditionalists cannot forgive what they consider as Master Ching Hai's "arrogance." "A woman cannot reach enlightenment," a monk once told me. As I walked out of the Palace of Fine Arts in San Francisco where Master Ching Hai lectured last November, several windshields of cars belonging to people attending the meeting had been broken. Rumors say that she has received death threats.

While I do not embrace most of my uncle's harsh criticisms of Master Ching Hai, I cannot ignore ambivalent feelings and thoughts I hold toward her group. Although Master Ching Hai says she does not want "to be treated as an adorable idol"[2] and asks her disciples not to kneel or pray to her personally, most of her followers do worship her, use her name in their everyday prayers, carry her picture around their necks, and live their lives according to her words. They treat her as a living Buddha and feel elevated from the rest of other human beings by virtue of being "saved from reincarnation." Master Ching Hai has said she was like a "mother" to her disciples, reducing them implicitly to children who may have difficulty thinking on their own. "I'd rather be a mother that gives than a monk that begs" she said.[3] "We are like a new person inside. We feel love for everyone around us. It went from hard times to good times. We want to help people. We feel so much happiness, a happiness we cannot explain. We feel young, we become children," my aunt Di Chin explains. She was not troubled but proud when her daughter once told her, "you are not our mother, Master Ching Hai is our mother." While these cultist aspects of the group deeply bother me, I admit I enjoy the present happiness of my two aunts and mother and their thirst for empowerment in their shifting sands of experience. But does "loving everyone" and feeling "happy" or being empowered, I wonder, contribute toward raising political awareness and questioning the unloving status quo of the United States? Could it help the three women of my family to identify the common destiny they share with their Asian "sisters"? Can, at last, Master Ching Hai be considered a feminist?

Master Ching Hai's use of simple language and everyday examples has permitted many Vietnamese refugees and immigrant women like my aunts and mother to have access to religious concepts generally reserved to a religious elite and veiled by rituals, habits, and chants they did not understand. "I went to the temple every week for thirty years since I was young. I learned a lot, but they didn't teach inside. We didn't really practice," Di Chin said. Master Ching Hai has reformulated for her disciples the existence of God in their country of resettlement and a sense of hope, self-worth, and meaning for their own uprooted lives. However, in contrast with liberation theology, which has been popular in Central America among the working class as a revolutionary force against dictatorship, Master Ching Hai's influence among the working class does not seem to challenge the dominant conservative political configuration. Master Ching Hai's teaching ferments the hope that her disciples no longer need to wait for their next life, as is sometimes implied by traditional Buddhists, to be successful. Having become a "mini-Buddha" by virtue of their initiation into the group, each disciple is left to harmoniously compete individually and slowly climb the ladders of enlightenment. "Look at me," Master Ching Hai said, "I am spiritual but I buy houses and property everywhere. One should not be one-sided, it would be fanatic." Though I can understand why certain Vietnamese Americans may embrace a "materialist Buddha," I also long for the modesty and simplistic lifestyle traditional Buddhist nuns and monks lead as an alternative model to heightened individualism and capitalist enterprise.

If Master Ching Hai's female disciples feel empowered as women, they may not always feel empowered as Asians. While ethnic solidarity among disciples is sometimes encouraged, it is at other times hindered. For example, all Master Ching Hai's disciples from around the world were invited to join forces, regardless of their ethnicity, to protest against Vietnamese refugees repatriation policies in Hong Kong. At a lecture Master Ching Hai held in 1994 at the Palace of Fine Arts in San Francisco, however, "Americans" were told to sit in the front rows, "Chinese" to sit behind them, and "Vietnamese" to sit in the back. In this case "Americans" meant whites, with the exception of two or three African Americans. How far away from the Master her disciples had to sit was extremely important to them, for the closer they sat to her, the more power they felt they received from her. Furthermore, although the vast majority of the audience was Asian, the majority of speakers who publicly testified about their experiences as initiates were also white. Could it be that Master Ching Hai weighs a white person's testimony more than an Asian one's? The head organizers were also white. During a lecture in San Jose in June 1994 Master Ching Hai praised "Americans" over Vietnamese: "I worship America for their work force, such a big and new country with so few people, and look, they are so successful. I feel pity for Vietnam who, with five thousand years of history and a lot of people, made nothing," she said, oblivious of history. This observation suggests that people with white skin may prevail over Asians in Master Ching Hai's teachings.

Whether Master Ching Hai has the divine power she claims to have or not, I can be no judge. What I have observed, however, are the changes the three women who are the most close to me have experienced in the last four years. As I described earlier, they each are in a new space in which they have found individual strength without having to disrupt the outer Vietnamese traditional structure. Master Ching Hai does not fit the stereotypical image of a self-effacing, self-sacrificing religious woman. If Master Ching Hai has "sacrificed" her happy marriage to a German doctor for the sake of all sentient beings, she does it in a grandiose manner by claiming her power of redemption.

> [M]any people may think I am talking a fairy tale. Therefore it is difficult to convey our message to the world at large, however much I am impatient to do so and however much my disciples are excited to do so. They still have to be patient and play down. This is very pitiful, but there is no remedy for it. Even when Jesus was there He did not save many people; not many people followed Him. Buddha was also the same; not many people followed Him. Only after they died did they become famous.[4]

In contrast to Jesus or Buddha, who had to resist temptation during their period of isolation to find their respective divine missions, Master Ching Hai never refers to such a struggle. At no time did she have to withstand the body of a woman as a sinful distraction from her almighty path. On the contrary, her disciples believe she was reincarnated on this earth in the form of a woman by choice. Women in her group do not feel they symbolize sin nor a distraction from men's goals, but on the contrary feel pride in their gender. Master Ching Hai, by affirming her gender and teaching Asian and Asian

American women the Quan Yin method she herself practices, has created the hope that, one day, they too will become saintly women, enlightened, beautiful, articulate, powerful, successful, and loved.

> Women and mothers are visible "objects" and very close to us, every day we know about them, still we forget this and always despise woman. So how could we know anything about God, who is so far away, so abstract, so metaphysical and whom we have never seen before? . . . The merit of women to this world is undeniable. Women are mothers of all the Buddhas and of all the saints in the past, present, and future. . . . If you can respect a woman just because she bore a saint [St. Mary] then why don't you respect a saintly woman?[5]

In this sense I do see Master Ching Hai as a feminist. But what kind of feminist is she? Like some white liberal feminists, Master Ching Hai confounds individual success with emancipation of the group. While she preaches love, compassion, and detachment, she encourages individual entrepreneurship and places great value on external appearances. A dress she has designed and worn can be sold for ten thousand dollars and marketed as "helping more sentient beings, and at the same time elevating people's perception of beauty."[6] She finds no contradictions in appearing on different occasions as a Chinese princess with long hair, a traditional Buddhist nun with a shaven head, a Thai or Korean queen with makeup, an Arabic woman with colorful veils, a Vietnamese bride without a groom, or a Santa Claus. "Dignified and beautiful clothing merely serves as an attempt to demonstrate the supreme dignity and splendor of the world on the other shore" she said.[7] She also sells "heavenly jewelry" to men that "can make them look beautiful and 'bright,' [and] will be reminders of spiritual practice."[8]

I often heard Master Ching Hai's disciples use this example to explain their practices: "Enlightenment, we get immediately. But that is only the starting, just like enrolling you know. The first day you enroll in the university, you become immediately the university student. But that has nothing to do with a Ph.D. After six years, four years or twelve years then you graduate. . . . Both sides have to cooperate."[9] Like university students striving for various degrees, Master Ching Hai's disciples can reach five levels of enlightenment. The first level is a place where their talents are developed, such as literary, artistic, or intellectual aptitudes and psychic faculties. These personal qualities are very likely, they are told, to correspond with career advancement. At the second level they gain the ability to debate and provoke miracles. At the third level "all the debts of this world" are erased. As for the fourth level, Master Ching Hai said human words are too limited to describe its extraordinary beauty. Finally, the fifth level is a unique place where only Masters can go. Master Ching Hai said that levels beyond this one are not to be sought because the power there is too great, both beautiful and ugly.

It is implicit in Master Ching Hai's teaching that she has reached the fifth level of enlightenment. She is an artist, an eloquent teacher capable of answering all questions with clarity, and she has a good sense of humor. She is able to quote from the Bible, Confucian teachings, or the Buddhist scriptures equally with ease. She also speaks five languages and is successful both in terms of her personal "career" and material gains (she is a multimillionaire). Although she was the daughter of a well-to-do doctor in Vietnam, had the opportunity to study languages abroad, was familiarized with the Western world, and once was married to a German physician, Master Ching Hai never attributes her spiritually derived abilities to her elite education and background.

If Master Ching Hai represents a model for her disciples, to be a Master also means to be an upper-class individual, a successful businesswoman, and an owner of many properties who can afford to engage in large-scale charitable work, undertake artistic activities, and take care of her appearance with taste and elegance—or with extravagance, depending upon the viewer's criteria of beauty. Though it might be true that without Master Ching Hai entering into their lives, my mother and my two aunts would have been on a path of self-destruction, it is also the case that Master Ching Hai's teachings affirm a conservative feminist middle-class ideology. Di Chin, now running her own small business in a black neighborhood, buys fake diamonds and wears fancy-looking dresses she has purchased at a flea market. My mother attempts to escape her imposed monotony as a housewife with artistic occupations, a déjà vu of a petit-bourgeois lifestyle. While Di Ut does not show off nor become an artist, she has found ways to better accept her lot as an exploited garment worker. Maybe Marx had a point when he stated that "religion is the opiate of the people." In a way Master Ching Hai's teaching can be seen as contributing to prevent the three women of my family from facing their economic reality and taking communal action that might lead to structural change.

For Master Ching Hai America is the country of opportunity where everyone can succeed equally regardless of their race, social class, or gender. This is a dream that has been fostered by many before her to control the American work force, and by many today to attack civil rights initiatives. Like them, Master Ching Hai emphasizes individual enhancement through hard work and discipline, favors nuclear-family values (in contrast to the traditional worshiping of ancestors), endorses the acquisition of private property, and ignores the various structural barriers imposed by societies. Master Ching Hai does indeed have much power. She has mastered the Supreme American Dream, never mind the fact that no matter how hard they work, or how disciplined or talented they might be, my aunts and mother will never become a "Master." In front of the altar, Di Chin has nonetheless placed bamboo branches standing in a pot filled with sand. On each of the branches, she has attached with safety pins the religious group's membership cards of her husband, two children, and herself. Although they stem from the same tree, they are now singled out as individuals, their respective pictures wrapped carefully inside plastic covers.

The brown Toyota is now far away, but as I write I see my aunt watching me type in a rearview mirror. My attention to Master Ching Hai began from the perspective of a niece sitting in the back seat of her aunt's car. My inquiry was initially guided by my concern about the involvement of my family in what may seem from the outside world as a sect, but also by the amazing transformation I saw my two aunts and mother undergo since their initiation with Master Ching Hai. I was also excited about the fact that this religious leader was a Vietnamese woman who had challenged the claim to Buddhahood. I decided to describe how Master Ching Hai had helped empower the three women in my family. As I listened, observed, and read more about the group, however, my enthusiasm was tarnished by the conservative elements I saw embedded in her teaching. I became increasingly troubled by what seemed to be a certain bias on the part of the Master regarding the issue of race. While I never wanted to question the reality of her divine power, I could not help but judge Master Ching Hai for what I considered her use of a privileged background to facilitate the reception of religious views. Being of a mixed heritage and having been raised in France, I was also highly aware of the fact that my analysis and inner gut feelings were for the most part not-so-Asian. I knew I was, and will always be, far from understanding the complexity that lay behind the three women's involvement in the group. How could they, I kept wondering, have so much fervor for a religious leader when they never seemed to have openly expressed any religious inclination in the past, other than performing rituals?

What became apparent to me in this process was that Master Ching Hai's success among my two aunts, my mother, and other Vietnamese women refugees and immigrants exemplified the void they experienced when resettling in their host country. In this context, the United States and France were no dream sites to be, but instead places where dreams were necessary in order to re-live.

BLINDSIDED
a zuihitsu

Kimiko Hahn

*t*hey *were always looking for some reason to kill us.*

My heart beats in my throat in vicarious terror. Have I ever felt such an extreme emotion?

The women's psychosomatic blindness could be something I identify with. Not that I willfully do not see, but also attempt to control the immediate.

The house was warm and quiet. I needed my mother's permission. I was standing right beside her and she couldn't hear me. "Are you listening?" I asked repeatedly.

The incidents of women turning what I will call *mad* in Asian American writings is very high: John Okada's *No-No Boy*, Milton Murayama's *All I Asking for Is My Body*, Maxine Hong Kingston's *Woman Warrior*, Hisaye Yamamoto's *17 Syllables*, Bharati Mukherjee's *Wife*, Wendy Law Yone's *The Coffin Tree*. Regardless of point of origin, date of arrival, age, etc. Not every one is first-generation. There is also Fae Ng's *Bone*, the sister's suicide propelling the narrative.

They were always looking for some reason to kill us.

My village had become a prison farm.

Of 170,000 Cambodian refugees living in the United States, half reside in Los Angeles. Local ophthalmologists noticed a high incidence of vision problems among women who arrived in the 1980s fleeing Pol Pot's Khmer Rouge. Approximately 150 have lost all or most of their sight, though there is nothing physically wrong with their eyes.

The Khmer Rouge took Chhean Im's brother and sister away. They killed her father and another brother *before her eyes.*

During the day they would take a person into a big meeting hall and beat them and beat them and we all sat in a circle and were made to watch.

I am surprised they speak to an interviewer. Or perhaps a relative told their story to the doctor who told the interviewer.

From his name I assume the writer is a white male, though he could be black or adopted or mixed. Like Winifred Eaton.

There is nothing wrong with their eyes. I am amazed the body can do this.

There was a draft. There was a draft from the crack in the window. I could see the curtain moving.

When the Vietnamese Army tried to liberate her village, the Khmer Rouge began massacring everybody in sight.

Perhaps there were men who lost their vision but it is unlikely any will ever be found since 80 percent of those killed were male.

The images consume me like a flame. My skin feels scorched, prickly, raw, and nauseous.

For the next two years the Khmer Rouge direct Lor Poy to dig children's graves.

On learning of my work he tells me when nuns interviewed Koreans in Hiroshima after the bomb, the survivors drew a blank. When inadvertently questioned in Japanese, one began to wail and recall the horrors. Others could also recall it in Japanese, but not in their mother-tongue.

The house was warm and too quiet. I couldn't avoid her any longer or wait for a better moment.

I was standing right beside her and she couldn't hear me. "Are you listening?" I asked repeatedly.

The body protects the spirit just as the spirit protects the body.

I was standing right beside him and he couldn't hear me. "Are you listening?" I asked repeatedly.

In prison camp the Khmer Rouge gave the family so little food her husband and daughter starved.

She watched her child starve. Watched her neighbor clubbed to death. Watched another disappear.

how the mind reacts to what the body perceives.

"Dissociation," a state of altered consciousness. If I am on a freeway of daydreaming and drive past the exit . . . If I . . .

The structure of *17 Syllables* reverses a chronological structure so we enter in the middle of the present, in the middle of an argument, so to speak. We do not discover the truth of the mother's past or of her first marriage until the last two pages where we find the mother, "damaged goods" as they used to say, married below her class to give her a future.

In 1919, Freud called his (physical) sacrifice "conversion disorder."

the student typed "sacriface"

What was reality for these women—how did the images affect their travel from country to country—

What of Thai children, male and female, daily prostituted, vagina and anus torn, bloody, swollen, feverish, bruised, lacerated with disease—who blame themselves for being sold. What of the men who permit themselves to wound these brown children? Are their faces still lustrous as my daughter's? Will they be allowed, even by themselves, to be human? We read about them as though this only happens to Thai children or only in Thailand.

conversion disorder

Are you listening?

To see socialism in its dialectical facets, to understand the extreme disfiguration by the Khmer Rouge who used anticolonialism as a subjective means to assert an order that destroys more than builds, to see the Vietnamese as a different force, I must also explore my attraction to the concept of a planned economy.

vision and revision

disassociation

To view phenomena in more than polarities. Blind but not blind.

The metaphor is not blindness. Not vision. Not hysteria. Then what? He knew a woman who brought a psychosomatic pregnancy to term. She gave birth. Then what? Psychosomatic nursing? Infanticide?

to term

The child prostitutes, rescued by a group of nuns, were telling their life stories for the first time. Mary, although sold by her parents, felt she and the other children must have been bad. It is not only in Thailand.

The virgins were naturally the most expensive. Their price diminished quickly. Considered less prone to AIDS by johns, in fact, their young bodies tear easily, the wounds an open invitation to disease.

dis / ease, dis / favor, dis / member, dis / possess, dis / rupt

Rape boys and girls. Sodomize neighbors. Club them. Skin them.

A vivisection of a text. A body of work.

I don't want to see this.

I don't want to see this.

I won't see it.

I do not see it.

I do not see.

The prisoners had nothing to eat except snakes, rats, worms, and the dead.

Close your eyes—*dream.*

At first a number of social workers thought the women were attempting to con the state for public assistance. But they behaved as the blind really do, relying on sound, air movement, a sense of *what a room is like.*

symptomatic

Ophthalmologists say their machines register sight, measure brain-wave activity picked up through sensors attached to the patient's head.

One of the Angka lifted an infant by the head and beat him to death against a tamarind tree.

Four of the Angka picked up a man (who had perhaps stolen a bit of rice, picked him up) by the arms and legs and threw him alive onto a big fire. After that (lesson) we all went back to work.

the need to engage with a text so personally the text becomes one's own, becomes part of one's own experience, one's own vision in fact

hysterical blindness

My heart beats in my throat as if attempting speech.

In 17 *Syllables* the three visit a family whose mother has gone mad. Of course the protagonist's father in a jealous rage takes away his wife's only pleasure, writing haiku. Apart from revealing her own history to her daughter she is completely isolated. She can speak but she will not speak.

In "The Legend of Miss Sasagawara" the woman rarely speaks to the others interned. When she finally speaks she is seen as "normal." Later in life, after the war, she is finally hospitalized and writes a long poem that refers to an authority figure who betrayed her with, ironically, his moral preoccupations. Her father, the Buddhist minister?

I was standing right beside her and she couldn't hear me. "Are you listening?" I asked repeatedly.

In one instance the terror brought on a person's immigration. In another, in glowing expectation, the immigrant arrives but experiences various forms of abuse from inside and outside the home. The mother's sister in *The Woman Warrior* immigrates to become reunited with her husband; in finding he has begun a new family she slowly goes crazy, which includes a paranoia—hearing figures who are coming for her.

garbage ghost, mailman ghost . . . as if turning the real less real? more, rendering them differently real, to marginalize the inhabitants of a more central existence?

It was too warm inside and too cold outside.

In cutting off sight how do their other senses remember?

Do the women remember more with their visual exile? as if replaying a film in a darkened theater? or do they not see *anything*?

If a person cannot see, what do they *see*? Is there an awareness of black? of gray?

When I shut my eyes I am exiled into my memories and imagination. I can only leave by admitting sight.

"See? See what I'm saying?"

The narrator read a poem written by Miss Sasagawara in the story's conclusion. We hear the poem is tantalizingly obscure, that the man's devotion to Buddha eclipses all human relations. In her version—

version, vision—

"Are you, are you—"

When the interview is complete she turns toward the draft whistling in beneath the door.

Note: Italicized quotes from "They Cried Until They Could Not See," by Patrick Cooke, *The New York Times Magazine*, June 23, 1991.

WARNING
(1980)

Mitsuye Yamada

*t*he voice of my father came to me
from a corner of his cell
(marked Dangerous Enemy Alien)

Do not sign your legal name
to anything not
on petitions for any cause
in the street
at meetings or rallies
not on receipts for orders,
special deliveries or C.O.D.s

I was my father's daughter
I had followed his advice assiduously
never left my thumbprints anywhere
never gave my stamp of approval
to anything
never cast my soulprint in cement
never raised my voice on billboards
and one day disappeared anyway
behind barbed wires.
They put up a sign on buildings
telephone poles and store fronts:
For all persons who never left a mark.

"My silences had not protected me."°

°Audre Lorde, MLA convention, Chicago, 1977

INHERITANCE

Brenda Kwon

*a*mong other things
I inherit her solitude; there are moments
when I, cutting
green beans into slivers, find
I have been chewing my tongue—
something I have seen her do
when alone. It is
the taste of loss and memory,
and I wonder which stories
she has yet to keep from me.
The picture I have is her face long before us; she
does not smile though
it's her eyes that will tell you
how she felt that day
after she pulled back her hair
put on her best blouse
the matching scarf, her fingers
knotting the ends. But for now she would stop,
her tongue at rest
in her mouth as she
anticipated the flash. You see,
she knew she was not alone.
There are words locked in
and beneath her tongue,
words I may never hear
nor understand. As I chew
my own tongue I want
it to taste to me
of words she has never said
secrets she has kept too well.
It isn't until I hear the sound
of my own breathing
that I understand
what she has given me.

PART 3

REFLECTION

*on the cusp
between
the old
and new*

VIRGINIA WONG'S WAY OF SEEING

Li Min Mo

i cut up a lot of old clothes into a thousand strips.
Scraps for a quilt start to take the shape of fantasy:
a feast of colors, abstract still-life
wild,
gardens like Impressionists' paintings.
Virginia looks at my handiwork and says,
"I love your original sunset, exotic plants,
the way you give new life to old memories."

I used to detest the arty types
who did things I didn't understand.
"An image is made of a single stroke or a thousand dots."
That kind of talk belonged to artists.
Being a housewife, part-time cashier at a supermarket,
my life is cluttered with the basics.
Since Lizzy and Julie took off to camp
the shelves in the fridge are getting empty.
It's the season for me to shape up at the
health club and time to stitch a quilt.

Lately I see things.
Maybe it's part of aging, or
because Virginia Wong has moved in
and paints on the porch every morning.
She winks at her canvas
as if there's something beyond,
the surface bleeding, blending,
shades of something bigger than life.
I guess she is exploring the abstract;
she screws her focus like a tiger stalking
in the dark, her pupils dilating,
drawing closer to the creature she's hunting,
in slow motion she springs forward,
shoots a pigment or two on the canvas.
And the image is awesome, mysterious.

THE BRILLIANCE OF DIAMONDS

Nora Okja Keller

*W*ith the birth of her only child, a daughter, my mother pulled jewels out of thin air, giving me a name that translates as "the Brilliance of Diamonds."

"I wanted to give you prosperity," she explained, "something that my family couldn't give to me."

My mother's family is dead, her parents from tuberculosis, her brothers from disownment. She renounced both the older and the younger brother when she "married" my American father. But they were the ones that broke into her room, shattering the bowls and cups their mother had given her and stealing the rice she had stored for the months that she would be too big with me to work at the American PX. They were the ones who wrote "dead" and "whore" in the dirt in front of her house.

"I thought a long time about your name," she told me. "A name can determine your life, who you will be. Each letter has a certain power, each person a special name, told in the stars. If you can find the secret of your name, you can unlock the universe."

In truth, though, I know my mother waited not because she was trying to decide on the best possible name, but because she couldn't get anyone to name me. In Korea, as she explained to me, the paternal grandfather is supposed to name his sons' babies. Since my mother didn't know the family of my absent father, and since her own father was dead, she had hoped a substitute grandfather, one of the *ajushis*, from the village would volunteer. No one did; naming, I suppose, is such a big responsibility.

She waited and hoped, however, long enough for several of the village gossips to start calling me Moo Myung: "Baby No Name." When my mother caught herself calling me that, she decided to read the stars and count letters herself, hoping to find—if not the right name—at least a name that wouldn't hurt me. Finally, she settled on Myung Ja, playing on the words for "name" and "sparking."

Perhaps it was because of that pun, a confusing word trick, or perhaps it was because I was cursed with that two-month namelessness, a rootlessness of body and soul, that we wandered through South Korea and finally crossed the Pacific Ocean. Whatever the reason, my name, unable to find a place for me, got me lost.

~~~~

When we first came to America, in search of my father, I was only four, but I was lost even then. My mother says that I stopped answering when she called for me, choosing instead to hide in the dirty laundry basket, under the dirty clothes of the family my mother kept house for.

~~~~

The lady was looking for smart, pretty Korean girls who knew how to speak English. "Sister," the woman said to my mother, "my sister-in-law in America is rich-rich now. Everyone who goes to America can be just like that!"

"Oh, really," my mother breathed, sitting forward, her back straight. She kept her eyes down, to show respect, but also to hide her eagerness. She watched her fingers stray to the edge of her dress and flirt with the rich tapestry of the couch, then willed them back into her lap.

"I can arrange for you to go there." The woman's voice was as soft, as insinuating and luxurious as the fabric and pattern of the couch. "And your baby, too, of course," she added. "Just think of what your girl can have if you work for my sister-in-law in America. My sister has her own business, a restaurant, a bar. She pulls in thousands, and in Hawai'i, no less."

"But Hawai'i is not America," my mother said.

"*Aigu*, Little Sister! Don't show everyone how uneducated you are! That's another thing about America; everyone is so smart!" When she spoke, the woman's face pulled into a scowl as, rolling the vowels from the back of her throat, she spat out each word. "You just cannot believe. It's like a miracle: everyone so so rich, everyone so so beautiful, everyone so so smart."

My mother wanted to go so badly she could feel it in her stomach like a hunger. "But, older sister," she said, "how can I go when I am none of those things?"

The woman squinted at my mother, lips pursed, and pretended to consider. "I will help you pass the interview. Can you say," she said, switching to English, "'You look nice man. You like buy drink?'"

~~~~

The woman's American sister-in-law sent her a paper-husband, a post-office worker who lived in downtown Honolulu and was in love with the sister-in-law. After eighteen months of visiting the Arirang's happy hours flirting with the sister-in-law who owned the bar, he had finally worked up enough courage to tell her, "I would do anything for you."

She had answered, "Marry my sister."

The man knew that my mother wasn't the owner's sister, but he came to get her anyway, because the owner had asked and because it was a free trip to Korea, his first time out of Hawai'i. He handed my mother a note from a bar owner. "Get married," it read, "and come in."

"After tonight," the man had said to my mother after they signed the papers, "you are American." After that night, with our new citizenship virtually guaranteed, we never saw him again.

~~~~~

During the time my mother worked for the American PX in Seoul, all she heard from everyone—including my father—was, "American Good, Best," so she was unprepared for the actual paradise America had to offer. When we got off the plane in Honolulu, my mother kept asking the bar owner, "This America? This America?" The wet wrap of heat, the smell of concrete and rain, and the smallness of the dilapidated apartments nestled between high-rise condominiums lining the streets reminded my mother of Korea during the war. Remembering the refugees from the North who lived in Seoul by hiding out in big wooden boxes, she said in English, "Look like *piramin*, look like broke house. No look like American!"

The sister-in-law, whom we called *Ajuma* out of respect, laughed. "Just wait," she said.

My mother waited, all the time looking, as *Ajuma*'s navy blue Cadillac silently cut through downtown, then knifed along the coastline highway where, on the right, my mother caught glimpses of ocean between palm trees, and, on the left, confronted the solid brown and green walls of mountain that stood out stark and clear against the white and blue of sky. The brightness hurt her eyes.

When the highway ended, we turned up a hill lined with a series of black iron fences and rock walls that encircled big houses and private swimming pools. More than anything else, it was those bright sapphire pools overlooking the dark ocean that started my mother humming. "Hmmm," she said. "Now this is a little bit American."

"Yes, here, Hawai'i Kai, is where all the best people live." *Ajuma* signaled and turned into a driveway, into a garage which opened, as if by magic, like a large mouth. "You can stay with me until you find an apartment of your own. That way you can watch my kids until your eight o'clock shift at the bar," she told my mother.

~~~~~

During the day my mother watched me and *Ajuma*'s two girls, whom I was taught to call sisters. They called me "dummy," telling my mother and me it meant "little cutie." When they played house, I was the pet, which I liked because I knew what was expected of me: barking and panting on all fours. "Dummy," they said to each other, "makes a good dog 'cause she can't talk right anyway." Once I tried to improvise, pretending to *shi-shi* on the floor. They rolled up a newspaper and hit me on the nose. The sisters liked that so much it became part of the script: "This bad puppy needs to be house-broken!"

I missed them when, after braiding their hair and packing their lunches, my mother drove them to school for the day. After dropping them off, my mother slept through the late mornings and early afternoons while I watched television. Whispering things like, "Please" and "thank you," and—more daringly—"Daddy," I pretended that Mr. Rogers was my father as I waited for the sisters to return home.

After their school and tennis lessons, having missed me all day, they would fly to pinch my arms and pull my hair. "Look!" Older Sister would say to Middle Sister. "She likes it! She doesn't even cry!" I learned to control pain, to look at it from outside of myself so that the sisters could admire my strength.

"Let me try!" Middle Sister reached for an arm. "Ugh, it feels weird," she said, as a chunk of skin folded and lodged underneath her fingernails. "I feel sick."

"Wow," Older Sister said, not unimpressed, as the three of us stood looking at the white hole in my arm, "dummy's tough." But when the blood started to ooze into the pinch-hole, she added, "If you tell on us, we'll beat you up and kick you out of our house!"

I slept with a butter knife under my pillow then, in case they jumped me while I slept, and became so tough that when visitors to the house knelt beside me to comment, "How sweet!" I spat in their faces and said, "I'll scratch your eyes out."

I never once told on the sisters, not only because I was afraid of them, but because they were my best friends. Though they weren't allowed to—because sweets were too expensive to give to nonfamily—they shared their after-school Ding-Dongs and Twinkies with me. Once we ate a whole box. Crouched in our bunk-bed cave, blankets from the top bunk hanging over the sides, we sucked the frosting out of the cylindrical cupcakes as they told me what they learned in school.

"Willy Kealoha said the F-word today. Miss Jenkins got so mad she jerked his arm and left a big Indian burn." Middle Sister held out her arm, twisting her elbow towards me. "All around her, like that. He was supposed to sit outside class until he was ready to come back and apologize, but all he kept saying was 'F-word, F-word, F-word.' The whole class heard, but Miss Jenkins made like she never."

"What's F-word mean?" I asked.

"F-word," said Older Sister, "means your daddy is going to die. F-word stands for . . . fuck." She whispered the word and then turned to hit Middle Sister, whose mouth had dropped open, on the arm. "I'm just explaining it, okay? I'm not really saying it."

Older Sister then mouthed what looked like the words, "Fuck you."

When Middle Sister and I sucked in our breaths, and Middle Sister started to yell, "I'm telling, I'm telling," Older Sister said, "I was only saying 'Vacuum,' you dopes." Middle Sister wasn't convinced. "Here," Older Sister said then, "have the rest of my Twinkies. I don't want them anyway."

As she watched us eat the last in the box, Older Sister added, "Besides, if I said it to Myung, it wouldn't matter anyway; she doesn't even have a father."

"I do, too," I yelled, ready to jump on her.

"Liar," Older Sister said.

"Liar," Middle Sister echoed.

"Yes, I do!" The Twinkie and Ding-Dongs made me feel sick.

"Where is he then?" asked Middle Sister, rolling her eyes at Older Sister who, not looking at her, scowled at me.

"I see him every day. . . ." I felt like I was going to throw up while the sisters began to sing, "Liar, liar, pants on fire—"

"Every day, on TV, he's famous." At least the lower bunk was Middle Sister's.

"On a telephone wire— Liar—"

Then, just before I threw up, I made the biggest mistake of my young life: "My dad," I said, "is Mr. Rogers!" For how much I had eaten, nothing really came out: mostly a frothy white mess of bubbles. But it stank.

"Gross!" The sisters screamed as they jumped out of our cave, pulling the blanket walls with them.

"Dumb-ass," yelled Older Sister. "Stupid dummy! Is that your name, huh? Dummy Rogers, huh? You're so dumb, you think TV is real. You think your name is Dummy Rogers."

"F-word, F-word, F-word," Middle Sister kept saying. "F-word, F-word, F-word." Then Older Sister asked, "Well, Dummy Rogers, do you know what a 'hapa bastard' is?"

~~~

It seems I spent most of elementary school trying on different names, popular names that the cheerleaders and May Day princesses had. In class, instead of copying down what was written on the blackboard, I'd write—in script—"Kelli," "Barbi," "Suzi," "Staci," making sure to dot each "i" with a heart. I'd pair those names with the last names of the cutest boys in class. I practiced for the time when I could transform—or at least mask—the abnormalities in myself.

Then in the summer before intermediate school, I met a boy who, though he wasn't the cutest boy in class, vaguely resembled Mr. Rogers. When I saw that his father looked even more like my role-model daddy, I decided that I had found the family I would marry into. My boyfriend belonged to a family, recently transplanted from Fort Pierce, Florida, that reminded me of the Brady Bunch, the Partridge Family, the type of family that I only pretended to belong to: the type of family that talked at mealtimes.

When I was invited to their house for dinner, his parents met me at the door, curious about the "new woman in their baby boy's life." "How nice! A Hawaiian girl," they said to me, and in whispers to each other: "Remember, Honey?"

Before me, my boyfriend had "made friends" with another Korean girl named Hyun Yi. "My baby likes Oriental girls," Tommy's mother smiled. "I try not to take it personally."

"Now, Mother," the father said. "The Oriental People are a fine people. Very respectful." He looked at me. "Isn't that right, Honey?"

I wasn't sure if he was calling me "Honey" as a form of endearment, or if he had me confused with his son's previous girlfriend. This was cleared up when his wife jabbed him and said, not quietly, "That's Monk Cha."

The rest of the evening, through the baked ham and gravied potatoes, through the mushroom soup, canned green beans, and Baco-bits casserole, through the apple pie with Cokes and Cool-Whip, my boyfriend's father continued to call me "Honey." Sometimes this was followed by a correction from his wife or an "excuse me," but for the most part it was as if no one noticed the mistake—not even my boyfriend. Each time I was called the wrong name, Tommy would look away, his face blank. I felt as numb as his face, unable to get up and announce, "My name is Myung Ja!"

I realized then that if I myself could not even say my name, that if when I whispered to myself, "My name is Myung Ja," my voice wavered, struggling in my throat as if with a lie, then my name was a lie. Myung Ja was not, could not be, my true name. My mother had made a mistake. I was not a diamond in America, just different.

After that visit with the parents of the boy I thought I would marry, I decided to find my real name, a name that matched the one he would give me, a name that would make me American.

~~~

"I tried my best," my mother said. "But, of course I didn't know anything about stars and numbers and letters. If I had money then, maybe I would have given it to a fortuneteller, a professional name finder." My mother shrugged, then smiled. "I can give you some money now, but . . ."

I wanted to tell her that I didn't blame her for the problems with my name, but because I did, I just said, "No, Mom, I think I have enough saved up myself."

She gave me the name and Kaimuki address of a "famous" Vietnamese numerologist, one that "all the stars go to." "Hundreds of people try to see her, that's how much in demand she is. Everyone lines up for her outside, for days, to speak with her. She charges five thousand dollars to find their true name. They pay because they know that, since they will make millions after they get the right name, what's five thousand now?"

"That's crazy!" I said. "We don't have that kind of money." I tried to calculate how long, how many years of birthday money it would take to afford a new name. "I won't go," I announced, but inside I was desperate, even more convinced of the pricelessness of a new name.

My mother patted my arm. "Don't worry," she said. "I already talked to her. Special price for me. And you. Fifty dollars. I told her we'll give her the rest when you make your fortune off it."

The house on Wilhelmina Rise was not packed with hundreds of people. In fact, as I opened the rusting wire gate to the weedy lot, it seemed no one—not even the fortuneteller—was there. I double-checked the faded numbers on the house, then walked through the yard, past a sun-bleached and molding three-foot plastic replica of the Virgin Mary and Christ Nativity scene, and up the front steps.

"Excuse me," I called through the screen door. "Hello? I have an appointment with the fortuneteller . . . my mother sent me."

When I thought I heard a "come in," I opened the door, slipped off my sandals, and stepped barefoot onto the straw-mat floor of her living room. After my eyes adjusted to the dim room, I saw Christ. He was everywhere. Huge black velvet posters of Jesus—his sad, teary eyes framed in a halo of long blond hair and beard—were thumbtacked onto the walls. In the spaces between the posters the fortuneteller had pasted various "Born Again" bumper stickers: "In God We Trust," "My Heart Belongs to Christ," "Honk If You Love Jesus."

She was on her hands and knees in the back of the room, wiping the mat floor with a dishrag. "Easier to clean than carpet," she muttered, then got up and shuffled into the kitchen. She was not what I expected, less . . . mystical. With her freckled scalp peeking through scanty grey hair, her fraying plaid shirt knotted over cotton drawstring pants, and her bumpy, stockinged feet thrust into rubber slippers, she just looked like anybody's old grandma-san.

The fortuneteller seated herself in a metal chair at one end of a two-person, fold-out card table and lit a stick of incense. "Keeps the flies away," she said, waving at the smoke pooling in front of her face. Behind her, next to the only window of the room, was a large gold-painted cross, beginning to peel, adorned with a particularly gruesome Christ. Gouged by the Crown of Thorns, his face dripped blood down onto his body. His chest, ripped open, revealed a blue and red heart. I tried not to look at it.

"First," she said, pushing a pad and pencil towards me, "write your name." When I did, she took the top paper, folded it into the palm of her hand, and said, "Now, tell me what you want."

I told her my story, beginning with before my birth, and explained why

I needed a new name. "I want to be an American now," I told her. "So please find me an American name."

The fortuneteller closed her eyes and, lifting the pencil, began to draw numbers on the writing pad. Seven, three, eight, nine, one, over and over again, some of the numbers overlapping and canceling the others out. My eyes, blurry with incense smoke, wandered up to the Jesus above the window. The heart began to beat each time I blinked. I imagined blood pulsating out of the body, dripping drop by drop like rubies down the kitchen sink.

After a few minutes, the fortuneteller put down the pencil and opened her hand. "That'll be fifty dollars," she said, as she handed me the paper on which I had written "Myung Ja."

"But!" I said, then swallowed. "I don't understand."

"Cash," she said. "No checks." She laid the paper flat on the table, smoothing the crease with the flat of her palm. "This name is your shining, your brightness, your heart and treasure. I am saving you a lot of money and trouble to let you buy it back from me . . . And tell you mama I said 'Hi.' Good woman, her." The old lady laughed, cackling like a chicken.

I frowned at her and swallowed again as, unable to stare her down, my eyes focused on the table top. "Old witch, old witch!" I thought to myself, over and over, like a mantra. As I continued my silent chant, willing myself not to blink, not to cry, a light from the window caught and reflected off the naming-paper she handed back to me. Its glare hurt my eyes, momentarily blinding me just like, it seemed to me then, the brilliance of diamonds.

CINEMAYA

Renee Tajima-Peña

i never went to film school. I'm always asked how and why I got into filmmaking and I never know how to respond. It simply happened, and it began happening as far back as when I was a little girl who thought that everyone in the world just had to be more interesting than I was. To be a Japanese girl in the homogeneous, Camelot-Pop-Insurgent-Disco America of the 1960s and '70s was to be nothing to no one in particular. I craved being an American, a *real* American—that alluring fraternity with all the glamor and perks of the insider. Along the way that hunger turned to anger, then curiosity. What does it really mean to be an American? Ironically, in my films I've always found the meaning in people who, on the surface, are the outsiders. The ordinary people, the "expendable" people. Among them Mrs. Lily Chin, Guitar John, Demetrio Rodriguez, Mike & Raf a.k.a. the Seoul Brothers, Pangku Yang and Shadow Love, all within whom I've encountered endless tales and extraordinary lives.

THE INVISIBLE GIRL

I always sit in awe at my husband's anecdotes from a childhood spent back in South Texas, just across the Rio Grande from Mexico. He remembers border days lived above the Cantina de la Florita, where his mother served beers and was twice taken away in a police car for some unknown infractions. Dreams and schemes hatched by young Galahads in their secret lair behind the old Alameda Theater, where *la carpa* troupes still came to perform.

As for me, I spent my first eight years living in a split-level tract house, anchored by a row of identical split-levels in a suburb outside of Chicago. I don't remember living so much as being an observer, a passive participant in the manufactured world around me. Nothing was old in our tract development—venerably named Mount Prospect, even though it was built astride the flattened prairies of Illinois. In spanking new Mount Prospect, there were no boarded-up aeries for secret societies of children at play. No magical woods or hidden caves. For castles, we made do with ping-pong tables draped with permanent-press sheets from Sears. Instead of real adventures, we lived vicariously through Big Hoss and Little Joe of *Bonanza*, Napoleon Solo and Illya Kuriyakan on *The Man From U.N.C.L.E.* I watched television constantly. It was company while Mom was at work, and surrogate to our own imaginations for spy games and heroic escapades.

I knew little of the trauma, or even romance of immigrant lives. I was third-generation Japanese American. My parents, as children of issei (first-generation) pioneers, had already weathered the trials of living between two cultures. They were raised with the ways of old Japan, the superstitions, and the legends of ancestors back home. By the time it got to me, most was lost in the translation. I didn't know from Nippon. There were no tales of a girlhood among ghosts, no long-lost brothers left behind during wartime, no midnight games of mahjong. Our evil spirits were real-life, all-American goblins like Richard Speck, infamous killer of six Chicago nurses. All siblings were accounted for, born and bred in the U.S.A., and my Presbyterian parents would not have looked kindly on mahjong or any other form of gambling.

Even my grandparents, Made in Japan as they were, seemed happy to leave the old country behind. My grandfather worked as a janitor until he was eighty, then spent the next two decades of life devoted to Roller Derby Demolition Derbies. He had a particular fondness for the women's teams. My grandmother remembered Japan only as a sad place where she was raised by an evil stepmother. Her real mother was banished from the village after she gave birth to my grandmother and her brother. In China, twins may be good fortune, but in Japan, a male child and female child born from the same womb was considered perverse, bad luck. At night, my great-grandmother use to sneak back to the village and stand below the window, to listen to the babies cry. When my grandmother was old enough, she and my Aunt Kawamoto dressed up in tennis clothes and snuck aboard an ocean liner bound for California. Years later, she was perfectly content that my mother abandoned Japanese traditions to raise us according to the teachings of Dr. Benjamin Spock.

Of course I had no interest in my grandmother back then, nor anything and anyone Made in Japan. For me, Japan during the 1960s was the home of poor relations, to whom we sent "care packages" of cast-off clothing and beef jerky every Christmas. It stood for nothing but shoddy goods, bad Godzilla v. Rodan movies, and the reason why I would never have the long legs and aquiline features of my classmates, not to mention my heroines Gidget and *That Girl*. I preferred to live in the reflected glory of televised America, even though that light never refracted on me or anything that even resembled me. While I was growing up, Asians simply did not exist on TV or anywhere in the public mind. Granted, there were fewer than than three million of us, only a speck on the U.S. census. And there were moments when we did surface. I remember one time—was it a floor wax commercial or an ad for Mr. Clean?—a lone, Asian actress appeared on screen, for less than a minute, and it created havoc in the living room. I spotted her first, but news traveled rapidly through the house. Mom left her roast in the kitchen. Dad ran in from the yard, and even Grandpa hobbled in behind his cane. "There's an Oriental on TV!"

An Asian sighting. You can't imagine what a thrill it was. Those were the days when you could drive across five states in America, and never catch a glimpse of another Asian face. And I had plenty of experience being the invisible girl on the road. Every summer my father would pack the six of us into the family sedan and head out for the American highway. Like millions of vacationers, we put the pedal to the metal down old Route 66 and in pursuit of Dinah Shore's beckoning call, "See the U.S.A. in your Chevrolet!" And we were invariably the only Asians in sight. I remember once in the backwoods of the Tennessee mountains we noticed a wizened, old Appalachian woman standing at a roadside grocery store. By her side, like an apparition, was a beautiful Japanese woman. Who was she? Where did she come from? My mother surmised that she must be a war bride, married to an American GI. All us kids were mesmerized, and we never forgot that vision, so bizarre and extraordinary on the road in America.

My parents were perfectly content to remain on the sidelines of the American scene. It was no wonder. My mother had grown up on Skid Row in downtown Los Angeles, home back in the 1930s to alcoholics and Japanese immigrants. Today, of course, it is home to alcoholics and Central American immigrants. My mother went to Japanese school there, spoke the language fluently, and wore a kimono for formal family photographs. But then the family spent World War II imprisoned in a Wyoming concentration camp for Japanese Americans. It didn't take much more for her to decide that being too Japanese wasn't a smart way to go in America. So when my mother had children of her own, she encouraged us to learn French and simply blend in.

Being invisible was something I hated. But I also hated being noticed, because it either meant an old codger pinching my cheek with a "what a little China doll!" line, or some kid blaming me for the Imperial Army's aerial attack on Pearl Harbor. I was basically a frustrated child, and it was apparent early on. As a toddler, I took to running out into the street and sitting myself down right smack in the middle of the white line on the road. When it was dark at night, I would cry that I couldn't see my hands, and therefore I no longer existed. Naturally my parents were mightily relieved years later when I decided not to become a doctor or a teacher, or someone responsible for the lives and well-being of others, and I became a filmmaker instead.

LOS ANGELES

Although I never went to film school, while an undergraduate at Harvard I did take a couple of production courses across town at M.I.T. But I never felt comfortable, again, being the only one. And then there was the time Ricky Leacock proclaimed of political filmmaking, "Dahling, it's passé." But at that time in the late 1970s, it was dazzlingly new to us Asian Americans. It was a first wave of Asian American independent cinema—an urgent, idealistic brand of filmmaking from collectives and media groups like Visual Communications in Los Angeles and Third World Newsreel in New York. I had come of age with the Asian American arts and political movements—fueled by the battle for ethnic studies, for social, economic, and cultural justice in our communities, and against the war in Vietnam.

It had all changed for me in 1966, when my family moved west. We left behind a homogenized Mount Prospect for Altadena, an integrated community in Los Angeles and home at one time or another to Sirhan Sirhan, David Lee Roth, and Rodney King. If my first filmmaking sensibilities had a source, it was here. Mainly, there was the anger. The social turmoil rocking America during the late sixties invariably swept through the schools. Even the children were mobilized. For me, the enemy of the people was embodied in Mrs. Counts, a blue-haired transplant from Nebraska and my sixth-grade teacher. Mrs. Counts was of the old school, of the days when both children and "Negroes" behaved. First, she had my best friend, Tracey, suspended for wearing her hair in an Afro. Then one day, I chose to write an oral report on the Japanese American concentration camps. There was little published at the time, so I based my research on interviews with my grandparents. As I delivered my report to the class, Mrs. Counts bellowed that the camps never existed, and that my grandparents had fabricated the entire episode. I discovered that the truth was dangerous.

By the age of fourteen, I had read *The Wretched of the Earth* and *The Autobiography of Malcolm X*. By sixteen, I had already led citywide student walkouts over dress codes, ethnic studies, affirmative action for teachers. I became a cultural nationalist of sorts. I cut neck and armholes in big bags of Asahi Premium Rice to wear over my jeans, as was the style among young Asian American rebels of the day. I took a stab at playing the Japanese koto, electrified of course, although no one was going to tear me away from R&B and the Doors. I discovered Yellow Power.

My exurban high school was, rather absurdly, regarded as an "inner-city school" for the mere fact that half the students were minorities. It was my good fortune, however, because it got me into a creative world I had never known before. I was assigned a still camera, a tape recorder, and an unlimited stock of film to document social problems in Los Angeles, which I then edited into multiscreen slide shows. I did shows on rape, children's poverty, race—any subject I felt passionately about.

I was still on the road, but this time traveling through Los Angeles' endless miles and neighborhoods. Invariably, I was drawn to Little Tokyo, Chinatown, Manilatown, anywhere where Asians ruled the streets. I became captivated by the faces of the old people, the issei, the *Manong*, the pioneers with paper names who came here to seek *gam saan*, the Gold Mountain. And the student activists who were in constant motion, galvanized to protect our communities from urban renewal—which in those days meant a slow death by corporate cleansing. Ironically, at the time, Asian American neighborhoods were in decline. The old people were dying out, their children were off to the suburbs, and there was no one to take their place. I thought I was documenting the last remnants of an era. I had no idea what was to come.

THE YELLOW MASSES

When I graduated from college in 1980 and set off to New York to become a filmmaker, the impending transformation of Asian America was only beginning to occur. Looking back, I realize that we were approaching an end of an era. At the time, Asian Americans were still considered a tiny, "invisible" minority, and fairly simple to define as a group. We were predominantly Chinese, Filipino, Indian, and Japanese, a majority of whom were American-born and English speaking. We shared a common history of labor immigration, exclusionary immigration laws, and racial discrimination. And this history was the crux of our political identity—as Asian Americans and as an aggrieved racial minority. At a time when the struggle for equality was focused on legal protections, the construction of this common identity was the political currency upon which gains in equality were achieved.

I first worked in Chinatown, as the first paid staff person for Asian Cine-Vision, the organizer of the annual Asian American International Film Festival. I found myself in a community of media-activist-filmmakers. In other words, as filmmakers we spent half of our time as activists fighting against Charlie Chan revivals and other assorted racist portrayals from Hollywood. The other half of the time was spent making up for lost time by documenting Asian American reality—something virtually excluded from the mainstream media and education.

But making films by and about Asian Americans struck me as problematic. How do you portray a marginal culture, with all its particularities and minutiae, to an untutored audience? How do you disrupt the center and realign the notion of universality? The theoretical underpinnings of such matters as "the other" and the like have been discussed ad infinitum. But for filmmakers, especially during the earlier days of Asian American cinema, it has very concrete repercussions. Let's say your drama centered on the Japanese American concentration camps, Filipino and Chinese bachelor societies of California, war brides, picture brides and the like. All the details and factual implications had to be carefully explained because the audience simply had no clue. This could put a mighty crimp into your storytelling style.

I didn't think you could follow the same rules as conventional filmmaking. I didn't really know those rules anyway, having had little in the way of a film education. It was all summed up for me when one film editor declared to me, "You have to cut on a move!" and another proclaimed, "You must never, never cut on a move!" What did I know? I did know television. I knew the songs in my head—the ones that connected me to certain times of my life, specific men or boys, roads or highways, even emotions. I knew I liked plays and stories. Fiction, basically, with memorable characters. In my high school, we were rarely assigned whole books to read—just chapters from a big textbook. But somehow, on TV I would imagine, I discovered Tennessee Williams, Lillian Hellman, southern authors of the decadent sort. I read their collected works back to cover.

And so as a documentary filmmaker, these influences seemed a natural way to get at my ever-present question, what does it mean to be an American? My first real directing effort, *Who Killed Vincent Chin?* (1988), investigates what keeps us apart, maneuvering the divided perceptions over race surrounding the murder of a Chinese American during the height of the auto recession in Detroit. In making the film, I began to explore two approaches to the documentary. Rather than look to other documentaries for inspiration, I wanted to find a literary voice for nonfiction filmmaking. Although *Who Killed Vincent Chin?* has no overt narration, I based its dramatic structure and fractured storytelling approach on *Rashomon*, the short story and film. By the same token, the structure, tone, and narrative for *The Best Hotel on Skid Row* (1990) was inspired by the short stories of Charles Bukowski and Raymond Carver (Bukowski is the film's narrator.)

Secondly, I have tried to locate the eclectic points of cultural intersection that Americans share, regardless of ethnicity. For Vincent Chin and his killer, Rob Ebens, it reverberates in Motown and Dinah Shore's exhortations to "See the U.S.A. in your Chevrolet"—the same imagery of America's go-go years I remember as a child, which is used impressionistically throughout the documentary. Rather than direct illustration, these musical and media themes emerge organically in the film as metaphors for memories and emotion. This kind of "cultural eclecticism"—which Coco Fusco has observed in her critique of Britain's black film workshops—is in contrast to the "roots" journeys of the 1970s which promoted racial validation by recapturing homeland traditions.

I have just completed a documentary road trip, which I call *My America . . . or, Honk If You Love Buddha*, coproduced with Quynh Thai. Again, I've looked for literary approaches in Jack Kerouac's *On the Road* and Carlos Bulosan's *America Is in the Heart*, stories that combine a certain all-American exuberance with the alienation of an outsider. In making the film I've been revisiting my past, those early days of being an Invisible Girl in America. And I've been contemplating our collective future as we move toward the twenty-first century. The United States is already reeling from the biggest single wave in immigration in its history, primarily from Asia and Latin America. As a result, the whole country is going through an identity crisis, which shows no signs of abating.

But by the time I set out to film *Fortune Cookies*, Asian America had undergone a tremendous upheaval. Between 1970 and 1990 alone, our population quadrupled in size—and it is expected to reach a staggering twenty million by the year 2020. We are now predominantly foreign-born, representing dozens of different nationalities. New immigrants speak countless dialects and represent every class stratum, from impoverished refugees to multimillionaires.

These huge demographic changes, apparent everywhere on the road, have challenged our identity as Asian Americans. Given our diversity in class, gender, and nationality, is the umbrella term "Asian American" still relevant? For example, what sense of allegiance would a Hmong refugee like Pang-ku Yang feel toward a suburban, third-generation Chinese American debutante, an eighth-generation Filipina from New Orleans, or a pair of Korean American rappers? And how will new immigrant groups approach traditional civil rights alliances with African Americans and Latinos that were forged during a previous generation of Asian American activism? And more significantly, it is anticipated that Asia will own the next century. A jarring thought: very soon, being Asian American will matter. When I was growing up, identity was always framed in terms of assimilation, "How do people become American?" Today the question is more aptly, "How has America become its people?"

THE PRESENCE OF LITE SPAM

Carolyn Lei-lanilau

*t*he Presence of Lite Spam—lingering in my psyche for a long time but oozing out after the (first) Rodney King verdict.

Anyone who is a darky—that is "who lives inside light or dark colored skin," poor or both, has eaten the forerunner of *paté*, spam. I wonder how the buggah's name "spam" was born? "Ham" in the "spa"? "Spit" plus "ham"? "the Sp(irit) in the present tense of the verb 'to be,'" communing in "am"? Or was it just military cordon bleu cuisine?

With the advent of yuppies in Hawai'i, a competition was devised among local wannabe yuppies to contest in a spam diversity competition. Spam paté, spam *musobi* (a kind of *sushi*) and delicious rewarding fresh from the can with jelly and cold white lard probably horse meat and fly-swappings in the spam staring *and* yuckking-it-up-at-you-in-the-face Third World Spam hands down authentic turn the silver key attached to the can spam incarnate gospel finally becomes legitimate. The poet sculptor painter activist gardener husband father cook visionnaire jokester Imaikalani Kalahele warned me about his now famous spam stew. Cringing, I begged, "What the hell do you put in it?" "A lot of potatoes, man!" he smacked.

Those "damn spam" sushi/musobis are enthusiastically bought and sold at every honorable *sushi* stand at home in Caliponi where everybody, everybody is cholesterol-conscious, at every Hawaiian event, there are the food booths with, of course, spam. In 1992, Lite Spam appears first in paper litcrature: the first art to be eliminated—becomes the prize introductory medium to premier Lite Spam followed by discretionary late night TV ads. What can this mean to a Naive Native? Aye! what's happening to us now? This is an example of deep counterculture adverse manipulation assimilation buffet à la carte in our butts. This lite spam is the new tool for exchange brokerage—the new nails. After a flash of *ha* and *'olelo* word power, I race to the telephone and dial 808. Know what that is? The area code to Hawai'i, man. In trouble, dial 808. On the coconut wireless, I shout the scandal to my chiefs of culture.

We are burned up, mostly we suffer from a kind of ancient pain: (Yea, Haunani: Tita—One. The Brilliant Screamer who rattled our McInerny three-piece vested brains and Hawai'i Visitors Bureau Hawaiian Telephone operator voices. That Ph.D. said that Something was wrong.—if you dunno who She is, better find out!)

Da tightshoe Madison Avenue execs (all kine color) who sell our land, our weather and get on the plane to *lu'au* in our backyard ain't factoring in the brahhss and sisstahs who put our big feet inside-out college departing with the *palapala*—before and after Civil Rights. No matter, mainstream-kind-scared American—Japan too—no gettum darkies: *akamai*—hip to double and triple talk hardcopy assessment deadline net worth. Some of us are white, some of us be village green. We have learned from Chinese to conquer people by marriage. Give you the best singing and sex in your no mo fun in lives. Aye Progressives, because we only in our developmental stages of processing bureaucratic white agenda and underneath it all, somewhere, yes sir, yess ma'am, we not logic by your instruments of measurement.

Some white folks, as much as we love you and you may have children by us: we didn't expect you and intelligent converted colored—yellow, red brown, sage, indigo, Florida Hawaiian folks would not know that we no get the verbs "to be" or "to have" in our wishes. Means, we no like compete an cut throat for success. *'a'ole*, NO.

Who asked Captain Cook come Hawai'i and insult us into Victorian habits and uniforms? You know what follows? Syphilis, false eyelashes, shoes, peanut butter and jelly sandwich, Miss Hawaii contest, Ala Moana Shopping Center. The otta day my fren Ivan the psychiatrist went said in pidgin rhythms, "Man, I have been having *angst*." Poorting, needed to say it in Nazi talk what he felt as a star trekking *kanaka*. (The greatest is when I was home and had to report a lost item to who? my favorite, the Honolulu Police.) When the Hertzgirl said that, "All security was involved in something and would be tied up for an hour."

I said, "What? Somebody was murdered?" The joke did not go over: we all knew the cops were eating dinner and did not want to bother with some tourist who lost something. Later on, at my mother's I call the cops and up drives this cute little meter maid cart and in it is a disarming local boy in a cop's costume. When he walks up to the house, I invite him in and he begins to unlace his shoes! Soo cute! (At that moment, I knew someday, I would move home just so that as an "old fut," I could push anyone around. Instead, I offer that he interviews me in the kitchen where he can enter through the back door and therefore leave his shoes on.) But as far as *kanaka maoli* and our lost kings and queens, before the missionaries and then Mackindly Mckinley screwed us, eh? Thee United States government—man, *haole*: how did Christians learn from their god to be so *makona*—so mean. How come *haole* love to hear our music and love to watch us *hula* but never let us—"forbid" was the word; how come *kanaka* were forbidden to *'olelo o Hawai'i*—speak Hawaiian. No wonder we real *da kine* and like beef or cry all da time—try-ing to reach our metaphors, man. When we *ali'i, we had ahupua'a*, system. Oh, it was *some system* and Ka'ahuamanu did her share to create even more complexity to it, but bottom line, it was Hawaiian. We had slaves and human sacrifice: it was not humanistic or maybe not even democratic but it was okay. And, along comes the whitebutts to embarrass our people to wear corsets and girdles around our throats. Exercise and Diets! Those English and those damn wigs? And while I'm *nuha—what is it with people who need to conquer people?* Talk about an inferiority complex! Must be something wrong. Whoa, now, after convincing us that our beloved and adopted spam not good for us, what is next?

Words: when I was born, my father—disappointed that I wasn't a boy—disguised my name to link with Charlemagne. My Hawaiian name is so common that I never used it before my friend Leialoha made it sound so pretty and sweet. All my life I have had impossible too much heaven in my body for this earth. Maybe because my Chinese and Hawaiian names both have heaven in them. Best thing that I have learned in life is to make a good life here and not worry about heaven. For a while, I changed my Hawaiian name to "Leilo'i" meaning "flowers in the mud terrace." I kept the "*lei*" part because it was half the name that my daddy gave me. And I *hanai*, adopted the "*lo'i*" part because that is where *taro*, our staple food, flourishes. That is where the *'oha*, the old root and the *kalo*, the first *taro* growing from the planted stalks and the *keiki*, the new shoots thrive. In the *lo'i*, the *'ohana*, the entire family of water, insects, mud, wind, salt air; the fish that wander in by accident; the hands that come to gather and plant *taro* within the *'aina*: which we are, belong: meaning. We are meaning. We cry, fight, and love each other. More is nevah enough passion. Sometimes we're like the birds and sometimes we are Pele. We like to go barefeet because in Hawai'i even dirt tastes good. Our earth is *Papa*; our mother, sweet. Our water is sweet and soft. In a way, we are kind of like babies. Maybe that is the shadow side of us as our skin wrinkles slowly—now the cosmetics industry doing test on us wondering how *kupuna* no mo wrinkles. We have a here and now kind of nature and that, in comparison to NYSE or NASDAQ, just doesn't cut it. If you want to come see and have fun, *hele mai*. Come look at us. See if you can find the Indians in the puzzle. See if you can tell we are standing in line behind and before you at the Safeway in your hometown. We will not appear in costume but just let your heart leak a little sweetness or laughter and we will balloon our *kolohe* bodies. If you go to the source of red dirt however, please, *kokua*. Ask first, and then no steal our bones and put your name on top of *the name* of our most loved *kupuna*. No make shame.

It has been long years to figure out how and who and what race and colors go good with my skin and ears. And then you have to throw it to the wind like a fisherman throwing the net out to sea. To catch crab, turtles, shoes, a husband, my kids, my bigbest family in the world or nothing. Maybe tears, maybe laughs.

And then, after I wrote testimony for *Ho'okolokolonui*, I changed my name back to
Lei-lani and then Lei-lanilau. And then, I made another list of windows to look out of or into.
THE LIST (for today)
The Slop Can Man
The Marriage Proposal in Hawaiian
Beatrice's Hernia
My Kona Hat
Manapua Man on Bicycle

'AUMAKUA: AN EXAMPLE OF HAWAIIAN THOUGHT PROCESSES

Lately (in the September/October 1992 issue of *Poet & Writers*) "some people" who want to be known as Hawaiian, have been leaking *'olelo* here and there like farts.

The latest in-concept among non-Us, has been the naive usage of the term *'aumakua*. For anyone who seems to imagine "doing Hawaiian" as the new frontier to conquer in translation: warning, *Beware*.
Those of us who are just peeking out of closets to sniff the air cautiously proceed with blessing from our *kupuna*, our *kumu* or our *'aumakua*. Unless you are truly skillful, dedicated, and gifted, no *kupuna* no *kumu*—the master teachers or caretakers of our culture would not accept a dilettante as an apprentice.
In the old way, you were *selected*. Like Kawena Pukui who was *hanai*. Every step of the way, Tested. Pukui was trained, tested. Watched and blessed, tested to be the carrier, voice, the vessel, song of our culture. You weren't chosen because of your family or you got a grant or because you could imitate *haole* real good; or because you look pretty good or because somebody could pay to be blessed. *'A'ole*, no. Not any old body was chosen. It was not "equitable." Only the best. With good ear power connected to the instincts and with a tongue that rivaled water, birds, fire, wind.

For a while things were completely outa hand in Hawai'i—getting like dat again—when everybody flying in wanted a piece of title so after being so nice and waiting for the *malahini* to adjust and being so *ho'omanwanui*, so patient, finally, Hawaiians stepped in: *'a'ole*, now you have to be certificated to be particular *kumu* or *kupuna*.
Still, only one Larry Kimura and one *Morning Dew*. Only one Pukui; only one Leialoha Apo Perkins. One Eric Enos. One David Malo.
Nonetheless, for those too impatient to bribe their way into Hawaiian

insiders; too disinterested to be possibly rejected, a way to *hanai* (adopt) oneself into the inner sanctum was to create one's own *'ohana 'aumakua*. The problem is that these very folks had no clue as to how fragile and volatile and mostly impractical this gesture was. Most adventurers of this type fail to know the concept of *'ohana 'aumakua*, and because in Hawai'i we refer to it simply as *'aumakua*, nouveau voyeur-participants casually refer to "my *'aumakua*" like it is their pet rock. What they don't realize is that one's *'aumakua* has the right to discipline you. Yell at you while you stay in front of the computer and squeeze the "badness" out of you to *Ho'opopono*—Get on the right path! I heard about some *haole* guys who had signs of menopause—nightsweats, inside-out vagina, breasts that ballooned and exploded just as they were delivering papers at the University of Hawai'i! They *delivered* those papers in pidgin! And then, you heard about the Japan American literati whose fingernails won't stop growing like conveyor belts?

Those of us who grew up with underground *'aumakua* know and expect— hope that our *'aumakua will* guide us. Cannot help (it), they are our ancestors—the combined force of rocks, geckos, sharks, owls—all our ancestors, which is why it is called *'ohana 'aumakua*. *Remember* when I mentioned my Hawaiian *tutu*? I expect my *tutu* to straighten me up by me having dreams; or maybe, I'll cry and be moody when it's not simply a matter of PMS. Sometimes, I cannot go somewhere or see certain people because of how the clouds appear or maybe, it could be a matter of the lack or presence of wind. *Remember* when I mentioned my cousin Robert Wilcox on page 3 or 4—the one that locals refer to as the "Maui Wilcoxes— the poor Wilcoxes. The one that went start the rebellion against annexation." What about my father and my sister? These are my *'aumakua*. No stuffed animal. My father scared the English language outa me and excited the dullness when I planned to water the backyard one day *while I was just going down the stairs* behind the outside deck.
You know what! before flying to a stupid nearby plum tree,
a fluff of wind
width of dirt,
an owl
my brown and white and grey feathers daddy was like making my deck *his hale* on the railing (well, to think like a *kanaka*, I guess it is his too).
Where were the neighbors' kids to show the owl?
Where were my artist and straight friends in the neighborhood?
I called my husband at Walnut Creek. He did not believe me. Then, he zipped home and he still demanded that it was not true. He shook his head, businessman as he is, refused to believe that an owl,

my father was introducing himself to the both of us in the most delicate intimacy.

Sacred and soft.
Wondrous and revealing a side unknown to anyone else: finally safe to be Hawaiian. Sweet and cool under the redwood branches.
My daddy, my daddy!
Anybody who is linked to their *'aumakua* could tell it was my father.
If you saw him, you would say "Aye Jackie Lau, *pe hea 'oe*? Howzit?"
Kanaka maoli—Hawaiians can tell by the way I tell this story (beyond merely the page) the intelligence of their antennae; ears sculpted to determine circumstance just by the sound of *ha*—that breath of life and how it is sounding at the moment. *Ha* and *'olelo*, the two most important clues on earth. A Hawaiian; that is, a practicing twenty-first centurion is not showing off the outward signs of *being Hawaiian*. Hattie could be captured with a net and skewered off to the Smithsonian. A true Hawaiian does not behave like those HVB hotel hula dancers. Like that nut Imai too. Hawaiians—the classy ones never show off and are always nice—like that prince Sonny Palabrica. Even when they're bad—they never swear because we have so much *kaona*—metaphoric ways of expressing the appropriate indirect meaning from our litany of proverbs. —Like that Japan American fake literati I mentioned earlier he is *Haumanumanu ka ipu 'ino 'ino*:
"A misshapen gourd makes an ugly container."
Instead of calling a human a "fuckup" or "asshole" how about this poetry?
As for me, my *'ohana* refer to me as "the sugar cane that makes the mouth raw when chewed." Home.

What was the logic behind this huge—phantom—owl in our yard?! And it stayed until my younger daughter came home from school. That owl hung around for hours and I was epileptic/tortured and joyous at the same time. Answer: This is a very common example of Hawaiian style *ha'ina 'ia mai ana ka puana*, explaining *'aumakua*: I "have to tell the story like it is." In the past, when I had other experiences and most of my life I was told I was crazy and believed I was insane. No, it was just my *'aumakua*—good thing I found out!
When I was a kid, so much *pilikia*, I had to walk over fire all the time.
It all began when I was a baby because my mother used to hang my diapers out while the funeral procession drove by our house.
When my mother hung the diapers at different hours and finished three days of chanting and carrying me over fire, my belly button stopped bleeding.
Later, I had to do it by myself while my mother and aunty chanted.

Oh I was scared, felt I was being punished because I was stupid.
It was kinda sexual too; like Pele teasing me.
When I had my own kids and they got sick, we just sat by the fire me
watching the comics burn to ash with the window open so the bad spirit
could fly out and their good one could step in at night before I put them to
bed if they needed the treatment.

They never had to walk over fire. That's the difference.
It's going to be longer and harder for them to be part of the tradition.
Everything is so/too rational.
But maybe not, they can separate their ethnic and psychic lives from their
public lives:
they know how to hide the psychic stuff in ways I don't know. I think the
technique is called "deflecting."
And I couldn't go into the ocean because *they* said that the *shark 'aumakua*
dreamed for me. So I don't know how to swim. You can imagine what
failure I feel like as a common Hawaiian. Little in common except our
beloved *'olelo*. When we hear our *'olelo* we cry and cry and cry. It's our best
friend, our therapy which binds us to nature, our mother and father. Can
you imagine, those damn *haole* missionaries! *illegally outlawing* our
beloved words! We sing and dance our *'olelo* of magic. Make you just want
to make love day and night. *Haole* used to only love to hear us sing the
songs night and day. But we have proverbs to work by and it's on the hard
drive. And we got girl groups that can really make you cry. Change yourself
silly. Ipo can get people to tattoo themselves in the old style of geometric
patterns with a bamboo! *Auwe!* Watch out for Ipo's eyebrow that wiggles
like ships when she convinces you about whatever Ipo wants.

And before I forget, I gotta mention that there are all kinds and shapes of
'aumakua. For instance, if it is impossible to be in a relationship with
anyone, maybe, it's because you already mated with your *'aumakua*. You
could even be married but have no interest with your partner. Probably you
and your *'aumakua* have something happening. This happened to me! I
was married. Got divorced. Had boyfriends galore. No, I only was
interested in things that were happening in the tenth century. William
Blake was my modern interest. So everybody I liked had to be an old soul
and I am not attracted to fuds. That was half my life. Enter my husband
from an ancient city after years of therapy climaxing with my near suicide.
And then the words from Sophie, a nun who taught me how to fold
laundry. She said, "Say good-bye to your father and your sister. Tell your
father you love him and to stop bothering you. Go to his grave and end it."
When I went to his grave, my mother talked to him out loud (I always
"thought" to him) and when I was leaving I turned and from my body,

unplanned, it was as though someone else said, "*A hui hou*," See you later. It was probably my entire *'aumakua* wishing me *aloha* and hello and protection. And I was so happy, loved, so certain that unless I'm writing a proposal where everybody's so uptight about the format and presentation, the grammar, vocabulary, and diaphragm of Good English, I will continue to live in the vigor of my mother's hometown in Kohala (with my *'aumakua*) guided by this *'olelo no'eau*

> He pa'a ko kea no Kohala, e
> kole ai ka waha ke 'ai.

"A resistant white sugar cane of Kohala which can make the mouth raw when chewed."
Imua!

FROM LATIN TO LATINO; FROM *NOPALES* TO *PANINI*

In between writing nonpaying articles; reading nearly as much Hawaiian history as I did Chinese history (and at my age starting all over again is like having sextuplets); in between begging for justice and hanging with my Oaktown homies (*imua* Oaktown!), I have to get this *kiawe*/mesquite (you noticed? I only italicized the Hawaiian part of the slashed concept because "mesquite"
is probably really "mosquito" or
"mescalito"; "mescara" or "mexicana" but "mesquite"?
Messs-keet—I hear shooting, I feel that horizontal anal verging on Southwest minimalism which hardly *sounds* ethnic.
Mesquite/esthete: no humidity, no loose muscles in my mouth.

> No cushion between my ankles and feet.
> No water under my eyebrows.
> No dirt in my pores.
> *'Aina* says, "Can not be our *'olelo*." But maybe before it was

BMW-ized   by the yups, maybe it is deep down darkness and therefore,
colored.

(as I was beginning about breaktime) . . . I have to set the relatives straight on this tradition of macadamian nuts: round cylinder cans which remind me of the cannery, clusters, chocolate, cream pie mess. *Please don't send any more macadamian nuts home to, with, or for me!*
Everytime. Everyvisit. Everybody—there is *Somebody* who bought some *on special*. Wrapped in thick cardboard, in the mail or suitcases along with guava or passion fruit juice, nonstop flights of macadamian nuts arriving and stored in the pantry.
"Oh, no, more of those 'gawddamn' nuts" the Little-Getting-Big daughter

sez. The other daughter just bats her eyelashes in philosophic acceptance of the larger system, the uninterrupted order of family ritual. On the other hand, if you were a family member AND *didn't* (after all these lifetimes) send, give, plague us with those nutty bombs
I wouldn't be normal.
I'd be doubting my worth and disappointedly hurt.
I never eat those things.
"Your neighbors will love it!" says my mother the Red Hen.
"Give some to the lady that drives Ana to school."
You never know when you have to shove a box or can in someone's face while smiling and mention that
"These just arrived from Hawai'i. Enjoy."
I used to like the unsalted kind so I could make that killer macadamian nut fatso pimples and so so flaky crust pie. Now, I don't dare become excited about the idea. But I can hardly wait to go home and eat one! Uuuuhh . . .
As a matter of fact, I'll admit that after complaining and lecturing about these nuts to my mother's face *and* informing her that I was going to write about it, she says
"They're on sale at Longs for $2.99."
I said, "Let's go."

But *kiawe* is something I can smell and want to burn in my fireplace— why not???
It smells so *ono*. Here on mainland, you got that potpourri crap sold everywhere from Payless to boutiques for every occasion in every place. I like burn some in my fireplace on a cold day or rainy night—I'm goin be the *pua'a*, the sacrificial *lu'au* pig.
You can eat me if I am cooked.
I will probably taste yummy. I have been enjoyed by most people most of my life, why wouldn't I taste delicious cooked?
I don't have to barbeque *something* just so that I can smell a combination of Hanauma Bay and fantasize one oversized pig, daddy ripping the crunchy greasy skin off for me. Some people burn incense; I like burning chunks of *kiawe*. Maybe, somedays I'll just burn some *kiawe* for the flavor in the air. When you grow up in the islands, you are really horny for smells all the time because everywhere, there is the salt air and maybe your aunty is drying some salted fish or meat in the backyard. You also got those flowers making you allergic to "purified air." I mean, your dreams are interfered with that ginger outside squeezing itself between your nostrils and your neurons. All my dreams have been forever altered because of that early childhood socializing with the plants and animals. And everywhere you go, *plumeria*.

And my family is so arrogant: we no mo *kala*, but we get bambula-size *pikake*. Everybody comes to beg or steal our *pikake*. Some people get big-size diamonds; our *pikake* big like potatoes.

When my mother was in labor with me and she had me by C-section in the middle of a tidalwave the day before April Fool's.
My daddy went hatchet the biggest *pikake* that he and my uncles could load into the truck. Then they went drive the truck to the hospital that had no anesthesia that day.
and daddy held ma's hand while the doctor cut with that *pikake* drowning out everybody's *pilikia*.
That's how I came into Kapiolani Hospital. That's why I gotta have smells but mesquite, non; *kiawe, si, si*

DEFINING GENEALOGIES: FEMINIST REFLECTIONS ON BEING SOUTH ASIAN IN NORTH AMERICA

Chandra Talpade Mohanty

*M*y local newspaper tells me that worldwide migration is at an all-time high in the early 1990s. Folks are moving from rural to urban areas in all parts of the Third World and from Asia, Africa, the Caribbean, and Latin America to Europe, North America, and selected countries in the Middle East. Apparently two percent of the world's population no longer lives in the country in which they were born. Of course, the newspaper story primarily identifies the problems (for Europe and the United States) associated with these transnational migration trends. One such problem is taking jobs away from citizens. I am reminded of a placard carried by black and Third World people at an antiracism rally in London: We Are Here Because You Were There. My location in the U.S.A., then, is symptomatic of large numbers of migrants, nomads, immigrants, workers across the globe for whom notions of home, identity, geography, and history are infinitely complicated in the late twentieth century. Questions of nationality, and of belonging (witness the situation of South Asians in Africa) are constitutive of the Indian Diaspora. This essay is a personal, anecdotal meditation on the politics of gender and race in the construction of South Asian identity in North America.

On a TWA flight on my way back to the U.S. from a conference in the Netherlands, the professional white man sitting next to me asks: (a) which school do I go to? and (b) when do I plan to go home?—all in the same breath. I put on my most professorial demeanor (somewhat hard in crumpled blue jeans and cotton t-shirt—this uniform only works for white male professors, who of course could command authority even in swimwear!) and inform him that I teach at a small liberal arts college in upstate New York, and that I have lived in the U.S. for fifteen years. At this point, my work is in the U.S., not in India. This is no longer entirely true. My work is also with feminists and grass-roots activists in India, but he doesn't need to know this. Being mistaken for a graduate student seems endemic to my existence in this country. Few Third World women are granted professional (i.e., adult) and/or permanent (one is always a student!) status in the U.S., even if we exhibit clear characteristics of adulthood like gray hair and facial lines. He ventures a further question: what do you teach? On hearing Women's Studies he becomes quiet and we spend the next eight hours in polite silence. He has decided that I do not fit into any of his categories, but what can you expect from a Feminist (an Asian one!) anyway? I feel vindicated and a little superior—even though I know he doesn't really feel put in his place. Why should he? He has a number of advantages in this situation: white skin, maleness, and citizenship privileges. From his enthusiasm about expensive ethnic food in Amsterdam, and his J. Crew clothes, I figured class difference (economic or cultural) wasn't exactly an issue in our interaction. We both appeared to have similar social access as professionals.

I have been asked the "home" question (when are you going home) periodically for fifteen years now. Leaving aside the subtly racist implications of the question (go home—you don't belong), I am still not satisfied with my response. What is home? The place I was born? Where I grew up? Where my parents live? Where I live and work as an adult? Where I locate my community—my people? Who are my people? Is home a geographical space, an historical space, an emotional, sensory space? Home is always so crucial to immigrants and migrants—I even write about it in scholarly texts, perhaps to avoid addressing it as an issue that is also very personal. Does two percent of the world's population think about these questions pertaining to home? This is not to imply that the other ninety-eight percent does not think about home. What interests me is the meaning of home for immigrants and migrants. I am convinced that this question—how one understands and defines home—is a profoundly political one.

Since settled notions of territory, community, geography, and history don't work for us, what does it really mean to be South Asian in the U.S.A.? Obviously I was not South Asian in India—I was Indian. What else could one be but Indian at a time when a successful national independence struggle had given birth to a socialist democratic nation-state? This was the beginning of the decolonization of the Third World. Regional geographies (South Asia) appeared less relevant as a mark of identification than citizenship in a postcolonial independent nation on the cusp of economic and political autonomy. However, in North America, identification as South Asian (in addition to Indian, in my case) takes on its own logic. South Asian refers to folks of Indian, Pakistani, Sri Lankan, Bangladeshi, Kashmiri, and Burmese origin. Identifying as South Asian rather than Indian adds numbers and hence power within the U.S. State. Besides, regional differences among those from different South Asian countries are often less relevant than the commonality based on our histories of immigration and our experiences in the U.S.

Let me reflect a bit on the way I identify myself, and the way the U.S. State and its institutions categorize me. Perhaps thinking through the various labels will lead me back to the question of home and identity. In 1977, I arrived in the U.S.A. on an F1 visa—a student visa. At that time, my definition of myself—a graduate student in Education at the University of Illinois—and the official definition of me (a student allowed into the country on an F1 visa) obviously coincided. Then I was called a foreign student and expected to go "home" (to India—even though my parents were in Nigeria at the time) after getting my Ph.D. Let's face it, this is the assumed trajectory for a number of Indians, especially the postindependence generation (mine) who come to the U.S. for graduate study.

However, this was not to be my trajectory. I quickly discovered that being a foreign student, and a woman at that, meant being either dismissed as irrelevant (the quiet Asian woman stereotype), treated in racist ways (my teachers asked if I understood English and if they should speak slower and louder so that I could keep up—this in spite of my inheritance of the Queen's English and British colonialism!), or celebrated and exoticized (you are so smart!, your accent is even better than that of Americans—a little Anglophilia at work here, even though all my Indian colleagues insist we speak English the Indian way!).

The most significant transition I made at that time was the one from foreign student to student of color. Once I was able to read my experiences in terms of race, and to read race and racism as it is written into the social and political fabric of the U.S., I was able to anchor myself here: racism and sexism became analytic and political lenses. Of course, none of this happened in isolation—friends, colleagues, comrades, classes, books, films, arguments, and dialogues were constitutive of my political education as a woman of color in the U.S.

In the late 1970s and early 1980s feminism was gaining momentum on American campuses—it was in the air, in the classrooms, on the streets. However, what attracted me wasn't feminism as the mainstream media and white Women's Studies departments defined it. Instead, it was a very specific kind of feminism, the feminism of U.S. women of color and Third World women that spoke to me. In thinking through the links between gender, race, and class in their U.S. manifestations, I was for the first time enabled to think through my own gendered, classed postcolonial history. In the early 1980s, reading Audre Lorde, Nassal el Sadaawi, Cherrie Moraga, bell hooks, Gloria Joseph, Paula Gunn Allen, Barbara Smith, Merle Woo, and Mitsuye Yamada, among others, generated a sort of recognition that was very inspiring. A number of actions, decisions, and organizing efforts at that time led me to a sense of home and community in relation to women of color in the U.S. Home not as a comfortable, stable, inherited and familiar space, but instead as an imaginative, politically charged space where the familiarity and sense of affection and commitment lay in a shared collective analysis of social injustice, as well as a vision of radical transformation. Political solidarity and a sense of family could be melded together imaginatively to create a strategic space I could call "home." Politically, intellectually, and emotionally I owe an enormous debt to feminists of color—and especially to the sisters who have sustained me over the years. Even though our attempt to start the Women of Color Institute for Radical Research and Action fell through, the spirit of this vision, and the friendships it generated, still continue to nurture me. A number of us, including Barbara Smith, Papusa Molina, Jacqui Alexander, Gloria Joseph, Mitsuye Yamada, Kesho Scott, and myself, among others, met in 1984 to discuss the possibility of such an institute. The Institute never really happened, but I still hope we will pull it off one day.

For me, engagement as a feminist of color in the U.S. made possible an intellectual and political genealogy of being Indian that was radically challenging as well as profoundly activist. Racialization and gender and class relations and histories became the prism through which I understood, however partially, what it could mean to be South Asian in North America. Interestingly, this recognition also forced me to reexamine the meanings attached to home and community in India.

What I chose to claim, and continue to claim, is a history of anticolonialist, feminist struggle in India. The stories I recall, the ones that I retell and claim as my own, determine the choices and decisions I make in the present and the future. I did not want to accept a history of Hindu chauvinist (bourgeois) upward mobility (even though this characterizes a section of my extended family). We all choose partial, interested stories/histories— perhaps not as deliberately as I am making it sound here. But consciously, or unconsciously, these choices about our past(s) often determine the logic of our present.

Having always kept my distance from conservative, upwardly mobile Indian immigrants for whom the South Asian world was divided into greencard holders and non-green-card holders, the only South Asian links I allowed and cultivated were with Indians with whom I shared a political vision. This considerably limited my community. Racist and sexist experiences in graduate school and after made it imperative that I understand the U.S. in terms of its history of racism, imperialism, and patriarchal relations, specifically in relation to Third World immigrants. After all, we were into the Reagan-Bush years, when the neoconservative backlash made it impossible to ignore the rise of racist, antifeminist, and homophobic attitudes, practices, and institutions. Any purely culturalist or nostalgic/sentimental definition of being "Indian" or "South Asian" was inadequate. Such a definition fueled the "model minority" myth. And this subsequently constituted us as "outsiders/foreigners" or as interest groups who sought or had obtained the American dream.

In the mid-1980s, the labels changed: I went from being a "foreign student" to being a "resident alien." I have always thought that this designation was a stroke of inspiration on the part of the U.S. State, since it accurately names the experience and status of immigrants—one's status as an "alien" is primary. Being legal requires identity papers. (It is useful to recall that the "passport"—and by extension the concept of nation-states and the sanctity of their borders—came into being after World War I.)

One must be stamped as legitimate (that is, not-gay-or-lesbian and not-communist!) by the Immigration and Naturalization Service (INS). The INS is one of the central disciplinary arms of the U.S. State. It polices the borders and controls all border crossings—especially those into the U.S. In fact, the INS is also one of the primary forces which institutionalizes race differences in the public arena, thus regulating notions of home, legitimacy, and economic access to the "American dream" for many of us. For instance, carrying a green card documenting resident alien status in the U.S. is clearly very different from carrying an American passport, which is proof of U.S. citizenship. The former allows one to enter the U.S. with few hassles; the latter often allows one to breeze through the borders and ports of entry of other countries, especially countries which happen to be trading partners (much of Western Europe and Japan, among others) or in an unequal relationship with the U.S. (much of the noncommunist Third World). At a time when notions of a capitalist free-market economy seem (falsely) synonymous with the values attached to democracy, an American passport can open many doors. However, just carrying an American passport is no insurance against racism and unequal and unjust treatment within the U.S. It would be important to compare the racialization of first-generation immigrants from South Asia to the racialization of second-generation South Asian Americans. One significant difference between these two generations would be between the experience of racism as a phenomenon specific to the U.S. versus the ever-present shadow of racism in which South Asians born in the U.S. grow up. This suggests that the psychic effects of racism would be different for these two constituencies. In addition, questions of home, identity, and history take on very different meanings for South Asians born in North America. But to be fair, this comparison is beyond the scope of this essay.

~~~~

Rather obstinately, I have refused to give up my Indian passport and have chosen to remain as a resident alien in the U.S. for the last decade or so. Which leads me to reflect on the complicated meanings attached to holding Indian citizenship while making a life for myself in the U.S.A. In India, what does it mean to have a green card—to be an expatriate? What does it mean to visit Bombay every two to four years, and still call it home? Why does speaking in Marathi (my mother tongue) become a measure and confirmation of home? What are the politics of being a part of the majority and the "absent elite" in India, while being a minority and a racialized "other" in the U.S.? And does feminist politics, or advocating feminism, have the same meaning and urgency in these different geographical and political contests?

Some of these questions hit me smack in the face during my last visit to India in December 1992 post-Ayodhya (the destruction of the Babri Majid in Ayodhya by Hindu fundamentalists on 6 December 1992). In earlier, rather infrequent visits (once every four or five years was all I could afford), my green card designated me as an object of envy, privilege, and status within my extended family. Of course the same green card has always been viewed with suspicion by left and feminist friends who (quite understandably) demand evidence of my ongoing commitment to a socialist and democratic India. During this visit, however, with emotions running high within my family, my green card marked me as an outsider who couldn't possibly understand the "Muslim problem" in India. I was made aware of being an "outsider" in two profoundly troubling shouting matches with my uncles, who voiced the most incredibly hostile sentiments against Muslims. Arguing that India was created as a secular state and that democracy had everything to do with equality for all groups (majority and minority) got me nowhere. The very fundamentals of democratic citizenship in India were/are being undermined and redefined as "Hindu."

~~~

Bombay was one of the cities hardest hit with the waves of communal violence following the events in Ayodhya. The mobilization of Hindu fundamentalists, even paramilitary organizations, over the last half century and especially since the mid-1980s had brought Bombay to a juncture where the most violently racist discourse about Muslims seemed to be woven into the fabric of acceptable daily life. Racism was normalized in the popular imagination such that it became almost impossible to publicly raise questions about the ethics or injustice of racial/ethnic, religious discrimination. I could not assume a distanced posture toward religion any more. Too many injustices were being done in my name.

Although born a Hindu, I have always considered myself a nonpracticing one—religion had always felt rather repressive when I was growing up. I enjoyed the rituals but resisted the authoritarian hierarchies of organized Hinduism. However, the Hinduism touted by fundamentalist organizations like the RSS (Rashtriya Swayamsevak Sangh, a paramilitary Hindu fundamentalist organization founded in the 1930s) and the Shiv Sena (a Maharashtsan chauvinist, fundamentalist, fascist political organization that has amassed a significant voice in Bombay politics and government) was one that even I, in my ignorance, recognized as reactionary and distorted. But this discourse was real—hate-filled rhetoric against Muslims appeared to be the mark of a "loyal Hindu." It was unbelievably heart-wrenching to see my hometown become a war zone with whole streets set on fire and a daily death count to rival any major territorial border war. The smells and textures of Bombay, of home, which had always comforted and nurtured me, were violently disrupted. The scent of fish drying on the lines at the fishing village in Oanda was submerged in the smell of burning straw

and grass as whole bastis (chawls) were burned to the ground. The very typography, language, and relationships that constituted "home" were quietly
but surely exploding. What does community mean in this context? December 1992 both clarified as well as complicated for me the meanings attached
to being an Indian citizen, a Hindu, an educated woman/feminist, and a permanent resident in the U.S. in ways that I have yet to resolve. After all, it is
often moments of crisis that make us pay careful attention to questions of
identity. Sharp polarizations force one to make choices (not in order to take
sides, but in order to accept responsibility) and to clarify our own analytic,
political, and emotional topographies.

I learned that combating the rise of Hindu fundamentalism was a necessary ethical imperative for all socialists, feminists, and Hindus of conscience. Secularism, if it meant absence of religion, was no longer a viable
position. From a feminist perspective, it became clear that the battle for
women's minds and hearts was very much center-stage in the Hindu fundamentalist strategy. Feminists in India have written extensively about the appeal of fundamentalist rhetoric and social position to women. (The journals
The Economic and Political Weekly of India and *Manushi* are good sources
for this work.)

Religious fundamentalist constructions of women embody the nexus of
morality, sexuality, and Nation—a nexus of great importance for feminists.
Similar to Christian, Islamic, and Jewish fundamentalist discourses, the
construction of femininity and masculinity, especially in relation to the idea
of the Nation, are central to Hindu fundamentalist rhetoric and mobilizations. Women are not only mobilized in the service of the Nation, but they
also become the ground on which discourses of morality and nationalism
are written. For instance, the RSS mobilizes primarily middle-class women
in the name of a family-oriented Hindu nation, much like the Christian
Right does in the U.S., but discourses of morality and nation are also embodied in the normative policing of women's sexuality (witness the surveil-
lance and policing of women's dress in the name of morality by the contemporary Iranian State). Thus, one of the central challenges Indian feminists
face at this time is how to rethink the relationship of nationalism and feminism in the context of religious identities. In addition to the fundamentalist
mobilizations tearing the country apart, the recent incursions of the International Monetary Fund and the World Bank with their structural adjust-
ment programs which are supposed to discipline the Indian economy are re-
defining the meaning of postcoloniality and of democracy in India.
Categories like gender, race, caste/class are profoundly and visibly unstable
at such times of crisis. These categories must thus be analyzed in relation to
contemporary reconstructions of womanhood and manhood in a global
arena increasingly dominated by religious fundamentalist movements, the
IMF and the World Bank, and the relentless economic and ideological colo-

nization of much of the world by multinationals based in the U.S., Japan, and Europe. In all these global economic and cultural/ideological processes, women occupy a crucial position.

In India, unlike most countries, the sex ratio has declined since the early 1900s. According to the 1991 census, the ratio is now 929 women to 1000 men, one of the lowest (if not the lowest) sex ratios in the world. Women produce seventy to eighty percent of all the food in India and have always been the hardest hit by environmental degradation and poverty. The contradictions between civil law and Hindu and Muslim personal laws affect women—rarely men. Horrific stories about the deliberate murder of female infants as a result of sex determination procedures like amniocentesis, and recent incidents of sati (self-immolation by women on the funeral pyres of their husbands) have even hit the mainstream American media. Gender and religious (racial) discrimination are thus urgent, life-threatening issues for women in India. In 1993, politically conscious Indian citizenship necessitates taking such fundamentally feminist issues seriously. In fact, these are the very same issues South Asian feminists in the U.S. need to address. My responsibility to combat and organize against the regressive and violent repercussions of Hindu fundamentalist mobilizations in India extends to my life in North America. After all, much of the money which sustains the fundamentalist movement is raised and funneled through organizations in the U.S.

Let me now circle back to the place I began: the meanings I have come to give to home, community, and identity. By exploring the relationship between being a South Asian immigrant in America and an expatriate Indian citizen in India, I have tried, however partially and anecdotally, to clarify the complexities of home and community for this particular feminist of color/South Asian in North America. The genealogy I have created for myself here is partial, interested, and deliberate. It is genealogy that underlies my self-identification as an educator involved in a pedagogy of liberation. Of course, my history and experiences are far messier and not at all as linear as this narrative makes them sound. But then the very process of constructing a narrative for oneself—of telling a story—imposes a certain linearity and coherence. But that is the lesson, perhaps, especially for us immigrants and migrants: i.e., that home, community, and identity all fall somewhere between the histories and circumstances we inherit and the political choices we make through alliances, solidarities, and friendships.

One very concrete effect of my creating this particular space for myself has been my recent involvement in two grassroots organizations, one in India and the other in the U.S. The former, an organization called Awareness, is based in Orissa and works to empower the rural poor. Their focus is political education (similar to Paolo Freire's notion of conscientization), and they have recently begun to very consciously organize rural women. Grassroots

Leadership of North Carolina is the U.S. organization I work with. It is a multiracial group of organizers (largely African American and white) working to build a poor and working people's movement in the American South. While the geographical, historical, and political contexts of these two organizations are different, my involvement in them is very similar, as is my sense that there are clear connections to be made between the work of the two organizations. In addition, I think that the issues, analyses, and strategies for organizing for social justice are also quite similar. This particular commitment to work with grass-roots organizers in the two places I call home is not accidental. It is very much the result of the genealogy I have traced here. After all, it has taken me over a decade to make these commitments to grass-roots work in both spaces. In part, I have defined what it means to be South Asian by educating myself about, and reflecting on, the histories and experiences of African American, Latina, West Indian, African, European American and other constituencies in North America. Such definitions and understandings do provide a genealogy, but a genealogy that is always relational and fluid as well as urgent and necessary.

HAMBUN-HAMBUN

Susan Ito

*t*he census form came today. I saw the dreaded instructions, the stern admonishment to *check only one box*. White. Japanese. Other. There is the blank space to fill in, a half inch in which to claim identity. I am other. Hambun-hambun, or half-and-half. *Hapa*. Biologically, genetically, I'm fifty percent Japanese, and fifty percent . . . unknown. Adopted as an infant into a Japanese American family, I have always had a heightened awareness of my "otherness."

"Your parents, they're so good, they treat you just like you were their own." I've heard this a lot.

Then is it true, that I am not "their own"? If not to them, to whom do I belong? From where do I come? From out there. From them, those phantom parents. Am I a part of this family, or not? I cling to their name, to *my* name, Ito, as one holds an amulet. I fasten it around my throat. Yes. *I do belong*. And yet, there is that question, that other name, burned into the black plastic of microfiche, buried in the catacombs of hospital storage like the name of a dead person. The life I never lived.

I've met the woman who gave birth to me; she is a nisei like my parents. I hunted her down when I was in college, searched the underground of buried information until I arrived at her door. She wasn't happy about being discovered, but when she learned that I had grown up a sansei, a third-generation Japanese American, something inside her softened. She had let me go into the world, destination unknown, and I could have turned up anywhere. But I grew up as the daughter of Masaji and Kikuko, who brought me to visit relatives in Japan when I was nine, who taught me to sing "Sakura," the cherry blossom song.

They get along well now, the three of them. They fall easily into a natural camaraderie, their shared culture, their linked parentage of me. We have all eaten sushi together, chopsticks clicking comfortably. None of them will mention that missing link, that *other* part of the equation, the one out of four parents who is not Japanese at all.

This invisible one, my nameless birth father, shows up to haunt me every time I look in the mirror. I see his freckles, his pink skin that doesn't tan easily. His dark furry forearms, and legs that need to be shaved every day. His nose, twice as long and more defined than my Japanese kin, is an unmistakable flag on my profile. But what color is that flag? What country? What people?

When my second daughter was born with blonde-red hair and blue eyes, those recessive genes surfaced like an earthquake in our family. Who are those fair freckled blondes, her great-grandparents? My birth mother has remained silent to my questions, and I have become tired of asking.

These questions of origin and identity have been circling around like stubborn moths in my head ever since I was small. They beat their wings, bumping up against my brain, dumbly searching for answers. What? Who? Why? I started writing when I was six, making up stories that always ended with astonishing surprises: The cat was really a turtle in disguise. A girl found a rabbit under her bed, and they became sisters. The questions and answers surfaced as fables in my green marbled notebooks before I knew how to speak them out loud. I wrote incessantly for years and years, words bleeding uncontrollably onto the page. When I searched for and found my birth mother, people would say, "You ought to make this into a story. Your life is such a soap opera." It seemed like a ludicrous idea to me; Japanese people don't show up on soap operas.

My adoptive parents, both nisei, are solidly cemented into the Japanese American community. They have their friends from half a century now, who all grew up together in New York City public schools, all with immigrant parents, mothers who were picture brides, fathers who didn't speak English. They stick together. I grew up between them, bolstered by their unflinching love for me, the way they never questioned my "authenticity." My parents' people took me in, called me "Susie-chan." Yet without my parents, I feel shy, self-conscious about joining the Japanese community in California. I worry that they'll look at me sideways, saying, "What is she doing here?"

Whenever I was out with one parent, new acquaintances would always assume that the other parent was white. And why wouldn't they? They were innocent questions, innocent assumptions, but the years of constant questions, the curiosity, the nosiness, have left me with a bitter taste that won't go away.

~~~

I am fourteen or fifteen years old, my body bursting into adolescence, all bright flowers and elastic in my new halter top. I am helping my father set up one of his merchandise booths and another salesman comes up, slaps him on the back.

"Mr. Ito! This is *your* daughter?"

My father beams and reaches out to ruffle my hair. "Yes, this is Susan."

"Why, you old dog. I never woulda known!" An elbow in the ribs, another slap, a wink. "Well, your wife must be *some beauty* then." Meaning: you snagged a white woman, you crafty little Jap.

My father and I busy ourselves with our work, not looking at each other.

~~~

I am thirty-five years old, teaching English at community college. A colleague invites me to join an Asian American faculty organization and, as I am introduced to the group, a nisei man does a double take, looks at me sideways.

"You don't *look* like an Ito."

What does an Ito look like? What does it mean to be Japanese American, to be "real"? I try to keep my voice steady, to find a balance between a humiliated whisper and outraged shouting. "Well, I am. I am." I don't offer an explanation.

~~~

I go to a conference of mixed-race people and am moved and astounded to see the hundreds of people who, in a peculiar way, all look like me, even as we are singularly different. It is a relief to be among so many who know this life, this *hapa* seesaw, but as I meet and share stories with other biracial people, I realize that once again I am on the periphery. Everyone seems to come from a family with two identifiable parents. Even those whose parents have split up, have photos, stories of the one that isn't around. They see themselves reflected in this dual mirror: "I get my blue eyes from *him* but my black hair is from *her*." They get to see the source of their mixture, their differences split by their blended roots. It is as if half of my mirror is covered up.

Even among this peculiar group of people with whom I have so much in common, I feel separate. They talk about the cultural wars between parents: Mom wanted to fix won tons, but Dad insisted on corned beef. I had none of that bifurcated experience. So maybe I'm not really a *hapa*, not really part of the club. It was a homogeneous front, my all-Japanese family. Yet sometimes, when I caught a glimpse of my own reflection, or saw a portrait of the three of us together, I felt dizzy.

My junior high school friend Cathy laughed when she saw the framed family photo on our piano. "What's wrong with this picture?" she giggled, pointing at me. It was like a children's puzzle, a song my own daughters have learned from *Sesame Street*: *One of these things is not like the others, one of these things just doesn't belong. . . .*

~~~

Not long after we met, my birth mother and I began to wage an emotional tug-of-war. I pulled and pulled at her, trying to extract information, stories, memories. *Tell me where I came from. Tell me who I am.* She begrudgingly let go of tiny fragments of her history, a small tidbit or anecdote every few years, but never much about that pale Midwestern man who helped to create me. Years of struggle, of tears and demands and refusal, and finally a silence that has turned into a stiff, saccharine cordiality. We don't bring it up any more.

Is information something that can be owned, hoarded, desired? Is it really possible to guard the truth as she has? After years of raging, pleading, begging, and threatening, I must finally accept the truth: We are not going to sit down together, a pot of green tea between us, talking about the past, flipping pages of a photo album, while I soak up a sense of identity. We are not going to appear on *Oprah*, an ecstatic mother-daughter reunion. If I am going to have a birth story, a chronicle of my roots, it is going to be up to me.

I write down all that I know of my beginnings, and these scanty notes barely fill one side of an index card. My birthdate. Birthplace. The place where they met. The few precious details that she has let slip into conversations, the small specks that I have been gathering like dust in my pocket.

I take my birthday, count back nine months, calculating my conception to be somewhere around Christmas in 1958. I close my eyes for several minutes, pulling myself back there. A cold month, a month full of snow. Then I begin writing. I imagine him, red-cheeked in the bitter wind, stomping ice from his boots. I see her in her cat's-eye glasses, a schoolteacher with black hair and red lipstick. The only Japanese woman in the tiny Midwestern town. I give them outfits, like paper dolls, and winter colds. He carries a linen handkerchief in his pocket. I write them closer and closer together, until their paths cross and I give them eye contact. This is the beginning of my story. This is where my life begins.

I write, not to provide a screenplay for *Days of Our Lives*, but to fill in the holes of this tale that I don't know, but which exists in my blood, my skin, my bones. Pages accumulate, and like the velveteen rabbit of childhood, I feel myself becoming real.

~~~~~

Five years ago, I had a bookshelf full of green marbled notebooks and a wild, aching need to write that I fed every day like a drug habit. The notebooks simmered on the shelf like radioactive material. A certain point came when it wasn't enough to produce chaos; I wanted to write a story. I took a class in creative writing, terrified of what I might find out. It would be a trite, predictable soap opera. I would be laughed out of the room.

Nobody laughed. The first story was published. Seeing the familiar letters of my own name, in black typography in a published book, was like seeing my birth mother's face for the first time. *There I am.*

Autobiography comes in different forms: the what-if of my creation tale, and then the this-happened-and-I-need-to-tell-it witness kind. It is different to take memory and to turn it into fiction, into the not quite tangible world of literature. This can be more vulnerable. Writing about actual life is a many-layered process. First you dig and dig with your pencil until something is unearthed. Is this what I was looking for? The dusting-off, the close examination. Yes, this is something I can use. Once its value is acknowledged, then comes the task of disguising it. Some memories must be enrolled in the witness protection program, given false mustaches and dyed hair. They pretend to live in cities that they have never visited.

I sweat as I write my author's bio for a particularly risky story, wondering who will see it. Someone suggests using a pseudonym, and my reaction is swift and furious: Unacceptable. My name was already taken from me once, and I won't let it happen again. I am not going to hide or lie about who I am.

But then the irony strikes me: in *some* ways it is fine, even necessary, to take on a disguise, to dress up the truth. This is what writing fiction is all about. But fiction is about being in control, about choosing the particular camouflage myself. When I sense a mask being fastened over my face by some external force, or a label slapped onto my shoulder, I balk. *Don't tell me who I am.*

A life once removed. It has felt, for much of these thirty-some-odd years, like a stigma, an unfair weight strapped to my shoulders. Always being held in question. Having that fear of not being whole, not being enough. Living a life neither here nor there, perpetually sitting on a fence and waiting to fall one way or another.

Yet this is what the essence of being a writer is; to remove oneself, to set a story down on a page and shape it from above. I am grateful to language, the place where I went in my greatest confusion, where the question "Who am I?" ricocheted around and around, making me dizzy. Writing became the ladder stacked of words, allowing me to climb hand over hand out of the chaos, out of the confusion. The answer is finally clear. I may be half-and-half of many other things, but I am entirely a writer.

Writers live in that space that is neither here nor there; that is both being and seeing at once. I used to be afraid of that space, for it offered no solid ground. But now I gladly step into it, as if I am letting myself out of the door of a moving airplane. I walk out onto a cloud that has no shape, and it doesn't feel like falling. I can see everything, and I'm flying.

FORTUNE

Priscilla Lee

*e*very year on the cusp between old and new,
  my grandmother kneels in front of the fireplace
  with her Tun Shu and bookmarks,
  tosses five quarters onto cold brick.
  She watches the order
  in which they fall, scratches my name
  with her brittle fingernail into the book's margin
  when she has matched
  their sequence to a fortune.

She is monitoring my progress.
  This year was a good year, next will be better,
  she always tells me after studying the characters.
  The warrior who has won the battle
  stands at a dark crossroad,
  and his horse is hungry.
  The carp attempts to leap
  the high wall, its scales
   a blistering glare
  above water. The fisherman
  catches the prize pelican
  with an oyster trapped in its long beak.
  The kirin, half tiger, half dragon, enters
  the forbidden city.

Year after year, she wants my fortunes to be set,
  offers assurances to drag me toward the coming year, but
  how can I be as certain as my grandmother
  that my life is good? The warrior has won a battle,
  but does he complete his journey
  if he has no horse, no food? Is the carp's leap
  a feat of transcendence
  or defiance? Which am I—
  the fisherman, the oyster, or the pelican?
  And the kirin, the long-awaited prince,
  to what political state is he born, and
  what does it mean to be born a prince and a woman?

The fortunes are ambiguities, a balancing
of possibility and limitation,
but my grandmother reminds me
that doubt can lead me away from the bright road.
Not even the gods can predict
how we will perceive our own lives.

RACE, CLASS, AND GENDER IN ASIAN AMERICA

Yen Le Espiritu

> The slit-eyed, bucktooth Jap thrusting his bayonet,
> thirsting for blood. The inscrutable, wily Chinese
> detective with his taped eyelids and wispy moustache.
> The childlike, indolent Filipino houseboy. Always
> giggling. Bowing and scraping. Eager to please, but
> untrustworthy. The sexless, hairless Asian male. The
> servile, oversexed Asian female. The Geisha. The sultry,
> sarong-clad, South Seas maiden. The serpentine,
> cunning Dragon Lady. Mysterious and evil, eager to
> please. Effeminate. Untrustworthy. Yellow Peril.
> Fortune Cookie Psychic. Savage. Dogeater. Invisible.
> Mute. Faceless peasants breeding too many children.
> Gooks. Passive Japanese Americans obediently marching
> off to "relocation camps" during the Second World War.
> JESSICA HAGEDORN, *Charlie Chan Is Dead*

*a*s is evident from the stereotypes of Asian American men and women listed above, representations of gender and sexuality figure strongly in the articulation of racism. Gender norms in the United States are premised upon the experiences of middle-class men and women of European origin. In the idealized American family, women are full-time homemakers and mothers and men are the breadwinners. U.S. culture aligns these gender roles—the bread-baker and the breadwinner—as complementary, ignoring the historical and political context of their constructions and gliding over questions of power and conflict.[1] This naturalized sexual division of labor engenders other sex-specific stereotypes: men are independent, capable, powerful, while women are dependent, ineffectual, and weak. As such, men become the protectors and women the protected. These Eurocentric-constructed gender norms form a backdrop of expectations for American men and women of color—expectations which racism often precludes meeting.[2] In general, men of color are viewed not as the protector, but rather the aggressor—a threat to white women.[3] And women of color are seen as oversexualized and thus undeserving of the social and sexual protection accorded to white middle-class women.[4]

For Asian American men and women, their exclusion from white-based cultural notions of the masculine and the feminine has taken seemingly contrasting forms: Asian men have been cast as both hypermasculine (the "Yellow Peril") and effeminate (the "model minority"); and Asian women have been rendered both superfeminine (the "China Doll") and castrating (the "Dragon Lady").

DUALISMS: GENDER, RACE, AND CLASS

The problems of race, gender, and class are closely intertwined in the lives of Asian American men and women. It is racial and class oppression against "yellows" that restricts their material lives, (re)defines their gender roles, and provides material for degrading and exaggerated sexual representations of Asian men and women in U.S. popular culture. Asian Americans have always, but particularly since the 1960s, resisted race, class, and gender exploitation through political, economic, and cultural activism. As a result, the objectification of Asian Americans as the exotic alien—different from, and inferior to, white Americans—has never been absolute.

On the other hand, in demanding legitimacy, some Asian Americans have adopted the either/or dichotomies of the dominant Eurocentric patriarchal structure, "unwittingly upholding the criteria of those whom they assail."[5] As an example, men who have been historically devalued are likely to take their rage and frustration out on those closest to them.[6] Having been forced into "feminine" subject positions, some Asian American men seek to reassert their masculinity by physically and emotionally abusing those who are even more powerless—the women and children in their families. In particular, men's inability to earn a family wage and subsequent reliance on their wives' income severely undermines their sense of well-being. Male unhappiness and helplessness can be detected in the following joke told at a Hmong family picnic: "When we get on the plane to go back to Laos, the first thing we will do is beat up the women!" The joke—which generated laughter from both men and women—drew upon a combination of "the men's unemployability, the sudden economic value placed on women's work, and men's fear of losing power in their families."[7]

While it is useful to view male tyranny within the context of racial inequality and class exploitation, it is equally important to note that this aggression is informed by Eurocentric gender ideology—particularly its emphasis on oppositional, dichotomous sex roles. The Asian American men who can see only race oppression, and not gender domination, are unable—or unwilling—to view themselves as both oppressed and oppressor. This dichotomous stance has led to the marginalization of Asian American women and their needs. Concerned with recuperating their identities as men and as Americans, some Asian American political and cultural workers have subordinated feminism to nationalist concerns. From this limited standpoint, they cast Asian American feminists who expose Asian American sexism as "anti-ethnic," criticize them for undermining group solidarity, and charge them with exaggerating the community's patriarchal structure to please the larger society. For example, when Maxine Hong Kingston's *The Woman Warrior* received favorable reviews, writer Frank Chin accused her of attempting to "cash in on the feminist fad."[8] In an analysis of the display of machismo among Mexican immigrant men, Pierrette Hondagneu-Sotelo characterizes these men's behaviors as "personally and collectively constructed performances of masculine gender display ... [which] should be distinguished from structurally constituted positions of power."[9] In other words, these displays of male prowess are indicators of "marginalized and subordinated masculinities."[10]

The racist debasement of Asian men makes it difficult for Asian American women to balance the need to expose the problems of male privilege with the desire to unite with men to contest the overarching racial ideology that confines them both. As Asian American women negotiate this difficult feat, they, like men, tend to subscribe to the either/or dichotomous thinking. They do so when they adopt the fixed masculinist Asian American identity even when it marginalizes their positions; or when they privilege women's concerns over men's or over other forms of inequality. Both of these positions advance the dichotomous stance of man or woman, gender or race or class, without recognizing the "complex *relationality* that shapes our social and political lives."[11] Finally, Asian American women enforce Eurocentric gender ideology when they accept the feminization of Asian men and its parallel construction of white men as the most desirable sexual and marital partners.

Traditional white feminists have likewise succumbed to binary definitions and categories when they insist on the primacy of gender, thereby dismissing racism and other structures of oppression. The feminist mandate for gender solidarity accounts only for hierarchies between men and women and ignores power differentials among women, among men, and between white women and men of color. Exclusive focus on gender makes it difficult for white women to see the web of multiple oppressions that constrain the lives of most women of color, thus limiting the potential bondings among all women. It further bars them from recognizing the oppression of men of color—the fact that there are men, and not only women, who have been "feminized," and the fact that white, middle-class women hold cultural power and class power over certain groups of men.[12]

In sum, Asian American men, Asian American women, and white women unwittingly comply with the ideologies of racialized patriarchy. Asian American men fulfill traditional definitions of manhood when they conflate might and masculinity and sweep aside the needs and well-being of Asian American women. Asian American women accept these racialized gender ideologies when they submit to white and Asian men or when they subordinate racial, class, or male concerns to feminism. And white women advance a hierarchical agenda when they fail to see that the experiences of white women, women of color, and men of color are connected in systematic ways.

BEYOND DUALISMS: CONSTRUCTING AN "IMAGINED COMMUNITY"

A central task in feminist scholarship is to expose and dismantle the stereotypes that have traditionally provided ideological justifications for women's subordination. However, ideologies of manhood and womanhood have as much to do with class and race as they have to do with sex. Class and gender intersect when the culture of patriarchy—which assigns men to the public sphere and women to the private sphere—makes it possible for capitalists to exploit and profit from the labor of both men and women. Because patriarchy mandates that men be the breadwinner, it pressures them to work in the capitalist wage-market—even in jobs that are low-paying, physically punishing, and without opportunities for upward mobility. In this sense, the sexual division of labor within the family produces a steady supply of male labor for the benefits of capital. The culture of patriarchy is also responsible for the capitalist exploitation of women. The assumption that women are not the main income earners in their families—and therefore can afford to work for less—provides ideological justification for employers to hire women at lower wages to perform jobs in poorer working conditions than exist for men.[13] On the other hand, in however limited a way, wage employment does allow women to challenge the confines and dictates of traditional patriarchal social relations. It affords women some opportunities to leave the confines of the home, delay marriage and childbearing, develop new social networks, and exercise more personal independence.[14] A Punjabi cannery worker said of her increased power within the family: "Now my husband, he listens to me when I say something; when I want to buy something, I do; and when I want to go in the car, I go."[15] As such, wage labor both oppresses and liberates women, exploiting them as workers but also sharpening their claims against patriarchal authority.[16] But this potential liberation is limited. As Linda Y. C. Lim points out, because capitalist employment and exploitation of female labor is based on patriarchal exploitation, "the elimination of these conditions may well bring about an elimination of the jobs themselves."[17]

U.S. capital also profits from racism. In the pre–World War II era, white men were considered "free labor" and could take a variety of jobs in the industrialized economic sector, while Asian men were racialized as "coolie labor" and confined to nonunionized, degrading low-paying jobs in the agricultural and service sectors. Asian immigrants faced a special disability: they could not become citizens and thus were a completely disfranchised group. As noncitizens, Asian immigrants were subjected to especially onerous working conditions compared to other workers, including longer hours, lower wages, more physically demanding labor, more dangerous tasks, and so on. The alien—and thus rightless—status of Asian immigrants increased the ability of capital to control them; it also allowed employers to use the cheapness of Asian labor to undermine and discipline the white small producers and white workers.[18] The post-1965 Asian immigrant group, though much more differentiated along social class lines, is still racialized and exploited. In all occupational sectors, Asian American men and women fare worse than their white counterparts. Unskilled and semi-skilled Asian immigrant laborers are relegated to the lower-paying job brackets or racially segregated industries. Due to their gender, race, and noncitizen status, Asian immigrant women fare the worst because they are seen as being the most desperate for work at any wage.[19] A white male production manager and hiring supervisor in a California Silicon Valley assembly shop discusses his formula for hiring: "Three things I look for in hiring [entry-level, high-tech manufacturing operatives]: small, foreign, and female. You find those three things and you're pretty much automatically guaranteed the right kind of work force. These little foreign gals are grateful to be hired—very, very grateful—no matter what."[20]

The highly educated, on the other hand, encounter institutionalized economic and cultural racism that restricts their economic mobility. The experiences of W. W. Tom, an electronics assembler, exemplify the lives of many under- and misemployed professionals. Once a physicist in China, Tom came to the United States in 1976. Because of language barriers, she was unable to find work in her profession. Regarding her predicament and that of others like her, she said, "We are all college graduates, but working in sewing or electronics factories. We all have taken a big step backwards in our profession or work, but we are lucky to find work—any work that we can do. I would be happy if I could just advance myself at my present job one step up. I have thought about this constantly . . . the day when I can work at a desk using a pen and not have to do menial labor."[21]

In sum, capitalist exploitation of Asians has been possible mainly because Asian labor had already been categorized by a racist society as being worth less than white workers' labor. This racial hierarchy then confirms the "manhood" of white men while rendering Asian men impotent.

Racist economic exploitation of Asian American men has had gender implications. Due to the men's inability to earn a family wage, Asian American women have had to engage in paid labor to make up the income discrepancies. In other words, the racialized exploitation of Asian American men has historically been the context for the entry of Asian American women into the labor force. Access to waged work and relative economic independence, in turn, has given women solid ground for questioning their subordination. But progress has been slow and uneven. In some instances, more egalitarian divisions of labor and control of domestic resources have emerged. In others, men's loss of status in the public and domestic spheres has placed severe pressures on the traditional family, leading at times to resentment, verbal or physical abuse, and divorce.

Moreover, Asian women's ability to transform traditional patriarchy is often constrained by their social-structural location in the dominant society. The articulation between gender discrimination, racial discrimination against (presumed or actual) immigrant workers, and capitalist exploitation makes their position particularly vulnerable. Constrained by these overlapping categories of oppression, Asian American women may accept certain components of the traditional patriarchal system in order to have a strong and intact family—an important source of support to sustain them in the work world.[22] Indeed, in this hostile environment, the act of maintaining families is itself a form of resistance. Finally, women's economic resources have remained too meager to maintain their economic independence from men. Therefore, some Asian American women may choose to preserve the traditional family system—albeit in a tempered form—because they value the promise of male economic protection. As Evelyn Nakano Glenn points out, for Asian Americans, the family is "simultaneously a unity, bound by interdependence in the fight for survival, and a segmented institution in which men and women struggled over power, resources, and labor."[23]

~~~

To recognize the interconnections of race, gender, and class is also to recognize that the conditions of our lives are connected to and shaped by the conditions of others' lives. Thus men are privileged precisely because women are not; and whites are advantaged precisely because people of color are disadvantaged. In other words, both people of color *and* white people live racially structured lives; both women's *and* men's lives are shaped by their gender; and *all* of our lives are influenced by the dictates of the patriarchal economy of U.S. society.[24] But the intersections among these categories of oppression mean that there are also hierarchies among women, among men, and that some women hold cultural and economic power over certain groups of men. On the other hand, the "intersecting, contradictory, and cross-category functioning of U.S. culture" also presents opportunities for transforming the existing hierarchical structure.[25] If Asian men have been "feminized" in the United States, then they can best attest to and fight against patriarchal oppression that has long denied all women male privilege. If white women recognize that ideologies of womanhood have as much to do with race and class as they have to do with sex, then they can better work with, and not for, women (and men) of color. And if men and women of all social classes understand how capitalism distorts and lessens all people's lives, then they will be more apt to struggle together for a more equitable economic system. Thus to name the categories of oppression and to identify their interconnections is also to explore, forge, and fortify cross-gender, cross-racial, and cross-class alliances. It is to construct what Chandra Mohanty calls an "imagined community"[26]—a community that is bounded not only by color, race, gender, or class, but crucially by a shared struggle against *all* pervasive and systemic forms of domination.

MAIDEN VOYAGE: EXCURSION INTO SEXUALITY AND IDENTITY POLITICS IN ASIAN AMERICA

Dana Y. Takagi

*t*he topic of sexualities—in particular, lesbian, gay, and bisexual identities—is an important and timely issue in that place we imagine as Asian America. There are at least two compelling reasons to think about sexuality and Asian American history.

One, while there has been a good deal of talk about the "diversity" of Asian American communities, we are relatively uninformed about Asian American subcultures organized specifically around sexuality. There are Asian American gay and lesbian social organizations, gay bars that are known for Asian clientele, and conferences that have focused on Asian American lesbian and gay experiences. But gay Asian organizations are not likely to view themselves as a gay subculture within Asian America any more than they are likely to think of themselves as an Asian American subculture within gay America. If anything, I expect that many of us view ourselves as on the margins of both communities. That state of marginalization in both communities is what prompts this essay and makes the issues raised in it all the more urgent for all of us—gay, straight, somewhere-in-between. For, as Haraway has suggested, the view is often clearest from the margins where "The split and contradictory self is the one who can interrogate positionings and be accountable, the one who can construct and join rational conversations and fantastic imaginings that change history."[1]

To be honest, the very act of including lesbian and gay experiences in Asian American history, which seems important in a symbolic sense, produces in me a moment of hesitation. Not because I do not think that lesbian and gay sexualities are deserving of a place in Asian American history, but rather, because the inscription of nonstraight sexualities in Asian American history immediately casts theoretical doubt about how to do it. But the recognition of different sexual practices and identities that also claim the label *Asian American* presents a useful opportunity for rethinking and reevaluating notions of identity that have been used, for the most part, unproblematically and uncritically in Asian American Studies.

The second reason, then, that we ought to be thinking about gay and lesbian sexuality and Asian America is for the theoretical trouble we encounter in our attempts to situate and think about sexual identity *and* racial identity. Just at the moment that we attempt to rectify our ignorance by adding, say, the lesbian to Asian American history, we arrive at a stumbling block, an ignorance of how to add her. Surely the quickest and simplest way to add her is to think of lesbianism as a minority within a minority. But efforts to think of sexuality in the same terms that we think of race, yet simultaneously different from race in certain ways, and therefore, the inevitable "revelation" that gays/lesbians/bisexuals are like minorities but also different too, is often inconclusive, frequently ending in "counting" practice. While many minority women speak of "triple jeopardy" oppression—as if class, race, and gender could be disentangled into discrete additive parts— some Asian American lesbians could rightfully claim quadruple jeopardy oppression—class, race, gender, and sexuality. Enough counting. Marginalization is not as much about the *quantities* of experiences as it is about *qualities* of experience. And as many writers, most notably feminists, have argued, identities, whether drawn from sexual desire, racial origins, languages of gender, or class roots, are simply not additive.[2]

NOT COUNTING

Writing, speaking, acting queer. Against a backdrop of lotus leaves, sliding *shoji* panels, and the mountains of Guilin. Amid the bustling enclaves of Little Saigon, Koreatown, Chinatown, and Little Tokyo. Sexual identity, like racial identity, is one of many types of recognized "difference." If marginalization is a qualitative state of being and not simply a quantitative one, then what is it about being "gay" that is different from "Asian American"?

The terms "lesbian" and "gay," like "Third World," "woman," and "Asian American," are political categories that serve as rallying calls and personal affirmations. In claiming these identities we create and locate ourselves in phrases that seem a familiar fit: black gay man, Third World woman, working-class Chicana lesbian, Asian American bisexual, etc. But is it possible to write these identities—like Asian American gay—without writing oneself into the corners that are either gay and only gay, or, Asian American and only Asian American? Or, as Trinh T. Minh-ha put it, "How do you inscribe difference without bursting into a series of euphoric narcissistic accounts of yourself and your own kind?"[3]

It is in vogue these days to celebrate difference. But underlying much contemporary talk about difference is the assumption that differences are comparable things. For example, many new social activists, including those in the gay and lesbian movement, think of themselves as patterned on the "ethnic model."[4] And for many ethnic minorities, the belief that "gays are oppressed, too" is a reminder of a sameness, a common political project in moving margin to center, that unites race-based movements with gays, feminists, and Greens. The notion that our differences are "separate but equal" can be used to call attention to the specificity of experiences or to rally the troops under a collective banner. But in the heat of local political struggles and coalition building, it turns out that not all differences are created equal.

There are numerous ways that being "gay" is not like being "Asian." Two broad distinctions are worth noting. First is the relative invisibility of sexual identity compared with racial identity. While both can be said to be socially constructed, the former are performed, acted out, and produced, often in individual routines, whereas the latter tends to be more obviously "written" on the body and negotiated by political groups.[5] Put another way, there is a quality of voluntarism in being gay/lesbian that is usually not possible as an Asian American. One has the option to present onself as "gay" or "lesbian," or alternatively, to attempt to "pass," or, to stay in "the closet," that is, to hide one's sexual preference.[6] However, these same options are not available to most racial minorities in face-to-face interactions with others. Put another way, homosexuality is more clearly seen as *constructed* than racial identity.[7] As Asian Americans, we do not think in advance about whether or not to present ourselves as "Asian American," rather, that is an identification that is worn by us, whether we like it or not, and which is easily read off of us by others.

A second major reason that the category "gay" cannot be comparable to the category "Asian American" is the very different histories of each group. Studying the politics of being "gay" entails, on the one hand, an analysis of discursive fields, ideologies, and rhetoric about sexual identity, and, on the other hand, knowledge of the history of gays/lesbians as subordinated minorities relative to heterosexuals. . . . Similarly, studying "Asian America" requires analysis of semantic and rhetorical discourse in its variegated forms, racist, apologist, and paternalist, and requires in addition an understanding of the specific histories of the peoples who recognize themselves as Asian or Asian American. But the specific discourses and histories in each case are quite different. Even though we make the same intellectual moves to approach each form of identity, that is, a two-tracked study of ideology on the one hand, and history on the other, the particular ideologies and histories of each are very different.[8]

In other words, many of us experience the worlds of Asian America and gay America as separate places—emotionally, physically, intellectually. We sustain the separation of these worlds with our folk knowledge about the family-centeredness and suprahomophobic beliefs of ethnic communities. And we frequently take great care to keep those worlds distant from each other. What could be more different than the scene at gay bars like "The End Up" in San Francisco or "Faces" in Hollywood, and, on the other hand, the annual Buddhist church bazaars in the Japanese American community or Filipino revivalist meetings?[9] These disparate worlds occasionally collide through individuals who manage to move, for the most part stealthily, between these spaces. But it is the act of deliberately bringing these worlds closer together that seems unthinkable. Imagining your parents, clutching bento box lunches, thrust into the smoky haze of a South of Market leather bar in San Francisco is no less strange a vision than the idea of Lowie taking Ishi, the last of his tribe, for a cruise on Lucas' *Star Wars* Tour at Disneyland. "Cultural strain," the anthropologists would say. Or, as Wynn Young, laughing at the prospect of mixing his family with his boyfriend, said, "Somehow I just can't picture his conversation at the dinner table, over my mother's homemade barbecued pork: 'Hey, Ma, I'm sleeping with a sixty-year-old white guy who's got three kids, and would you please pass the soy sauce?'"[10]

That the topic of *homo*-sexuality in Asian American studies is often treated in whispers, if mentioned at all, should be some indication of trouble. It is noteworthy, I think, that in the last major anthology on Asian American women, *Making Waves*, the author of the essay on Asian American lesbians was the only contributor who did not wish her last name to be published.[11] Of course, as we all know, a chorus of sympathetic bystanders is chanting about homophobia, saying, "She was worried about her job, her family, her community. . . ." Therefore, perhaps a good starting point for considering lesbian and gay identities in Asian American Studies is to problematize the silences surrounding homosexuality in Asian America. While it may seem politically efficacious to toss the lesbian onto the diversity pile, adding one more form of subordination to the heap of inequalities, such a strategy glosses over the particular or distinctive ways sexuality is troped in Asian America. One way that homosexuality may be seen as a vehicle for theorizing identity in Asian America is through the missteps, questions, and silences that are often clearest in collisions at the margins (identities as opposed to people). In the following discussion, I describe two such confrontations—the coming out of a white student in an Asian American Studies class and the problem of authenticity in gay/lesbian Asian American writing. Each tells in its own way the awkward limits of ethnic-based models of identity.

THE COMING-OUT INCIDENT

Once, when I was a teaching assistant during the early 1980s, a lesbian, one of only two white students in my section, decided to come out during the first section meeting. I had asked each student to explain their interest, personal and intellectual, in Asian American Studies. Many students mentioned wanting to know "more about their heritage" and "knowing the past in order to understand the present." The lesbian was nearly last to speak. After explaining that she wanted to understand the heritage of a friend who was Asian American, she said, "And, I guess I also want you all to know that I am a lesbian." In the silence that followed I quickly surveyed the room. A dozen or so Asian American students whom I had forced into a semi-circular seating arrangement stared glumly at their shoes. The two white students, both of whom were lesbians, glanced expectantly around the circle, and then they, too, looked at the ground. I felt as though my own world had split apart, and the two pieces were in front of me, drifting, surrounding, and at that moment, both silent.

I knew both parts well. On the one side, I imagined that the Asian American students in the class recoiled in private horror at the lesbian, not so much because she was a lesbian or white, but because she insisted on publicly baring her soul in front of them. I empathized with the Asian American students because they reminded me of myself as an undergraduate. While my fellow white students chatted effortlessly in section about readings or lectures, I was almost always mute. I marveled at the ease with which questions, thoughts, answers, and even half-baked ideas rolled off their tongues and floated discussion. For them, it all seemed so easy. As for me, I struggled with the act of talking in class. Occasionally, I managed to add a question to the discussion, but, more often, I found that by the time I had silently practiced my entry into a fast-moving exchange, the discussion had moved on. In my silence, I chastised myself for moving too slowly, for hesitating where others did not, and alternately, chastised the other students for their bulldozing, loose lips. I valorized and resented the verbal abilities of my fellow classmates. And I imagined how the Asian American students who sat in my class the day the lesbian decided to come out, like me, identified the ability to bare one's soul through words as "white." On the other side, I empathized as well with the lesbian. I identified with what I imagined as her compelling need to claim her identity, to be like the others in the class, indeed to be an "other" at all in a class where a majority of the students were in search of their "roots." I figured that being a lesbian, while not quite like being Asian American, must have seemed to the intrepid student as close to the ethnic model as she could get. Finally, I thought she represented a side of me that always wanted, but never could quite manage, to drop the coming-out bomb in groups that did not expect it. Part of the pleasure in being an "outsider" can be in the affirmation of the identity abhorred by "insiders." I imagined that she and her friend had signed up for my section because they *knew* I too was a lesbian, and I worried that they assumed that I might be able to protect them from the silence of the closet.

In the silence that followed the act of coming out, and, indeed, in the ten weeks of class in which no one spoke of it again, I felt an awkwardness settle over our discussions in section. I was never sure exactly how the Asian American students perceived the lesbian—as a wannabe "minority," as a comrade in marginality, as any White Other; or perhaps they did not think of it at all. Nor did I ever know if the lesbian found what she was looking for, a better understanding of the Asian American experience, in the silence that greeted her coming out.

More important, the coming-out incident suggests that marginalization is no guarantee for dialogue. If there is to be an interconnectedness between different vantage points, we will need to establish an art of political conversation that allows for affirmation of difference without choking secularization. The construction of such a politics is based implicitly on our vision of what ought to happen when difference meets itself—queer meets Asian, black meets Korean, feminist meets Green, etc., at times all in one person.[12] What exactly must we know about these other identities in order to engage in dialogue?

THE QUESTION OF AUTHENTICITY

What we do know about Asian American gays and lesbians must be gleaned from personal narratives, literature, poetry, short stories, and essays. But first, what falls under the mantle, *Asian American gay and lesbian* writings? Clearly, lesbians and gays whose writings are self-conscious reflections on Asian American identity and sexual identity ought to be categorized as Asian American gay/lesbian writers. For example, Kitty Tsui, Barbara Noda, Alice Hom, and Merle Woo are lesbians who write about themselves as lesbians, which grants them authorial voice *as lesbians*. But they also identify as *Asian American* and are concerned with the ways in which these different sources of community—lesbian and Asian American—function in their everyday lives.

But what then about those who do not write explicitly or self-consciously about their sexuality or racial identity? For example, an essay on AIDS and mourning by Jeff Nunokawa, while written by a Japanese American English professor, does not focus on issues of racial and sexual *identity*, and, as such, is neither self-consciously gay nor Asian American.[13] What are we to make of such work? On the one hand, we might wish to categorize the author as a gay Asian American writer, whether he wishes to take this sign or not, presuming of course, that he is gay, since his essay appears in an anthology subtitled, "gay theories," and, in addition presuming that he is Asian American, or at least identifies as such given his last name. On the other hand, we might instead argue that it is the author's work, his subject matter, and not the status of the author, that marks the work as gay, Asian American, or both. . . . In this case, we might infer that since the topic of the essay is AIDS and men, the work is best categorized as "gay," but not Asian American.

The university is filled with those of us who, while we live under signs like gay, Asian, feminist, ecologist, middle-class, etc., do not make such signs the central subject of our research. And what about those individuals who write about gays/lesbians, but who identify themselves as heterosexual? In the same way that colonizers write about the colonized, and more recently, the colonized write back, blacks write about whites and vice versa, "we" write about "them" and so on.

Not only is marginalization no guarantee for dialogue, but the state of being marginalized itself may not be capturable as a fixed, coherent, and holistic identity. Our attempts to define categories like "Asian Amerian" or "gay" are necessarily incomplete.

A politics of identity and whatever kind of politics ensues from that project—multiculturalism, feminism, and gay movements—is first of all a politics *about* identity. That is, about the lack of a holistic and "coherent narrative" derived from race, class, gender, and sexuality. . . . Because no sooner do we define, for example, "Japanese American" as a person of Japanese ancestry than we are forced back to the drawing board by the biracial child of a Japanese American and African American who thinks of herself as "black" or "feminist."

RETHINKING IDENTITY POLITICS

The gist of this essay has been to insist that our valuation of heterogeneity not be ad hoc and that we seize the opportunity to recognize non-ethnic-based differences—like homosexuality—as an occasion to critique the tendency toward essentialist currents in ethnic-based narratives and disciplines. In short, the practice of including gayness in Asian America rebounds into a reconsideration of the theoretical status of the concept of "Asian American" identity. The interior of the category "Asian American" ought not be viewed as a hierarchy of identities led by ethnic-based narratives, but rather, the complicated interplay and collision of different identities.

At the heart of my insistence on a qualitative, not quantitative, view of difference is a particular notion of subjectivity. That notion of the subject as non-unitary—that is, the notion that each of us has multiple identities—stands in sharp contrast to the holistic and coherent identities that find expression in much contemporary talk and writing about Asian Americans. At times, our need to "reclaim history" has been bluntly translated into a possessiveness about *the* Asian American experience (politics, history, literature) or perspectives as if such experiences or perspectives were not diffuse, shifting, and often contradictory. Feminists and gay writers offer an alternative: to "theorize" the subject rather than assume its truth or, worse yet, assign to it a truth.

To theorize the subject means to uncover in magnificent detail the "situatedness"[14] of perspectives or identities. The politics that result will be marked by moments of frustration and tension, because the participants will be pulling and pushing one another with statements such as, "I am like you," and "I am not like you." But the reward for an identity politics that is not primarily ethnic-based, or essentialist along some other axis, will be that conversations like the one which never took place in my Asian American studies section many years ago will finally begin.

PART 4

CONTESTATION

*tell this story
to America
and the
whole world*

STORYTIME

Anu Gupta

*T*here once was a woman. She was the daughter of fire; fury and anger incarnate. She would be the cause of the destruction of the universe and the beginning of a new era, a darker era, the era in which we now live.

The wise men, *rishis*, had predicted that she would marry the great Arjuna of the Pandav family. I doubt she knew she would be married to the greatest archer in all of India. All she knew was that men from across the country had been invited to compete for her hand. She was the prize in a test of strength and skill of the rulers of all the lands, the "property" of the man with the most virility. This competition, a *swymber*, was the way in which all princesses were married. To make Draupadi his wife, the suitor had to use the great bow of Shiva, the god of destruction, and shoot the eye of a revolving fish, hanging from above, while looking below at its reflection in a pool of oil.

I was a very little girl when I first heard this story. I can still remember watching the fan above me, imagining one of its blades to be the fish that Arjuna had to shoot at, as my grandmother wove her tale. On those hot and humid nights in India, I would lie on a cot, waiting patiently for my grandma and grandpa, Naniji and Nanaji, to lock up their section of the *havali*. Our family house was similar to a fortress, only round, not square. Big iron gates guarded its occupants from thieves, and the only things stolen that summer were clothes Nani hung out to dry on the roof by the monkeys who refused to be kept out. They would make off with *saris* and *chunnis*, and once in a while, to my Nani's chagrin, one of the baby monkeys would grab her brassiere and scamper across the rooftops, holding it like a safety blanket. This was my mother's house, and now I, the eldest daughter of the eldest daughter, had come to remember her memories and relive her childhood.

My Nani knew some English and would tell me these mythological stories before we all went to sleep. She had lived in the capital, Delhi, and studied Shakespeare when she was young, before India got her Independence. Her family was one of the few that actually benefited from the British occupation. She went to convent school every day to learn how to be "English." 1947 changed all that, including the life of my Nani. As Independence came to India, the Goddess Laksmi, bearer of wealth, left my Nani's home, and she was married off as soon as possible to someone beneath her status.

She went through great pains to tell me about all of the gods and goddesses. Every day there was a new tale, a remarkable adventure, a forbidden love story, a battle for honor. The words filled my ears, and later the dreams filled my head. I was quizzed when we went to temple about all the idols before me, and only correct answers earned me the right to eat the *prasad*, or holy food, on the way home. Perhaps my Nani was afraid that her "Amerikan" granddaughter would grow up to be a bad "Hindu," not knowing why she prayed to the gods that she did pray to, having no understanding of her deep religious heritage, questioning and doubting the existence of the Being who gave her life. For me, the connection between temple and tale was a confused one, and I only listened to learn the magic. These tales weren't stories I could borrow from the public library, or learn in any of my classes. These were stories of good and evil, of my past and my future. I learned about my culture this way, through the myths which were truths for my Naniji.

Arjuna, being the son of god, shot the arrow straight into the center of the eye of the revolving fish. He won the tournament, and also won the hand of Draupadi, the daughter of fire, the destroyer of mankind.

~~~

I have five lovers. One from my past—the mistake, the crush, the lust relationship. The other is from my present; he is my comforter, my friend, my hearer, my "rebound-man-turned-boyfriend." The third is my forbidden lover. She is beautiful, passionate, sensual—the one I want to be with but can not. The man of my dreams is the fourth. Sexy, intelligent, romantic, compassionate, he occupies my fantasies and my daydreams. My last lover comments as I walk down the street wearing a miniskirt, offers to buy me a drink or two or three at bars, comes to me only at night, and leaves me in a sweat with a lump in my throat and rage and shame in my soul. He is the lover of my nightmares, the one who prank-calls me, who defies restraining orders. The fifth lover is the one I have murdered a hundred times—the one who refuses to die.

Arjuna returned home with his new wife and his four brothers. Upon entering, he proclaimed joyously, "I have a surprise for you, Ma."

His mother, Kunti, was finishing her morning prayers. Without looking to address her son, she responded, "That's nice, share it amongst all of you." Quite pleased with herself she finished her chants. "What a good mother I am," she thought to herself. Anything that was hers, she always gave to her five sons. Little did she know what she had done.

I wonder how Draupadi must have felt. Leaving her own home, she arrives at her new one to have her mother-in-law tell her that she should be shared. She's a woman, not a doe, that can be carved and eaten by everyone. I am sure she expected Arjuna to clarify the situation to his mother. "No, Ma, you don't understand. Come look, I have brought you a daughter-in-law. Isn't she beautiful?" That is what I would have expected.

Arjuna hung his head in shame. You see, all five brothers had never ever disobeyed Kunti's orders. She was like a goddess and her wishes were obeyed without a second thought. They could not disobey her now. If Kunti told them to share Draupadi, then they all must share her, all five of them. And so, Draupadi went from having one husband to having five husbands.

She would have five masters to serve. She would have five different hands stroke her hair, caress her breasts, and explore her *yoni*. Five different men, all brothers, would make love to her. She would be passed from one man to the other, night after night. If she wasn't a queen, she would be called a prostitute.

I have always wondered how this part of the story is condoned by Indians. If I had five husbands, I would be ostracized, called a whore, and, in this country, thrown into jail for polygamy. In a culture where lovemaking is done only to have sons, where the *Kama Sutra* is depicted as an "instruction book" to combat infertility, where does this rampant defiance of the normal monogamous marriage fit? How could the queen be shared by the brother-kings? Everything has its explanation, even this. You see, the Pandavs were all sons of different gods. Their mother, Kunti, was impregnated by five different gods to give birth to the Pandavs. And those gods are just different forms of the same god. So, in essence, Draupadi was married to a god who took the form of five different men. She had only one husband, god. As such, my five lovers, past, present, forbidden, dream, and night, are not sanctioned. I am engaging in sexual prostitution of the soul; I turn the same five tricks, day in and day out.

Draupadi lived the rest of her life with her five husbands. When they were banished, she accompanied them. When any one of them was sad, angry, or upset, she would go to him, comfort and console him. She liked Bheema the best, after Arjuna, for he understood and shared her anger and rage. Yudhistra was her opposite. His patience incensed her beyond belief. The twins were the youngest of the five. They were followers of Yudhistra and Bheema. Finally there was Arjuna, the man who had won her, her first husband. She loved him more than anything, and he her. It is rumored that after a while each brother built a castle and Draupadi stayed with each one for a year. During that time, no other brother was allowed to visit her. Arjuna broke this rule and visited Draupadi while she was at Yudhistra's castle. He was banished for a year by Yudhistra. As much as they loved each other, it was some other woman who would give birth to Abimanyu, Arjuna's son, and the "grandfather" of all the men and women who now live on Earth.

~~~~~

"Am I a slave, or am I free?" Draupadi asked. But what answer can deaf ears give? She was neither free nor a slave, but no one had the courage to point that out.

Draupadi was boiling with rage. How dare her husband Yudhistra use his wife as a wager during a game of dice. She wasn't his prized horse, or his favorite castle. Yudhistra, however, had already lost all those things to his cousin-brother with whom he was playing. A desperate man, he then bet and lost all four of his brothers. Finally he bet himself. Now, the question arises: If he bet himself, how could he then bet his wife Draupadi? A man who has bet himself, lost, and is now a slave, can not bet anything else, because he does not own anything else to bet. According to some, however, that was a moot point. Draupadi, as his wife, is his property and, as such, if he is a slave, she is one as well. Others believed that once he became a slave, Yudhistra had no right to bet anything else, including his wife.

"Am I a slave, or am I free?," she asked the crowd of men once again. No one, not even Yudhistra, would give her an answer.

Almost every woman in the history of mankind has asked this question. Draupadi was just the first. How many women have told their husbands that they do not own them. How many have fought to be independent, to go where they please, to study, to get a job. And how many of them were beaten, raped, and silenced, told that they were in essence slaves to their husbands.

When I told my boyfriend that I could do whatever I wanted, he grabbed both my arms and threw me against the wall. Even though he was five inches taller than I am, I could see the whites of his eyes right in front of mine. I was a slave in that relationship. He told me how to dress, whom to talk to, and what to say. He is now my ex-boyfriend.

Lessons of childhood are learnt well. I watched my aunt get raped on her wedding night. I saw my uncle's hand grabbing her exposed breast; the red and the gold of the sari being ripped while the other hand muffled her screams and protests. The hair that my mother had so lovingly braided that morning came undone in the struggle. This is what my aunt had saved herself for, this was the night that she had dreamed about for years. No one but me could understand why she wanted an abortion when she found out she was pregnant. After all, she was married, she should be overjoyed. Now I ask you, was my aunt a slave, or was she free?

I never understood why Draupadi bothered to ask that question. Even if they had told her an answer, would it have mattered to her? Draupadi would have followed Yudhistra and the others wherever they went. That was part of her duty as a wife. It was the way of the *dharma*, the pact by which all the *kystria* or ruling class lived. As a wife, Draupadi would always be a slave. As a woman, she would always be free.

~~~~

He had violated her by touching her sacred hair. How could he touch her purified hair, in front of all these men. She was a queen, Queen Draupadi. He didn't care; she was a slave. That is what the men had decided. She was a slave, and her new master had a right to see the "goods." So, if she wasn't going to undress herself, he would have to. Dragging her by the hair, he pulled her to the center of the room. He grabbed one end of her sari and started pulling.

Once upon a time there was a princess. As she was traveling through her kingdom, she came upon a little boy with a flute. He played so well that all the village girls stopped whatever they were doing and began to dance with him. When she heard his music, she joined the dance as well. It is said that over a hundred girls danced that day to the notes of that flute and none of them made a mistake. As the boy with the flute was helping the princess back into her carriage, he cut his pinky finger on the edge of her chariot. The princess ripped a piece of her sari off and tied it around his finger to stop the bleeding. He promised her that one day he would come to her aid when she most needed him. The boy's name was Krishna; the princess was Draupadi.

The cousin-brother began tugging at her sari. The crowd looked on with horror, but no one stopped him. Even her husbands were helpless. She placed her hands together and raised her head to the sky.

"You once promised to come in my time of need, Lord Krishna. Please do not fail me now."

Miraculously, the sari became longer and longer. Yellow turned into green into red into blue. It was endless. Pretty soon, he became tired and sat down. Draupadi was saved from shame and dishonor. He had failed to unclothe her in public.

I wish he had tugged on my hair. I wish he had bruised and beaten me; it would have made it so much easier to accept. Instead, he caressed it, told me how beautiful and silky my hair was. He leaned over to inhale its scent as he wrapped the ends of the wavy strands around his fingers and pushed the sides behind my ears. I told myself that this wasn't happening, that I would just go home and wash away his filthy residue. From my hair he moved to my face, caressing it, scanning it, looking for some mysterious treasure. I smiled, trying to create conversation. My hair was not purified in holy waters, but it was still my hair.

I wish I had been as lucky as Draupadi. There was no second shirt under the one that he had begun to unbutton. There was no magical pair of panties under the ones he yanked off from underneath my hitched skirt. I hadn't tied any piece of clothing to the bleeding finger of a human god. There was no miracle for me to save me from shame. I was let down in my time of need. Yes, just one set of clothes for me. They came off so easily. At least he didn't rip them; he was good about that. I had them to put on again once he left. How do I wash my soul?

~~~~

"After the cousin-brothers had tried to shame Draupadi, the Pandavs all took an oath to destroy them. This pledge led to the war that destroyed all those who lived in that eon. When the gods make a promise, it must be fulfilled, no matter what the consequences. Everyone who had maligned and assaulted her died a brutal death at the hands of Arjuna and Bheema."

"But what happened to Draupadi, Nani?" Even though I was sleepy, I hadn't forgotten about the daughter of fire.

"Draupadi died of old age and accompanied the Pandavs to heaven after the world was destroyed and reborn."

As a child I thought that my Nani was tired and made up that lame ending so that I would go to sleep. I now realize, however, that Draupadi becomes a forgotten figure in the tale. She had served her purpose of being the spark for the *Mahabartha*, and after the war began, there was no other role she could play. As a woman she could not be a warrior. The fighting was left to the men, the gods, and the rest of the tale is devoted to the triumph of good over evil. There was nothing else Nani could have told me about Draupadi; she had to assume that sooner or later Draupadi died like everyone else. For me Draupadi was not so easily forgotten. My Draupadi could not die such an insignificant death. Even now I dream about her, her beauty, courage, intelligence, and strength.

~~~

I smiled and brushed my granddaughter's hair away from her sleepy eyes. "No, Chand, I didn't forget about Draupadi. She gave birth to many, many daughters. She told them that they were beautiful and special. Draupadi taught them to be strong and courageous. She gave them the tools to survive the hardships that a new, darker era would bring. She helped them understand the injustices they would face as women. Draupadi made her daughters believe in themselves. Lastly, she made them promise to always remember that they were the daughters of fire, just like their mother. And those daughters gave birth to more daughters, who gave birth to more daughters . . . who gave birth to me and you."

A PORTRAIT OF THE SELF AS NATION, 1990–1991

Marilyn Chin

> Fit in dominatu servitus
> In servitute dominatus
> In mastery there is bondage
> In bondage there is mastery
> LATIN PROVERB
>
> The stranger and the enemy
> We have seen him in the
> mirror.
> GEORGE SEFERIS

*f*orgive me, Head Master,
but you see, I have forgotten
to put on my black lace underwear, and instead
I have hiked my slip up, up to my waist
so that I can enjoy the breeze.
It feels good to be without,
so good as to be salacious.
The feeling of flesh kissing tweed.
If ecstasy had a color, it would be
yellow and pink, yellow and pink
Mongolian skin rubbed raw.
The serrated lining especially fine
like wearing a hair-shirt, inches above the knee.
When was the last time I made love?
The last century! With a wan missionary.
Or was it San Wu the Bailiff?
The tax collector who came for my tithes?
The herdboy, the ox, on the bridge of magpies?
It was Roberto, certainly,
high on coke, circling the galaxy.
Or my recent vagabond love
driving a reckless chariot, lost
in my feral country. *Country,* Oh I am
so punny, so very, very punny.
Dear Mr. Decorum, don't you agree?

It's not so much the length of the song
but the range of the emotions—Fear
has kept me a good pink monk—and poetry
is my nunnery. Here I am alone in my altar,
self-hate, self-love, both self-erotic notions.
Eyes closed, listening to that one hand clapping—
not metaphysical trance, but fleshly mutilation—
and loving *it*, myself and that pink womb, my bed.
Reading *Ching Ping Mei* in the "expurgated"
where all the female protagonists were named
Lotus.
Those damned licentious women named us
Modest, Virtue, Cautious, Endearing,
Demure-dewdrop, Plum-aster, Petal-stamen.
They teach us to walk headbent in devotion,
to honor the five relations, ten sacraments.
Meanwhile, the feast is brewing elsewhere,
the ox is slaughtered and her entrails are hung
on the branches for the poor. They convince us, yes,
our chastity will save the nation—Oh mothers,
all your sweet epithets didn't make us wise!
Orchid by any other name is equally seditious.

Now, where was I, oh yes, now I remember,
the last time I made love, it was to you.
I faintly remember your whiskers
against my tender nape.
You were a conquering barbarian,
helmeted, halberded,
beneath the gauntleted moon,
whispering Hunnish or English—
so-long Oolong went the racist song,
bye-bye little chinky butterfly.
There is no cure for self-pity,
the disease is death,
ennui, disaffection,
a roll of flesh-colored tract homes crowding my imagination.
I do hate my loneliness,
sitting cross-legged in my room,
satisfied with a few off-rhymes,
sending off precious haiku to some inconspicuous journal
named "Left Leaning Bamboo."

You, my precious read, O sweet voyeur,
sweaty, balding, bespeckled,
in a rumpled rayon shirt
and a neo-Troubadour chignon,
politics mildly centrist,
the *right* fork for the *right* occasions,
matriculant of the best schools—
herewith, my last confession
(with decorous and perfect diction)
I loathe to admit. Yet, I shall admit it:
there was no Colonialist coercion;
sadly, we blended together well.
I was poor, starving, war torn,
an empty coffin to be filled,
You were a young, ambitious Lieutenant
with dreams of becoming Prince
of a "new world order," Lord
over the League of Nations.

Lover, destroyer, savior!
I remember that moment of beguilement,
one hand muffling my mouth,
one hand untying my sash—
On your throat dangled a golden cross.
Your god is jealous, your god is cruel.
So, when did you finally return?
And . . . was there a second coming?
My memory is failing me, perhaps
you came too late
(we were already dead),
Perhaps you didn't come at all—
you had a deadline to meet,
another alliance to secure,
another resistance to break.
Or you came too often
to my painful dismay.
(Oh, how facile the liberator's hand.)
Often when I was asleep
You would hover over me
with your great silent wingspan
and watch me sadly.
This is the way you want me—

asleep, quiescent, almost dead,
sedated by lush immigrant dreams
of global bliss, connubial harmony.

Yet I shall always remember
and deign to forgive
(long before I am satiated,
long before I am spent)
that last pressured cry,
"your little death."
Under the halcyon light
you would smoke and contemplate
the sea and debris,
that barbaric keening
of what it means to be free.
As if we were ever free,
as if ever we could be.
Said the judge,
"Congratulations,
On this day, fifteen of November, 1967,
Marilyn Mei Ling Chin,
Application # z-z-z-z-z-,
you are an American citizen,
naturalized in the name of God
the father, God the son and the Holy Ghost."
Time assuages, and even
the Yellow River becomes clean . . .

Meanwhile we forget
the power of exclusion
what you are walling in or out—
and to whom you must give offence.
The hungry, the slovenly, the convicts
need not apply.
The syphilitic, the consumptive
may not moor.
The hookwormed and tracomaed
(and the likewise infested).
The gypsies, the sodomists, the mentally infirm.
The pagans, the heathens, the non-
denominational—

The coloreds, the mixed-races and the reds.
The communists, the usurous,
the mutants, the Hibakushas, the hags . . .

Oh, connoisseurs of gastronomy and *keemun* tea!
My foes, my loves,
how eloquent your discrimination,
how precise your poetry.
Last night, in our large, rotund bed,
we witnessed this fall. *Ours*
was an "aerial war." Bombs
glittering in the twilight sky
against the Star-spangled Banner.
Dunes and dunes of sand,
fields and fields of rice.
A thousand charred oil wells,
the firebrands of night.
Ecstasy made us tired.

Sir, master, Dominator,
Fall was a glorious season for the hegemonists.
We took long melancholy strolls on the beach,
digressed on art and politics
in a quaint wharfside cafe in La Jolla.
The storm grazed our bare arms gently . . .
History has never failed us.
Why save Babylonia or Cathay,
when we can always have Paris?
Darling, if we are to remember at all,
Let us remember it well—
We were fierce, yet tender,
fierce and tender.

Notes:
Second stanza: *Ching Ping Mei* is a Chinese erotic novel.
Sixth stanza: Exclusion refers to various "exclusion acts" or anti-Chinese legislation that
    attempted to halt the flow of Chinese immigrants to the U.S.
Hookworm and tracoma are two diseases that kept many Chinese detained and quarantined
    at Angel Island.
Hibakushas are scarred survivors of the atom bomb and their deformed descendants.

ASIAN PACIFIC AMERICAN WOMEN AND RACIALIZED SEXUAL HARASSMENT

Sumi K. Cho

> I'll get right to the point, since the objective is to give
> you, in writing, a clear description of what I desire. . . .
> Shave between your legs, with an electric razor, and then
> a hand razor to ensure it is very smooth. . . .
>   I want to take you out to an underground nightclub . . .
> like this, to enjoy your presence, envious eyes, to touch
> you in public. . . . You will obey me and refuse me
> nothing. . . .
>   I believe these games are dangerous because they
> bring us closer together, yet at the same time I am going
> to be more honest about the past and present
> relationships I have. I don't want you to get any idea that I
> am devoting myself only to you—I want my freedom
> here. . . . The only positive thing I can say about this is I
> was dreaming of your possible Tokyo persona since I met
> you. I hope I can experience it now, the beauty and
> eroticism.

*t*he above passage comes from a letter written by a white male professor to a Japanese female student at a major university.[1] The more unsavory details referring to physical specifications and particularly demeaning and sadistic demands by the professor have been edited. In her complaint against him, the student stated that the faculty member "sought out Japanese women in particular" and "uses his position as a university professor to impress and se-duce Japanese women." The professor had a history of targeting Japanese women because "he believes they are submissive and will obey any parame-ters he sets for the relationship," according to the student's complaint. "He said that he wants sex slaves, that he considers and treats women as dispos-able. . . . He rarely takes precautions in a sexual relationship."[2]

Another Japanese female student and former officer of a campus Japa-nese student organization recalled that the same professor had approached her outside of a 7-11 store near the campus and asked for her phone number, stating that he was interested in meeting Japanese females. "I gave him my number because I was the vice-president [of the Japanese student organiza-tion] and felt I should be gracious." Through the course of their conversa-tions, the professor told the woman that he "hangs around campus looking for Japanese girls" and asked "where [he] could meet them." By his own admission, "[he] stated that he was not popular in high school and college." However, "when he went to Japan he found out that he was popular" and was now "making up for lost time." The professor told the student that "[h]e liked Japanese females because they were easy to have sex with and because they were submissive."[3]

I have long been haunted by the unsuccessful resolution to this case due to the effective intimidation of the courageous student and those who sought redress.[4] Victims of sexual harassment often fear coming forward because of precisely the type of administrative, legal, and community discouragement or intimidation that constituted the "secondary injury" in this case. Here, the secondary injury was inflicted by the university's affirmative action office, which claimed to find no evidence of an actionable claim worth investigating,[5] the self-proclaimed "feminist law firm" in town that defended the predator-professor,[6] and the university counsel that bolstered the intimidatory tactics of the professor's lawyer.[7]

What I hope to reveal in this article is how converging racial and gender stereotypes of Asian Pacific American women help constitute what I will refer to as "racialized sexual harassment." Racialized sexual harassment denotes a particular set of injuries resulting from the unique complex of power relations facing Asian Pacific American women and other women of color in the workplace. More specifically, this article explores how race and gender combine to alter conceptions of both the "primary injury" (the offending conduct legally recognized as sexual harassment) and the "secondary injury" (the actions of employers and institutions that ally with the harasser). In two cases that I discuss, stereotypes of Asian Pacific American female plaintiffs and the racial and gender politics of the plaintiffs' work environment are determining factors in the harms suffered and systemic responses thereto. The law's refusal to recognize and address the compoundedness of racialized sexual harassment lets flourish converging stereotypes and the oppressive structures that give rise to such injuries.

CONVERGING STEREOTYPES:
THE MODEL MINORITY MEETS SUZIE WONG

Asian Pacific American women are at particular risk of being racially and sexually harassed because of the synergism that results when sexualized racial stereotypes combine with racialized gender stereotypes. The "model minority myth," a much criticized racial stereotype of Asian Pacific Americans, has been shown to paint a misleading portrait of groupwide economic, educational, and professional super-success. In addition, the mythical model minority is further overdetermined by associated images of political passivity and submissiveness to authority. But despite the many critical articles written by Asian Pacific Americans on the model minority stereotype, few have theorized specifically how it relates to Asian Pacific American women.[8] Model minority traits of passivity and submissiveness are intensified and gendered through the stock portrayal of obedient and servile Asian Pacific women in popular culture.[9] The repeated projection of a compliant and catering Asian feminine nature feeds harassers' belief that Asian Pacific American women will be receptive objects of their advances, make good victims, and will not fight back.

Similarly, the process of objectification that affects women in general takes on a particular virulence with the overlay of race upon gender stereotypes. Generally, objectification diminishes the contributions of women, reducing their worth to male perceptions of female sexuality.[10] In the workplace, objectification comes to mean that the material valuation of women's contributions will be based not on their professional accomplishments or work performance but on men's perceptions of their potential to be harassed.[11] Asian Pacific women suffer greater harassment due to racialized ascriptions (exotic, hyper-erotic, masochistic, desirous of sexual domination) that set them up as ideal-typical gratifiers of Western neocolonial libidinal formations. In a 1990 *Gentleman's Quarterly* article entitled, "Oriental Girls," Tony Rivers rehearsed the racialized particulars of the "great Western male fantasy":

> Her face—round like a child's, . . . eyes almond-shaped for mystery, black for suffering, wide-spaced for innocence, high cheekbones swelling like bruises, cherry lips. . . .
>
> When you come home from another hard day on the planet, she comes into existence, removes your clothes, bathes you and walks naked on your back to relax you. . . . She's fun you see, and so uncomplicated. She doesn't go to assertiveness-training classes, insist on being treated like a person, fret about career moves, wield her orgasm as a non-negotiable demand. . . .
>
> She's there when you need shore leave from those angry feminist seas. She's a handy victim of love or a symbol of the rape of third world nations, a real trouper.[12]

As the passage reveals, colonial and military domination are interwoven with sexual domination to provide the "ultimate Western male fantasy."[13] Asian Pacific women are particularly valued in a sexist society because they provide the antidote to visions of liberated career women who challenge the objectification of women.[14] In this sense, the objectified gender stereotype also assumes a model minority function as Asian Pacific women are deployed to "discipline" white women, just as Asian Pacific Americans in general are used against their "nonmodel" counterparts, African Americans.

The "ultimate Western male fantasy," part of colonial sexual mythology based on Western perceptions of women in Asia, is applied to Asian Pacific

American women in an international transfer of stereotypes through mass media and popular culture. Military involvement in Asia, colonial and neo-colonial history, and the derivative Asian Pacific sex tourism industry establish power relations between Asia and the West which in turn shape stereotypes of Asian Pacific women that apply to those in and outside of Asia.[15] As his article continues, Rivers suggests that the celluloid prototype of the "Hong Kong hooker with a heart of gold" (from the 1960 film, *The World of Suzie Wong*) may be available in one's own hometown: "Suzie Wong was the originator of the modern fantasy. . . . Perhaps even now, . . . on the edge of a small town, Suzie awaits a call."[16]

Given this cultural backdrop of converging racial and gender stereotypes in which the model minority meets Suzie Wong, so to speak, Asian Pacific American women are especially susceptible to racialized sexual harassment. The university, despite its well-cultivated image as an enlightened, genteel environment of egalitarianism, unfortunately does not distinguish itself from other hostile work environments for Asian Pacific American women. I now turn to two cases in which Asian Pacific American women faculty were subjected to quid pro quo and hostile environment forms of harassment.[17] Although racialized sexual harassment experienced by professionals should not be assumed to be identical to that facing women of color employed in blue- and pink-collar jobs, there is commonality in the social construction of the victims.

QUID PRO QUO: THE ROSALIE TUNG CASE

Rosalie Tung joined the University of Pennsylvania Wharton School of Business (hereinafter, "Business School") in 1981 as an associate professor of management. In her early years at the Business School, she garnered praise for her performance.[18] In the summer of 1983 a change in leadership brought a new dean and new department chair to the school. According to Tung, "shortly after taking office, the chairman of the management department began to make sexual advances toward me."[19] In June 1984 the chair awarded Professor Tung a twenty percent increase in salary and high praise for her achievements in research, teaching, and community service.

However, when Tung came up for tenure review in the fall of 1984, her chair's evaluation of her performance changed dramatically.[20] "After I made it clear to the chairman that I wanted our relationship kept on a professional basis," she stated in her charge, "he embarked on a ferocious campaign to destroy and defame me. He solicited more than thirty letters of recommendation from external and internal reviewers when the usual practice was for five or six letters."[21] Although a majority of her department faculty recommended tenure, the personnel committee denied Professor Tung's promotion. Tung later learned through a respected and well-placed member of the faculty that the justification given by the decision makers was that "the Wharton School is not interested in China-related research."[22] Tung understood this to mean that the Business School "did not want a Chinese American, an Oriental [on their faculty]." Of over sixty faculty in the management department, there were no tenured professors of color and only one tenured woman. At the entire Business School, with over three hundred faculty, there were only two tenured people of color, both male.

Tung filed a complaint with the Equal Employment Opportunity Commission (EEOC) in Philadelphia alleging race, sex, and national origin discrimination. She also filed a complaint with the university grievance commission. Tung's file and those of thirteen faculty members granted tenure in a recent five-year period were turned over to the grievance commission. During this process, the peer review files revealed that despite the many letters the department chair had solicited, only three negative letters were in her file—two of which had been written by the chair himself! One of the chair's negative letters was written only six months after his rave review in June 1984. Professor Tung's file contained over thirty letters consistently praising her as one of the best and brightest young scholars in her field, including one from a Nobel Prize laureate. Her impressive list of achievements and contributions had been acknowledged by her peers in her election to the board of governors of the Academy of Management, a professional association of over seven thousand management faculty. Tung was the first person of color ever elected to the board. Following forty hours of hearings, the university grievance commission found that the university had discriminated against Tung. Despite a university administrative decision in her favor, the provost overseeing the matter chose to do nothing. Professor Tung suspects that race and gender stereotypes played a role in shaping the provost's inaction: "[T]he provost, along with others in the university administration, felt that I, being an Asian, would be less likely to challenge the establishment, because Asians have traditionally not fought back. In other words, it was okay to discriminate against Asians, because they are passive; they take things quietly, and they will not fight back."[23]

Tung also noted the comments of one of her colleagues, describing her in a newspaper article as "elegant, timid, and not one of those loud-mouthed women on campus." Her colleague continued, "[i]n other words, [Professor Tung was] the least likely person to kick over the tenure-review apple cart."[24]

In light of the university's nonresponse to its own internal committee's findings, Rosalie Tung pursued her EEOC claim. In order to investigate, the EEOC subpoenaed her personnel file along with those of five male faculty members who had been granted tenure around the same time she had been denied. The University of Pennsylvania refused to turn over the files, and the case, known as *University of Pennsylvania v. EEOC*, eventually reached the U.S. Supreme Court.

Among its claims, the university argued that one of the essential First Amendment freedoms that a university enjoys is the right to "determine for itself on academic grounds who may teach."[25] The Court rejected the university's contention and handed down a unanimous decision in favor of Tung's EEOC investigation. The conservative Rehnquist Court set an important precedent in establishing baseline procedures for Title VII claims in academic employment. *University of Pennsylvania v. EEOC* represents the Court's willingness to alter, at least slightly, its long-standing tradition of absolute deference to higher education's decision-making process in the face of egregious discrimination and harassment. The Tung case exposed and rejected the "academic freedom trumps harassment and discrimination" rationale that served to hide the evidence of wrongdoing in tenure denials.[26]

HOSTILE ENVIRONMENT: THE JEAN JEW CASE

Dr. Jean Jew arrived at the University of Iowa in 1973 from Tulane University along with another physician and her mentor, who had just been appointed chair of the anatomy department in the college of medicine. Almost immediately, rumors circulated about her alleged sexual relationship with her mentor. These rumors persisted for the next thirteen years. Despite the increased number of incidents of harassment and vilification Jew experienced after joining the anatomy department, she was recommended by the department for tenure in December 1978. Her promotion, however, did not quiet her detractors. In a drunken outburst in 1979, a senior member of the anatomy department referred to Jew as a "stupid slut," a "dumb bitch," and a "whore."[27] Jew and three other professors complained separately to the dean about the slurs.

Jean Jew's tenure promotion not only failed to quiet her critics, it apparently further fueled the rumor mill and provided colleagues with an opportunity to air personal grievances and exploit departmental politics. Jean Jew was the only woman in the anatomy department and one of a few Asian Pacific American women among the University of Iowa faculty. In this homogeneous setting, stereotypes flourished to such an extent the faculty did not even recognize the difference between jokes and racial slurs. One faculty member who referred to Dr. Jew as a "chink" contended that he was merely "using the word in a frivolous situation" and repeating a joke.[28] The model minority stereotype of competence and achievement fed existing insecurities and jealousies in a department that was already deeply polarized.[29] In responding to these insecurities, a traditional gender stereotype informed by racialized ascriptions acted to rebalance the power relations. Gender stereotypes with racial overtones painted Jew as an undeserving Asian Pacific

American woman who traded on her sexuality to get to the top. To Jew, this stereotyping and her refusal to accede to it played a large role in the "no-win" configuration of departmental power relations:

> If we act like the [passive] Singapore Girl, in the case of some professors, then they feel "she is [unequal to me]." If we don't act like the Singapore Girl,[30] then [our] accomplishments must have derived from "a relationship with the chair." There were quite a few people that felt that way to begin with. They thought because I was working with the chair, I was his handmaiden. Many faculty testified that in inter-collaborative work, I was doing work that led to publication but that he was the intellectual, with Jean Jew as his lackey. The term used was that I was the collaborative force, but not independent.[31]

This construction of Dr. Jew is perhaps most evident in the continued attack on her credentials. One of her primary harassers, whose advanced degrees were not in anatomy but in physical education, may have felt the need to attack Jew's professional standing and personal character out of his own academic insecurities. Among the many incidents, this faculty member intimated to a lab technician that Dr. Jew held a favored status in the department because of her willingness to engage in a sexual relationship with the chair in exchange for economic and professional gain. Overall, this faculty member made more than thirty-three demeaning and harassing statements about Jean Jew in an attempt to discredit her professional and personal reputation.[32]

Other colleagues also denigrated Jew. After he was denied tenure in 1991, one doctor filed a grievance with the university stating that his qualifications were better than those of Jew, who had been tenured. To support his case, the doctor submitted an anonymous letter to the dean, indicating that Jew's promotion was due to her sexual relationship with the chair. The letter stated, in fortune-cookie style, "[b]asic science chairman cannot use state money to . . . pay for Chinese pussy."[33] Another doctor who held administrative responsibilities in the department frequently posted obscene drawings outside his office, where students congregated, which depicted a naked copulating couple with handwritten comments referring to Jew and the department chair.[34] On the very day that the senior departmental faculty were to evaluate Jew for promotion to full professor, the following off-color limerick appeared on the faculty men's restroom wall:

> There was a professor of anatomy
> Whose colleagues all thought he had a lobotomy
> Apartments he had to rent
> And his semen was all spent
> On a colleague who did his microtomy.[35]

The faculty voted three in favor, five against Jean Jew's promotion, and she was denied full professorship.

Following her denial, Jew registered a complaint of sexual harassment with the university affirmative action office, the anatomy review and search committee, and the university's academic affairs vice-president. No action was taken on her complaint. In January of 1984, her attorney, Carolyn Chalmers, submitted a formal written complaint alleging sexual harassment to the vice-president. In response to the written complaint from legal counsel, a panel was appointed to investigate Jew's charges. The panel found in Jew's favor, yet the university took no meaningful action in response to the panel's findings. In utter frustration at the university's unwillingness to remedy the hostile work environment, Jew and Chalmers took the case to court.

Jean Jew's first suit in federal district court alleged that the University of Iowa failed to remedy the hostile work environment from which she suffered. After fourteen days of testimony, the judge issued a ruling, finding inter alia that the University of Iowa had failed to respond to Jew's complaints. According to the judge, the faculty in the anatomy department displayed "a pattern of verbal conduct which sexually denigrated Dr. Jew . . . in a concerted and purposeful manner."[36] He reasoned that "Dr. Jew has conducted herself throughout her employment at the university as a serious and committed teacher, scholar and member of the academic community."[37] The judge also found that sexual bias played a significant role in her denial of promotion to full professor in 1983. He found that four of the five professors who voted negatively on her promotion had displayed sexual bias. Judge Vietor ordered the university to promote Jew to full professor and awarded over $50,000 in back pay and benefits dating back to 1984, a rare remedy given the federal courts' historic deference to university academic personnel decisions.

Jew also filed a second defamation suit in state court in October 1985. The suit alleged that she was sexually harassed by another member of her department. The six-woman, one-man jury unanimously found for Jew and awarded $5,000 in actual damages, and $30,000 in punitive damages. Jew had won her second legal battle, but her adversarial relationship with the University of Iowa was not over.

The university stated that it would appeal the federal judge's decision on First Amendment grounds in October 1990. The Iowa Board of Regents governing the university provided the public rationale for the appeal, stating that Vietor's decision made the university responsible "for policing the statements and behavior of faculty members in ways that appear inconsistent with academic life and constitutional protections."[38] "In an academic community this is extremely disturbing," the statement continued. "The effect of chilling speech in a community dedicated to the free exchange of ideas and views—even unpleasant ones—requires that the board and the university pursue the matter further."[39] Jew's attorney Carolyn Chalmers interpreted the board's comments as a defense of the university's freedom to promote faculty members without judicial intervention even when it engages in sexual discrimination. As for the free speech claim, Chalmers observed that "[w]hat they're arguing is that academic freedom protects gutter talk."[40]

Only when considerable community criticism surfaced did the university decide to cut its losses and accept the validity of the verdict. In an editorial criticizing the university's strategy for appeal, Professor Peter Shane of the University of Iowa College of Law wrote:

> No proper concept of academic freedom . . . could immunize the public denigration of Dr. Jew as a "slut," a "chink," a "bitch" and a "whore"—all this by people actually permitted to vote on her qualifications for promotion! Neither should academic privilege protect the circulation of unfounded rumors about any person. . . . The only connection between academic freedom and Dr. Jew's experience is that university officials essentially ostracized her for insisting that promotions be evaluated in a way that does not disadvantage women. That ostracism and the consequent chill on her sympathizers' expression surely did compromise academic freedom.[41]

Faculty and staff supporting the federal judge's finding of sexual harassment brought added pressure against the university appeal effort by forming the Jean Jew Justice Committee and distributing the judge's order and findings of fact to the campus community.[42]

The university's unwillingness to accept responsibility for the racialized sexual harassment of Jean Jew extends beyond the attempt to appeal the decision. That the University of Iowa paid for the legal expenses to defend the offending professor's defamation suit for over five years, as well as the $35,000 judgment entererd by the court in his guilty verdict, reveals the depth of complicity between the university and the adjudged harasser. Clearly, the administration sided with the wrongdoer after its own internal investigative panel supported Dr. Jew's claims and even after a verdict was returned against him. The university's adversarial treatment of Jew, its inaction following the internal committee's findings, its futile appeal attempt, and its shouldering of the harasser's individual civil liability reflect a disturbing pattern whereby academic institutions circle the wagons to protect the harasser against the harassed. One wonders to what extent the university's persistent litigiousness in the face of adverse administrative and legal findings reflects the prevalence of racial and sexual stereotypes that led it to side with the harasser and formulate an aggressive legal strategy to "bully" a plaintiff perceived to be politically weak and passive. As Professor Martha Chamallas, former University of Iowa law professor and founding member of the Jean Jew Justice Committee, observed:

> . . . the rumor campaign against Jew was successful and persistent because it drew upon deep-seated and harmful stereotypes about professional

women and about Asian academics in American universities. In contrast to the official fact-finders who were constrained to base their judgment solely on the evidence presented, many within the University community making less considered judgments may have allowed stereotypes to influence their views.[43]

CONCLUSION

In light of the prevalent and converging racial and gender stereotypes of Asian Pacific American women as politically passive and sexually exotic and compliant, serious attention must be given to the problem of racialized sexual harassment revealed by the two cases discussed. On a theoretical level, new frameworks that integrate race and gender should be developed to take account of the multidimensional character of racialized sexual harassment that occurs and is challenged across races, social classes, and borders.[44] The law's current dichotomous categorization of racial discrimination and sexual harassment as separate spheres of injury is inadequate to respond to racialized sexual harassment. On an advocacy level, women's and Asian Pacific American organizations should affirmatively address racialized sexual harassment and seek ways to counter the compounded vulnerability[45] that Asian Pacific and Asian Pacific American women face in confronting both the primary and secondary injuries. Finally, on an international level, insofar as the problem of racialized sexual harassment of Asian Pacific American women, even in elite employment sectors such as institutions of higher education, derives in part from international stereotypes that feed upon unequal power relations, military history, and uneven economic development between Asia (especially in the Philippines and Thailand) and the U.S., it is important for critical race feminists to commit to eradicating the sources of racialized sexual harassment not only in the U.S., but also in the lives of sister counterparts overseas.

EPILOGUE

Following her Supreme Court victory in which access to the comparison files of her colleagues was granted, Rosalie Tung entered into a confidential settlement with the University of Pennsylvania. She currently holds the only endowed chair in the School of Business at Simon Fraser University in Vancouver, British Columbia.

Jean Jew continues to research and teach at the University of Iowa as a full professor. She remains active in women's issues on campus and recently had a university-wide award named in her honor.

HOW TO ARTICULATE THE INARTICULABLE I

Hershini Bhana

*a*s i try to give voice to that which is tattooed on breasts / vagina / thighs with the white / green ink of semen and blood, i know that this night will forever remain outside articulation, outside the soft-cushioned rooms where i stammer out testimony, outside the borrowed manuals that tell me how to recover in forty easy steps, outside literary metaphorization and colonial analogies—outside with empty bottles in a vacant, dark parking-lot. Instead this night becomes evidence without trial, a witness to my collapsing subjectivity and growing wordlessness (me who has always been so good with words). my silence is empty / unveiled / transparent: a bell without a clapper, a hull-less ghost ship whose sails fill with the echo of the wind. i interrogate only that which is supposed to encompass all my lack, those four letters that signify an oil-seed, that skinny / flat word named 'rape,' that sits on my chest at night separating my language from desire.

Often, inside my bed, inside my body, i wrap the sheets and blankets tightly around me as if to suffocate the desert blossoms of pain and glass that flower profusely under my skin, like bougainvillea against black iron grilles. my memory betrays me continuously in its remembering and my t-ongue is pierced, as if by thorns.

HOW TO ARTICULATE THE INARTICULABLE II

Hershini Bhana

                    raining never ending and this tree / park bench / bridge
not offering much   more
                    home / less; sound of teeth traffic—standing at some corner,
hoping to hide muddy shoes   life / less:
mildew of dank un-being covering left eye. married,
always marr-ied with houses emptied of wives—she's visiting her
mumwhat brown skin you have chatting a-way
        mildew spreads lovingly down left leg, and he's huffing and angry and
its time for me to moan - moan - moan   head back, teeth bared, close to
catatonia, close.   close and he pays me for the whole
night and i'm glad to be in here as it's rain-ing, rain-ing and my shoes will be
ruined and
                            i'm cold, aching-ly cold   home / less
he comes   he comes back, my head is thrown back and i hear the
plumbing- upstairs- bad plumbing like in all these old english houses and
he's shooting lead and i'm cold - cold and it's rain-ing in here too,   rain-
ing inside insideoutsideinsideoutsidein   out
                    breathe   exhale   moan - moan -
moan

HOW TO ARTICULATE THE INARTICULABLE III

Hershini Bhana

        genre gene-rating own logic . . . i refuse, i your author(ity) words
set in mo-
                             tion
my hands are of tongues—mauve / gold and wet, sing-ing   singing
perfect, round semibreves of humiliation.
        i refuse refuge / refuse but graduate, get a job, write a
narrative, writewrite   punctuate
silence bit-ter orange s(t)inging and
i'm afraid to blink, afraid of the dark and of buttonholes empty of buttons.
Starvation gene-rating own logic, passed down   mouth to mouth to mouth
to mouth to mouth to mouth to mouth to m uth to m th to m h to h
        messages, f etched to the gods, in stones, in seeds, in sl o
w   mo-
                       tion
diving hungering
                           transcoding and

my hands are of tongues—mauve / gold / perfect   round.

THEY DEFILED MY BODY, NOT MY SPIRIT: THE STORY OF A KOREAN COMFORT WOMAN, CHUNG SEO WOON

Dai Sil Kim-Gibson

The term "comfort women" is a euphemism for women who were forced to serve as sexual slaves for Japanese soldiers under the pretext that they were joining Jungshindae, *literally "Voluntarily Committing Body Corps," a Japanese-coined term meaning devoting one's entire being to the cause of the emperor. The more precise term is* Jungun Wianbu *(military comfort women) in Korean and* Jugunianfu *in Japanese. Because the term itself is an indication of the complexity of this issue, I use it advisedly.*

From the early 1930s, when Japan launched a war of aggression on mainland China, the Japanese military established "comfort houses (stations)," i.e., military brothels for the Imperial Army. After the outbreak of the Sino-Japanese War in 1937, the system was firmly established and the comfort women were treated as military supplies. The number of these women is disputed; estimates usually range from 100,000 to 200,000. They were drafted from Japan's prewar colonies and a wide range of Japanese-occupied territories. Korea was the single major source. It is generally agreed that 80 to 90 percent of the women came from Korea.

Comfort women were only a fraction of the human resources Japan appropriated from Korea. Expansion of the war caused a severe domestic labor shortage, a predicament the Imperial government sought to solve by mobilizing "peninsula people" (Koreans). Since 1910, Japan sought to complete Japanization and annihilation of Korean culture and history. The concentrated wartime draft of Korean men and women was consistent with Japanese colonial policy. Comfort women were recruited under the pretext of "work" opportunities or simply coerced. Korean villages were raided to seize women. Toward the end of the war, schools were pressured to identify and provide girls.

Until recently, the issue has been confined to buried memories of a shamed past. Even since it became public, the investigation has met numerous obstacles, including Japan's initial denials and refusal to disclose relevant documents. Bit by bit, like nightmares unraveling, some facts were uncovered and Japan was forced to deal with it. According to the Washington Post *(February 7, 1996), a key United Nations investigator, Radhika Coomaraswamy, in her report for the fifty-three-nation U.N. Human Rights Commission, recommended that in addition to apologies and compensation, Japan must identify and punish those responsible for this crime. However, Japan still denies its legal responsibility and refuses to fully disclose all the facts.*

Why am I writing about Korean comfort women?

I am a Korean American woman who came to the United States as a graduate student. I was born in northern Korea while Japan ruled our country, made us change our names to Japanese, speak their language, and worship their emperor. In the spring of 1945, my chest bubbling with the happy feelings of an enthusiastic first grader, I was playing a popular game with five small stones, throwing them into the air and placing them in sets. The animated chatter and laughter of girls, as I recall, spread through the schoolyard like a symphony of spring.

A Japanese teacher suddenly grabbed my arm and jerked me to my feet. "You are speaking Korean!" "Of course, I am!" I said, fearful but with pride. She took me to a huge teacher's room. I was ordered to stand by a window where everybody could see me, stretch my arms upward like a surrendering soldier, and repent! One by one, the teachers went home. When the evening dusk started to set in the sky, I was told to go home. On the way, I was met by my mother, who ran toward me from a distance. Only at the touch of her hand and the sound of her gentle voice did I begin to cry.

Living in America, I, like many others, decided to let my past be. The war and the colonial experience of both victims and victimizers has been largely repressed, buried with anger or sorrow. Most Americans of Asian roots whose ancestors experienced the horrendous atrocities committed by Japan do not know about that "uncomfortable past" and perhaps they don't care to learn. We were born in America, what do we have to do with that? Let's deal with the pressing issues here.

This is, however, one of the pressing issues of America and indeed of the world. The story of the Second World War is not just about problems between the European/American powers and Japan; it was not just a war between yellow and white. It was also yellow against yellow. It was about what Japan did to fellow Asians and others under the pretext of emancipating the Asian race from Western imperialism. This is a neglected story. Further, if America is truly a nation of immigrants from different roots, we Americans must attempt to understand each other's roots, each other's history.

The story of comfort women is a neglected aspect of war, of human rights violations, and of human brutality. Equally important, it is an ignored issue of gender. Further, it is a story of mostly Asian women from predominantly poor and uneducated families, a case of triple discrimination and neglect.

In August 1995, I went to the NGO Forum on Women in China held in conjunction with the Fourth World Conference on Women to help place the issue of Japanese military secual slavery before the eyes of the world. On the fourth of September, I attended the International Symposium on Violence Against Women in War and Armed Conflicts and was honored to translate the testimony of a former comfort woman from South Korea, Chung Seo Woon.

At age seventy-five, with lines of aging on her face, she still exuded dignity and beauty. As she went to the podium, I disappeared into a translation booth. "I was born an only daughter with no sons in a family of a well-to-do landowner in southern Korea," she started. Her voice flew out like a quiet stream. I listened to her every word and put them into English with my heart's devotion. "Half a century has passed since the time when every day was a dreadful nightmare for me, but

Japan still tells lies and avoids responsibility. How can they do that in the presence of myself and many others like me, victims who are alive and kicking? The seed the Japanese planted, the evil seed, they must harvest no matter how dreadful if they wish to be part of the human race. Don't you believe so?" Loud applause. "Then they say, 'For all those poor Asians, we will raise private funds and help.' I have a message for you. I might be poor, but not that poor. I demand the compensation that is rightly due to me, even if I would burn the money after it's in my hand. It is not a matter of money but of principle. The Japanese defiled my body but not my spirit. My spirit is strong, rich, and proud." With the thunderous applause, I took off my headphones and stepped out of the booth. She stood by the podium with her head lifted high in front of the people who honored her with a standing ovation. With my arms around her, we came down together and sat in the front row of seats side by side. It was a moving moment, a moment that stood above time, an eternity.

The next day, I went to her hotel in Beijing at her invitation. When I knocked at her door, she was still in her pajamas, frantically trying to communicate with a Chinese cleaning woman. Her face, exhaustion hovering, brightened up at seeing me. "Oh, I am so glad to see you. I was so tired that I stayed in bed until a while ago but I had to get up because my stomach grumbled for food. I was trying to tell that woman to get me some food. Everyone is out; no one is around." "Not to worry anymore. I will go and grab some food. Go back to bed and rest. You don't need to change, either." We sat by the window, she still in her pajamas, looking out at the ancient city of Beijing with food and Coke bottles between us. "You saved me. It is a kind of sickness. I can't function unless I put some food in my stomach when I feel this hungry." Slowly, color came back to her face, accompanied by a smile. "Thanks for inviting me to come. Yesterday your testimony was painful but moving. I felt as if my chest was choked with sadness even while I was so intensely translating," I said. "Thank you. In the evening, I had to go see a Japanese government official. That's why I am in this shape. It was awfully intense." I chewed my food and waited. "Last night, I asked him how he felt to see all these women from around the world demanding justice from Japan, many of them from the countries which Japan had victimized; if he felt ashamed about what Japan did to us. I took off my glasses and showed the scars on my face and said, 'If you were a woman, I would take off my clothes and show the numerous scars all over my body, but I can't do that. I was taught not even to roll up my sleeves in front of a strange man. So you can imagine how I felt when the Japanese officers and soldiers tore apart my clothes and humiliated me, doing the most unthinkable things to my naked body. It is bad enough that Japan committed such a horrendous crime against humanity but it is even worse to avoid responsibility for the wrong you committed. When is Japan going to face up and render justice to us, not that you can ever bring my life back to age fifteen.' He said, 'I feel sorry,' but his voice was hardly audible." Her hand holding a Coke bottle to her mouth shook a little. "It must be hard on you to talk about such a painful past all the time, especially at the public meetings." "Oh, but I have lived for these opportunities. In any case, my past is never over whether I talk *about it or not. I am still in the battle every day. So often my dreams are battlefields in which I am desperately fighting the Japanese soldiers. In the darkness of the night, I scream and yell. Then, my husband wakes me up and gently wipes away the cold sweat pouring over my body." I did not have to ask her to tell me her story. In fact, there was no stopping. We talked until the sun set in the sky of that ancient city and shared dinner at a hotel restaurant. Alas, space does not allow me to present her full story, but this is her story in the first person.*

THEY DEFILED MY BODY, NOT MY SPIRIT

i was born as the only daughter without sons in the family of a wealthy landowner in southern Korea. I know that the majority of the women who suffered my fate came from poor and uneducated families but I was a protected child of a well-to-do family. Like many of my friends, I wanted to go to school but my father would not let me. He said, "What's the use of learning Japanese language and history before you know your own?" He kept me at home and taught me Chinese characters, written Korean, and calligraphy. My father was adamantly opposed to changing our names into Japanese. So we never did. In those days, the Japanese took all of our brassware to use for the war, for weapons, etc. My father dug a deep hole in our rice field and buried all of our brassware. He said that it wasn't because we had such an attachment to them but he was opposed in principle to contributing to the Japanese war effort. One day police came and took my father away. I learned that the police took my father to the hiding place and made him dig it up. When they found all that brassware, they kicked and beat my father. I don't know how they found out about it. My father was put into a prison. We asked to see my father every day but each time we were refused. One day, however, a Japanese official came and asked if I wanted to visit my father in the prison.

When my father saw me coming to his cell, he almost fainted. Gathering himself, he said, "You should never have come here. This is not a place for a girl like you. Please don't come back at all and, whatever you do, please don't tell your mother what you saw today." I stood there with tears streaming down my cheeks. My father looked so frail; he looked as if I could blow him away. Going closer to him, I grabbed his hands but he groaned. Frightened, I pulled my hands away, and saw his hand covered with bandages. "I didn't realize . . . What happened to your hands?" I saw blood marks around his fingernails. I demanded to know what happened to him. He told me, "They pulled all my fingernails. They did the same thing to my toes." "Do they torture you every day like this? What else did they do to you?" "You don't want to know and you should not trouble yourself anymore. I wish you hadn't come but don't tell your mother." "Is it because of the brassware that they torture you?" I asked. "It is more than that but I can't tell you. Please go back and take good care of your mother." My feet would not move but I had to leave him there in that horrible prison cell. Then the same Japanese official who took me to my father's cell came to our house. "There is a factory in Japan where you could go and work for two years. If you go there, I will see to it that your father is released from prison. Immediately after you leave, he will be released." After seeing my father, I didn't think I had a choice; I was only glad that I could do something to save my father.

My mother was horrified. She said I couldn't go. She pleaded and begged. "You are the only one I have left. How do you expect that I can live if you also leave me? Besides, you are only fifteen and you have never been anywhere. Two years in a Japanese factory! It's unthinkable." Of course, she didn't know the true state of my father. It was bad enough to leave, but to persuade my mother was something else. Finally, resigned to the situation, my mother quietly packed clothes made of fine materials, occasionally stopping to wipe her tears and pointing to some as special items she had prepared for my wedding someday. I can't tell you how I felt when I followed the Japanese man, leaving my mother behind. Every step away from home was prompted by the image of my father, especially the bandaged hands and feet. His pain was mine; we were so close. Even if I was a girl, I was the only child. I was my father's baby. This stubborn man whose facade was as stern as rock had unlimited love for me. Do you know what my name, Seo Woon, means? It means 'feel empty/sorry' [no English equivalent]. My parents were sorry that I wasn't a boy but I didn't care. You know why? My father loved me to death, I knew that. On a ship headed to Japan, there were many girls and women, some even bubbling with hope that they would earn lots of money for their poverty-stricken families. A Japanese woman introduced herself as the person responsible for taking us to a factory. I closed my eyes and blocked my fear, thinking only about my father who by then would be home under the tender care of my mother.

Upon arrival in Japan, we were made to wait a few days. Finally, one day, my number was called out. They didn't bother to use our names; we were numbers. I thought we were going to a factory but again they ordered us to get on a huge ship. I still thought we were traveling within Japan. When the ship pulled in some place, I didn't know then but later learned that it was Taiwan. After leaving some girls there, we moved on to Bangkok, Saigon, Singapore, and Jakarta, at each place leaving girls. When we arrived in Bangkok, I felt a strange sensation, knowing that we were not going to a factory in Japan. You understand all these names became clear to me much later. At the time, I didn't know what was happening. I was a prisoner on a ship that kept going. By then, I was devoid of any sense of time—time just felt endless.

It was in Jakarta—and I did know this name—that something totally unexpected and dreadful happened. There were twenty-three of us left and we were taken to a hospital. A doctor came in, inspected my body below there, and did something. I had never felt such piercing pain in my life; I felt as if my entire inside shrank into a small bundle and my body rolled like a ball with the whole world's pain compressed in it. I cried and bled for three days. I didn't know then but, of course, they operated on me to prevent pregnancy.

Now changed to abrupt and coarse manners, the Japanese took us to a city called Semarang [*a coastal city of Indonesia, about 250 miles east of Jakarta and occupied by the Japanese from 1942 to 1945*]. Within the military compound, there were rows of barracks. I was ordered into one of the rooms. Night fell in a strange land, so far away from my father and mother. A Japanese officer in uniform came in, sat down, looked at me, and gestured to me to take off my clothes. Then, he started to undress himself. I crawled into a corner of the room, hid my face between my legs, and wished that I could shrink myself into nothing. The officer yelled, he jerked me to my feet, grabbed my clothes, and tore them off. I stood in my underwear, trembling like crazy. He took out his sword and used it to tear my underwear. I was sixteen, the only daughter in a family without sons.

From the next day onward, five or six soldiers a day came, and the number increased to forty and fifty. Every time I fainted, they poured water over me and did the same thing all over. Much of the time, both body and spirit felt numb but when the bodily pain became unbearable, I screamed. Then they would give me shots, sometimes several times a day. Each time the shot soothed my pain and I was again under those soldiers. I didn't know it then but they made me an opium junkie.

Beginning at nine at night, officers came. In comparison with them, the soldiers were harmless. Because there were always lines outside the door and because they were not given much time, the soldiers had to hurry and go, but the officers—they were something else. They had more time, and those high-ranking ones, they could stay overnight. They demanded such unspeakable and weird things. When I didn't obey them, many of them took out swords, threatened me, and used them on my body. When they did, they made sure that I bled. Did you know that the Japanese believed that once the sword was out, unless it saw blood, it would not fit back into its case? Such strange people . . . [*She asked me this question and looked out of the window, her eyes gazing far away*]. To this day there are so many scars on my body from the sword wounds.

I attempted suicide. I saved, every chance I got, strong pills for malaria. When I had forty of them, I swallowed them, no longer able to endure the pain and humiliation. However, two of my friends, who also saved the pills for the same purpose, could not go through with it and discovered me. They reported it and all I remember is that water came out from every part of my body—my mouth, nostrils. . . . They revived me. It was then that I made up my mind to survive and tell my story, what Japan did to us. It was that determination that kept me alive until the day when some Indonesian women who did our laundry informed me that Japan had lost the war. Of the twenty-three of us, only nine were alive at the war's end. When our bodies could not be used, we were killed. They cut the women's throats in front of our eyes, warning us that we would be subject to the same fate if we disobeyed. The same Indonesian women informed the Allied soldiers about us, and they came to take us to Singapore and put us in a camp. I heard that the Japanese had been ordered to kill all of us to wipe away all trace of their atrocities.

I had to wait almost a year before I was put on a ship home. When I returned home, our house was full of dust and spiderwebs, completely deserted. The neighbors came with brooms and cleaned the house. They told me about my parents. My father was never released; he died in prison. The Japanese came to the house and tried to rape my mother. Humiliated, holding a piece of iron between her lips, she killed herself. Then, the Japanese took the house and used it to entertain important visitors from Japan.

Did I cry? No, I didn't. I held back tears with so much love and pride for my parents—my father, thinking back, who was undoubtedly involved in the independence movement, and my mother who chose death rather than be defiled by the Japanese. You know, we die once, only once. It matters how we die. I was immensely proud of the way my parents died. The Japanese took our country away but they could not take the spirit of my parents. The Japanese defiled my body through and through but not my spirit. I locked up the house and decided to get rid of the opium addiction. It was my personal battle to regain my dignity as a Korean woman, as a human being. I gnashed my teeth so much that my gums bled and I could not eat. I crawled around the room, ripping off the floor paper until only the mud underneath showed. Then, I dug the mud. I chewed off all my fingernails. It was a desperate scream to be free of the opium and to be human. It was an eight-month struggle.

I was never able to have a normal sex life, but I met a kind man who wanted a companion more than anything else. He was a medical doctor who served in the Japanese army and had a nervous breakdown. He understood me. He is the one who wakes me up when I fight the Japanese soldiers in my dreams. I never hid what happened to me in Semarang. Why should I hide? I am not the one who should feel shame; it is Japan who should carry all the shame on its shoulders. Help me tell this story to America and to the whole world.

"BAD WOMEN":
ASIAN AMERICAN VISUAL ARTISTS
HANH THI PHAM, HUNG LIU, AND YONG SOON MIN

Elaine H. Kim

I

*n*ames. Names imposed by slave owners and immigration officials who could not and would not pronounce a person's given name. Names changed or adopted for use in a new land. Names taken on as part of an effort to forge a new self, a new life. Growing up, I learned that most Korean peasant women my mother's age didn't have given names. They were called "baby" or "pretty" until they married, whereupon they could be called "so-and-so's wife."

I figure that my grandmother fled Korea for Hawaii, either alone and pregnant or with a small infant, sometime between 1903 and 1905, the period during which Korean laborers were being recruited to work on the sugar plantations of Hawaii. She told my mother that she had had other children, who died. She said that she had left because she became "fed up" with her husband, an inveterate gambler, when he threw a blanket over my mother to muffle her crying. Fearful lest her only remaining child be smothered to death, she decided to run away to Hawaii, thereby fashioning a narrative of protective motherhood that pinned their exile on my mother. Then again, the story of her becoming a "bad woman" because she was a "good mother" could have been created by my mother to cope with not having known her father. There's no way for me to find out now.

Although they cannot be said to have conquered the social barriers they faced, I like to think of both my grandmother and my mother as bravely stepping forth to meet them. They were blamed both for circumstances beyond their control and for the choices they made—for responding to the violation of their bodies by leaving home to start a new life. No doubt they would both be considered "bad women" in a community that does not recognize female sexual desires, condemns single motherhood, especially among unmarried women, discourages the woman who runs away from a violently abusive husband, and criticizes the woman who wants to live alone or focus on her work for placing her individual well-being over the needs of family members. They became female transgressors.

It turns out that most of us are probably descended from a long line of "bad women," and it seems to me that we need to reexamine just what is meant by "badness," so that we can claim the term for quite different uses.

Unofficial Asian American history is replete with "bad women." They may not be acknowledged or much written about, but their legacies branch into the present. In the novel *Thousand Pieces of Gold* (1981), Ruthanne Lum McCunn immortalized the legend of Polly Bemis, the Chinese pioneer woman who became a homesteader in the American West in the latter part of the nineteenth century, after having been sold into prostitution by her impoverished family in the early 1870s, held as a Chinese saloonkeeper's mistress, and finally won in a card game by a white man who eventually became her husband. But most of the nineteenth-century Chinese women in America who had been lured, sold, or kidnapped into prostitution to meet the demand for sexual services in the predominantly male West Coast culture remain anonymous, except as statistics used to fuel the massive movement to end Chinese immigration to the U.S. Some suggestion of the individual agency of early Japanese prostitutes in Hawaii and on the Pacific Coast do remain, since in their public discussions, Japanese government officials and Japanese American community leaders, fearing harm to the reputation of Japan in the West, publicly expressed their indignation that these women deliberately chose prostitution over much less lucrative but more "honorable" agricultural labor.[1] Little has been said about Japanese and Korean picture brides who ran away from their husbands in the early decades of this century, but desperate notices from deserted husbands in the Japanese vernacular press provide clues that such incidents were not infrequent. Another group of "bad women," divorced second-generation Chinese American women, were talked about mainly in immigrant Chinese families, where they stood for the evils of "Americanization." Rose Hum Lee points out that although comparable numbers of immigrant Chinese women left their husbands, little was said about them.[2] Asian women, some of whom worked as bar girls on U.S. military bases in their homelands, built power bases for themselves by marrying U.S. citizens and then sponsoring family members as immigrants. Another group of "bad women" includes Filipino and other Asian women who immigrated to this country as so-called "mail order brides" and then started catalogue companies of their own. Finally, Asian American lesbians, artists, and activists have challenged patriarchal stories with their own lives.

Asian American female "badness" is particularly unruly because it so often challenges both Western patriarchal racism and patriarchal attitudes and practices in Asian American families and communities, which are profoundly influenced by Western concepts and customs.

One arena where "bad women" seem to abound is the visual arts, where illusions are challenged and the possible is imagined and made palpable. In their quite different ways, Asian American women activists-artists Hanh Thi Pham, Hung Liu, and Yong Soon Min are most certainly "bad women" who remember and celebrate other "bad women" as they uncover the past buried by the winners of History and place the woman's body in world history. And in doing so, they gesture toward both the history and the politics of the possible.

II

Among contemporary Asian American "bad women," Vietnamese American photographic installation artist Hanh Thi Pham ranks high. At a time when movements against affirmative action are enthusiastically taking up the notion that Asian Americans are a diligent, docile "model minority" that makes other people of color look lazy and threatening, Hanh places her own dark Asian body into photographs that stage racism in U.S. history and the arrogance of Americans during the Vietnam War. As a member of the Vietnamese refugee community in the U.S., where people suspected of harboring favorable attitudes towards Vietnam have been mysteriously killed, she places Ho Chi Minh in her art work and challenges the right-wing political views that predominate among many of her fellow refugees. In a world where heterosexism is a given, where men control almost all of the power and resources, where the female body is generally allowed to function only for procreation and male sexual pleasure, she focuses on women and celebrates female sexual desire with images of her own nude body.

In 1985, in collaboration with sculptor Richard Turner (who attended high school in Vietnam when his father worked for the South Vietnamese government), Hanh created *Along the Street of Knives*, an installation of eight large multiple-exposure color photographs. Although each photograph is a self-contained entity, the series makes up a narrative drama. Using "set design" drawings on acetate to create the scenes, Hanh and Turner situate themselves on the sets, performing in different costumes and poses. The set is lit in sumptuous, symbolic colors. Filtered theater spots, dissolving details into white or black background areas, impart the feeling of being caught in a dream or trance. The two artists act out the scenes, creating an allegorical "movie" of successive still shots that is actually a performance of history. Each photograph is created with between two and thirteen exposures compacted into one negative or transparency.

In "Asking Questions of Mr. Sky" (from the 1990 installation *A Different War: Vietnam in Art*), the American men in Hawaiian print shirts and shorts need their television and their beer as they recline on their lawn chairs, peering at Vietnam through dark glasses and binoculars. As viewers, we look at them looking at Vietnam. We identify with them, but also with the woman who could be both a Vietnamese woman and an Asian immigrant woman as she climbs a Jacob's ladder that leads nowhere. She may be striving towards the imperialist culture, or she may be trying to escape the de-

ABOVE: © Hanh Thi Pham and Richard Turner, "Reconnaissance," 1985. Ektachrome print, 20×24 inches. From the installation *Along the Street of Knives*. BELOW: © Hanh Thi Pham, "Asking Questions of Mr. Sky," 1985. Ektachrome print, 20×24 inches. From the 1990 installation *A Different War: Vietnam in Art*.

© Hanh Thi Pham, "Misbegotten No More." From the 1991–92 installation
Expatriate Consciousness.

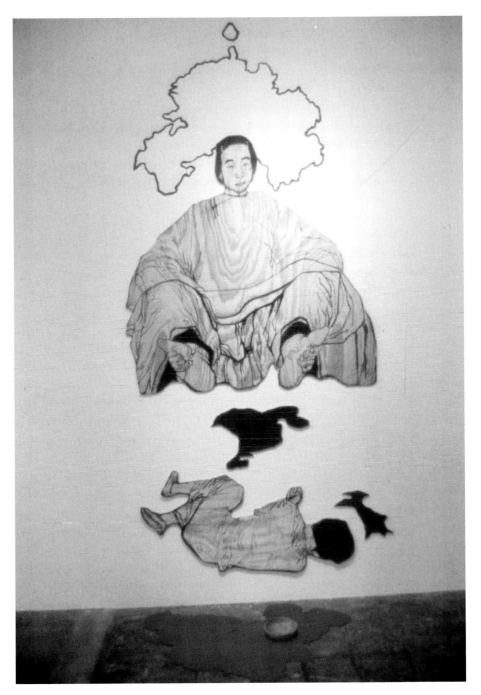

© Hung Liu, "Trauma," 1989. Ink on wood, felt, and clay. From the *Chinese Pieta* mixed media installation, Women's Building, Los Angeles, CA. Courtesy Steinbaum Krauss Gallery, NYC.

LEFT: © Hung Liu, *A Third World*, 1993. Oil on canvas, gold leaf, wood, 92×96 inches. Collection of the Santa Barbara Museum of Art, Santa Barbara, CA. Courtesy Steinbaum Krauss Gallery, NYC. BELOW: © Hung Liu, *Odalisque*, 1992. Oil on canvas, lacquered wood, antiques, and mixed media, 52½×95×8 inches. Collection of Barbara and Eric Dobkin, New York. Courtesy Steinbaum Krauss Gallery, NYC.

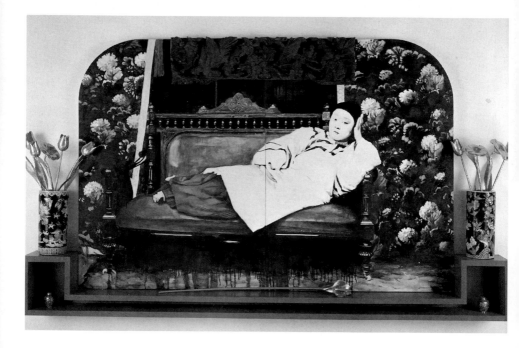

© Hung Liu, *Jiu Jin Shan (Old Gold Mountain)*, 1994, mixed media installation at the M. H. de Young Memorial Museum, Golden Gate Park, San Francisco, CA. Courtesy Steinbaum Krauss Gallery, NYC.

© Yong Soon Min, "Talking Herstory," 1990. Lithograph.

LEFT: © Yong Soon Min, "Defining Moments," 1994, developed during a 1992 Light Work Residency in Syracuse, New York (photographed by Allan de Souza).
BELOW: © Yong Soon Min, "Dwelling," 1992. Sculpture, detail (photographed by Erik Landsberg).

© Yong Soon Min, photograph and detail from the 1991 *deCOLONIZATION* installation at The Bronx Museum of Art.

structive and voyeuristic gaze of the white men as she balances precariously on the suspension bridge, moving in the direction of the question marks in the sky, but the bridge ends in black space. Still, her apparent destination is marked only by question marks suspended in empty space.

The installation is also meant to draw attention to the brutalizing effects of the war itself on both Americans and Vietnamese. The photographs focus on the possibly dark results of differences and misunderstandings between the two cultures. Both Americans and Vietnamese, especially uprooted Vietnamese like Hanh herself, are victims of war and undergo a "process of mutual humiliation," for "no one . . . has been able to follow his or her ideals without being destructive, from Ho Chi Minh down to the rank-and-file American GI."[3] In one photograph, Hanh pictured herself as a Vietnamese girl wearing long braids and Vietnamese clothing, a sinister rifle propped beside her as she peers at an American couple. While we see them through her eyes, we are somehow made complicit in the possibility that she will take up arms and drive them from Vietnam. In another, she is drowning an American man in a tub of water, and in still another, she assumes the role of the South Vietnamese general shooting a suspected Viet Cong in the head in the well-known news photograph, except the person being executed is an American.

Hanh's performance of Vietnamese womanhood disrupts the Orientalist fetishization of Asian women as what she calls "nice smiling submissive" exotic sex objects or pitiable victims of Asian patriarchal practices.[4] Her art work challenges aesthetic and political modes that privilege Americans over Vietnamese, men over women, and heterosexuals over queers. In "Misbegotten No More," one of nine photographs in a photographic installation titled *Khong La Nguoi O [Expatriate Consciousness]* (1991–92), Hanh's image is seen in profile in the center of a collage of transparencies and color xeroxes, handwriting, newspaper photographs, and Vietnamese poetry, flexing her right arm in an "up yours" gesture. Her image is superimposed over an upside-down, crossed-out image of Buffalo Bill, that quintessential Wild West "hero" and enemy of not only the buffalo but also the Native Americans whose land he invaded. The accompanying text contains the Vietnamese phrase that means "not the person who lives here," which Hanh says means refusing to be a servant, since in Vietnamese "a person who lives here" means a servant. "[It stands for] 'not as your servant.' I am speaking to Americans."[5]

> . . . in the picture, I no longer want to be a servant of the system, and I can be my own self. I'm a lesbian. I'm very proud of myself as a woman. I'm very proud of my body, the muscles of my body, and my intentions as a person. [This is] my empowerment, given to me by myself.[6]

Hanh came to the U.S. in 1975, when she was twenty-one years old and settled in southern California with her family. Fourteen years later, she came out as a lesbian. "I was a very 'good' and dutiful female before," she has said. "I remember my marriage to a man, and living as a housewife [for twelve and a half years], while trying to be a role model daughter. . . . I tried always to blend in with the expectations of family and femaleness." Stimulated by her divorce to start "taking charge of [her] life," she experienced a "new birth: bringing out the man within the woman."[7] The change was not without pain, because, although she tries to identify herself as a strong lesbian, Hanh calls herself a transsexual, a man in the body of a woman.

> I have . . . remained lonesome. Males mistake me for a female, then females decipher the male aspect of me as not being like themselves. . . . They know I am not one of them, and that bothers me. . . . I always value females to be superior to males, and transsexuals. I still feel very sad that I cannot completely be a woman.[8]

In general, the Vietnamese refugee community has responded to Hanh's work with what she calls "outrage." Some are angry about her work about Vietnam because they want "positive" images to enhance their businesses and therefore the community's economic advancement. Others, in the guise of objecting to her public display of "in-house" community issues, disapprove of her left-leaning political orientation. Through the 1980s, many Vietnamese Americans who seemed tolerant of the communist government in Vietnam were murdered. "You're not supposed to address these issues," says Hanh. "If you live in Orange County [in Southern California, where the largest Vietnamese refugee community in the U.S. is located], you are supposed to support the right wing. . . . If you're otherwise, then you're a leftist. There's nothing in the middle."[9]

> Long time ago, I did not want to be associated with the term "radical." But afterwards I say, "Yes! I am radical!". . . If you don't do anything, nothing changes the world.[10]

While Hanh may be dismissed by some as too "bad" a woman to be dealt with, for others it is precisely her badness that inspires and empowers, by challenging social injustices such as racism and patriarchy, by insisting on the centrality of female identity, and by assertively acknowledging the validity of female desire and sexual pleasure.

III

"Bad Women," a 1991 San Francisco exhibit of Hung Liu's paintings of young Chinese prostitutes from the early decades of this century, has nothing to do with female desire and sexual pleasure. Liu discovered the photographs that inspired the images at a public archive while visiting Beijing earlier that year. They were arranged in two books that had apparently served as catalogues for wealthy male customers. Liu had been searching for old photographs that recalled China before the 1949 Revolution, which effaced signs of social life before communism, especially when they seemed to suggest Western influences.

Born in 1948, Liu is a first-generation product of Chinese communist culture; like other artists of her generation, she has at times been obsessed with a desire to uncover what was forbidden to her, particularly as a result of the Cultural Revolution of the 1960s. She has often painted from her own family's photographs, as well as from a collection of photographs of urban scenes, landscapes, temples, and families that she found in 1987 in a catalogue of a traveling American exhibition: *The Face of China As Seen By Photographers & Travelers 1860–1912* (Aperture, 1978). Fascinated by erasures of the past, she found that painting from third-generation reproductions and faded photographs was like dealing with memory loss. It was difficult to locate private collections because so many family photographs had been destroyed during the Cultural Revolution, when people blotted out traces of their past so as not to be suspected of bourgeois backgrounds or aspirations. Trying to unearth the buried past itself marks Liu as a possible traitor to Chinese nationalism, and shining floodlights into the dark corners of Chinese patriarchy so that it is revealed before Western eyes makes her a truly "bad woman."

Discovering these photographs was immensely important to Liu for a number of reasons: first, because of her desire to uncover pre-communist Chinese life; second, because of her keen interest in unexpected connections between China and the West; third, because of her wish to document in her art the forgotten lives of anonymous people, especially women, who have most often been the victims rather than the victors of History; and fourth, because of her focus on the interplay of illusions and gazes as she painted the photographs of women posed in front of paintings so that contemporary Western viewers might look at her looking at what the Chinese used Western technology to look at.

Liu has said that for her, painting from photographs constitutes a defiant act of sorts, since artists in communist China were exhorted to paint from life to better represent the true human condition. Painting from pictures was considered "cheating," even though artists were supposed to create illusions from life. Liu recalls how Chinese teachers criticized her for painting pale, unhappy-looking people instead of ruddy-cheeked heroes and heroines of the revolution.[11] But she suggests that copying an image, which requires focusing one's physical and emotional attention like a scientist on every square inch of its minutest details, is to pay homage to it. "I communicate with the characters in my paintings," she has said, "with reverence, sympathy, and awe." In a sense, by painting their images, Liu is worshipping her forgotten sisters, who were known only by trade names like Little Apple, White Lily, Sweet Orchid. She wants to acknowledge them, to reclaim, recover, and reinterpret them, these anonymous "sisters for sale" who were not allowed to have names or even, she imagines, their own children. "I don't want their stories to be forgotten; I don't want them to disappear without a trace."[12]

Liu presents Chinese female pariahs, whose identities had been buried and denied, on altars and at the center of a theater stage. Instead of being downcast as might be expected in Chinese society, their eyes stare brazenly and Westernly at the viewer. But their gaze expresses accessibility rather than agency or even insolence. That their images are captured by Chinese men using Western technology is important to Liu, who often equates colonization with rape, the camera with the rapist, and Chinese land with Chinese women.

Exposing Chinese patriarchy, bringing "bad women" and private shame into the public, and criticizing Chinese officialdom constitute the work of a "bad woman," as does the artist's insistence on inscriptions of her own very female image, whether as communist soldier, green-card holder, "guerrilla girl," Buddha, or Third World woman with a Mao button on her shoulder and a gold map of San Francisco in the middle of her forehead.

Having settled in America, she began to view herself as a Chinese artist working outside China: "My responsibility as a classically trained Chinese artist in America is to express my Chineseness as clearly as I can."[13] At the same time, she distinguishes between Chinese and Chinese American artists: "Maybe the . . . images [in my work look] Chinese. But this doesn't mean I'm a Chinese painter, because I never would have painted this way in China."[14] In 1995, after having visited China again and having seen the influence of the West everywhere, Liu declared that she no longer had to "confine [herself] to only Chinese imagery" and began to focus on the absence of "fixed origins" and her "collaged identity" as a cross-cultural, hybrid artist.[15] "I do not feel obligated to be Chinese anymore," she recently said.[16] Indeed, her installation at the San Francisco DeYoung Museum in 1994, *Jiu Jin Shan* [*Old Gold Mountain*], focuses on Chinese America, with its asymptotic railroad tracks, which lie like a false promise over a huge mountain of fortune cookies. Believing that America was the "mountain of gold," early Chinese immigrants came and found themselves working on the transcontinental railroad, digging tunnels through snow drifts and blasting rock cliffs with dynamite at half the white man's wages. Though they had perished by the thousands by the time the railroad was completed in 1869, their role in creating America's wealth has never been fully acknowledged. Thus the fake gold is the fortune cookie, a joke invented in America: it doesn't really contain fortunes and it isn't even really Chinese.

Yong Soon Min also works with cultural and aesthetic collage. Like Liu, she insists on the centrality of women, focuses on concepts of self and nation-hood and on her own female body and its place in global politics, and chal-lenges Eurocentrism in her work. And, like Liu, she is interested in using photographs to dismantle the truth-claims of representation. But although she uses photographs and videotapes, they are usually part of large, complex installations in which written text plays an important role. "The installation is a Godsend for me," Min has said. "Installations help the artist break out of the constraints of the wall. They also serve as a receptacle for my own collec-tion of materials."[17]

Because she is concerned with the oppositional, the personal, with "talking about the banished" and helping to create a culture of resistance,[18] Min grapples with perspectives, themes, and images traditionaly kept hid-den in the Korean American community: not only the notion that women are central to history and nation, with images of the naked female body as the site of nationhood and global politics, but also antiimperialist politics. Her work challenges the old Korean concept of *sadaejui* [reliance on the powerful] by exploring the affinities among people who have suffered op-pression in the West, such as Native Americans ("Home Be Coming," 1992); countries that Americans overlook, like Palestine ("Two States Now," 1989); and societies that have survived Western military onslaught, like Vietnam ("DMZXING," 1994).

Like Hanh and Liu, Min places her own image in her work, where her personal history, the history of Korea, and global context are brought to-gether. In the lithograph "Talking Herstory" (1990), her face is featured in profile on the bottom of the print. The celadon-colored forms that seem to sprout from her lips are a collage of torn pieces of a map of Korea, arranged to suggest branches of a family tree from which hang various snapshots from the 1940s and 1950s. The tree branch and the snapshots float on a blue rect-angle that represents a strip of sky. On the margins are pale images from news photographs of statesmen from the U.S. and the U.S.S.R., which parti-tioned Korea after World War II. Roosevelt, Stalin, Truman, Nixon, and Khrushchev shake hands and smile at one another as they negotiate the fate of the nation and Min's family.

In *Writing Self/Writing Nation: Four Essays About Theresa Hak Kyung Cha's DICTEE* (Third Woman Press, 1994), a book Min designed, she presents a variation of a six-part photo ensemble titled "Defining Mo-ments," in which the artist connects crucial moments in Korean history to important dates in her own life. Opposite the title page is a negative of Min's abdomen and forearms, with "occupied" written on one arm and "territory" written on the other. Emanating from the navel are four dates: 1953; April 19, 1960; may 19, 1980; and April 29, 1992. The book's sections are divided by images of Min's face and torso, over which she has printed photographs from the Korean War, which ended in the year of her birth, 1953; the April 1960 student revolution, which Min witnessed as a child; the 1980 Kwangju massacre, which marked the awakening of her own political consciousness; and the April 1992 Los Angeles uprisings, a defining moment for her as a Korean American, which occurred on Min's birthday. In each visual, the letters "DMZ" for "demilitarized zone" are written across her forehead, and the word "Heartland" is inscribed across her chest. Just as the words are carved into her flesh, the scenes from Korean and Korean American history are tattooed onto her body. In the final visual at the end of the book, Min superimposes a shot of Paekdusan, the fabled mountain in North Korea; it is the mythical birthplace of the Korean people, the supposed birthplace of the late North Korean leader Kim Il Sung, and the site considered both by the opposition movement and later by the South Korean government as a symbol of hope for reunification of North and South Korea. The back cover of the book features a photograph of her arms crossed over her naked torso, onto which is superimposed interlocking maps of Korea and the United States, the webs of rivers and mountains like the veins and blood vessels of her body through which her Korean and American blood courses.

Like the partitioned nation, Min's Korean and "Third World"[19] body is occupied and divided. It is also a site of contestation as we reclaim our decolonized bodies for sexuality and desire. The lines, "Where is my demilitarized desire? Where is my decolonized body politic?" appear frequently in her work. Several collaborative works with her artist husband Allan deSouza address the artists' "double and triple colonization": he, a Goan born in Kenya who immigrated first to England and then to America, and she, the child of cold war politics, born in divided Korea, which endured Japanese colonialism and then U.S. neocolonialism, who immigrated to the U.S., where she finds herself being asked, "What are you doing here? Why don't you go back to where you belong?" "We are," Min says, "like errant children disowned for bad behavior by their foster parents because we don't belong in the model American family."

Min's installations are richly complex, the format allowing her to respond to her "compulsion to try to say everything in each and every work." It is here that she can engage in autobiographical work—telling stories and uncovering buried histories, while exploring the continuum between the personal and the political, between personal and official memory.

In *deCOLONIZATION* (1991), "bad women" are featured on one side of the room, where Min places an enlarged black and white photograph of Min's mother and some other Korean women on a U.S. army base, standing in front of an American-made car. The women work on the base, unaware that they are working for those who contribute to the death of their men. Layers of frosted mylar create a sense of distance, fragmentation, and burial. The images flicker unevenly beneath material opaque and obscuring, like tracing paper or gauze. For Korean women, association with the U.S. military suggests prostitution, economic need, betrayal of nation—"badness." The text reads "OK, GI Joe, Checkpoint Charlie, I'm your first, your second, your third world girl, your mama-san, geisha, *ayah*, Miss Saigon, war-bride, mail-order bride, I'm yours."

Korean female identity is symbolized by the diaphanous Korean traditional dress that floats down in the center of the room, the *moshi* [flax] *ch'ima* [skirt] elongated. The dress envelops the female form, hiding even the pregnant body's curves with its own graceful lines, concealing with the illusion of fragility the resilience and fortitude of the bodies it encloses. The female strength suggested by the dress is represented again by the image opposite the doorway to the installation. Situated in a separate corner is photo documentation of dancer Lee Ae Ju performing at an antigovernment rally in South Korea. She is splitting a piece of cloth by running through it. This image is mirrored in the corner so that she seems to be bursting forth from the constraints of a black cross that frames her image in red. Splitting the cloth cathartically releases *han*, the Korean word for sorrow and anger that grow from accumulated experiences of oppression.

Here, Min has given us several layers of "bad women": herself as the Korean American artist, Lee Ae Ju as the contemporary Korean activist dancer, and the traditional Korean *mudang*. The dancer, herself a "bad woman" because she uses her body in social movement activism, recalls the healing ritual movements of the quintessential "bad woman" of Korea, the female *mudang* [Korean shaman]. With the onslaught of Western imperialism and what Min views as its "handmaiden," the massive Christian missionary efforts in Korea (thus Min's use of the cross, which the dancer symbolically breaks from and transcends), the *mudang*, the mostly female pre-Confucian, pre-Buddhist traditional spiritual healer, became almost universally despised as a symbol of non-Western, premodern superstition and ignorance. Even those who (usually furtively) utilized their services viewed the female *mudang* as "bad women" because they were thought to prioritize their calling over their husbands and children, to infantilize their husbands with their superior earnings, to curse their social superiors, including men and their mothers-in-law, while in a trance, and to be highly sexed and sexually expressive. Young nationalists today recognize them as representing indigenous cultural practices all but obliterated by Korea's encounter with modernity. But, in my view, their symbolic importance lies in the fact that, though Korean official culture usually ignored the psychic and spiritual needs of women and the poor, the *mudang* traditionally ministered to the everyday needs of common people. For example, Confucian rituals for the dead traditionally excluded children who died before marriage and parent-hood and women who died childless. The souls of such people, having no one to perform ancestor commemoration ceremonies for them, would have been condemned to roam the earth but for the *mudang*, who performed rites for them. By bringing back the *mudang*, tying her to the politics of re-sistance, and suggesting her triumph in the victorious dance, Min forces us to see "badness" in new ways, thereby giving us art to live by.

ANNA MAY SPEAKS

Lisa See

This chapter from On Gold Mountain, *a nonfiction book about my family, gives actress Anna May Wong the fictional chance to address her fans and her detractors. The words here are culled from various sources, including interviews with Anna May, studio press releases, interviews with people who knew her, and old family stories.*

*n*obody asked me what I thought. Nobody asked me if I liked it when my brother used to brag to his classmates about me, hoping it would rub off on him. Nobody explained that even after I was dead my family would try to keep me a secret. Nobody said there would be others who would say I created bad stereotypes. Nobody said that there would be these people with their "fanzines" and their fantasies. Nobody asked me what *I* thought, but I'm going to tell you and you can believe it or not. I don't care. Because whatever *I* say you will change anyway.

You say to me, *What is your home? Is it California?* I ask you back, how could it be the United States where I cannot buy property? Where I cannot marry a white man? This is how American I am. One time I was asked to umpire a baseball game in a floor-length *cheongsam*. *Could it be Chinatown?* This is what I know about Chinatown: They didn't want me unless they thought they could profit from me. So they want to raise money for China Relief. They hold a Moon Festival. They say, "We need a grand marshal. We need a star." They know in their filthy hearts there is only one person to ask. "We will ask Anna May." Of course I go, knowing that the day after the Moon Festival they will go back to their old ways and I will go home alone to Santa Monica.

What of Europe? Surely this is where you are most comfortable. This is where you have had so much fame. This is what I know. I couldn't get a decent job in America and I wanted to be a star. When I'm in London, someone asks me, "Why did you leave America?" This is what I say: "I think I left America because I died so often. I was killed in virtually every picture in which I appeared. Pathetic dying seemed to be the thing I did best."

Another time they ask me that same question and I answer, "When I left Hollywood I vowed that I would never act for film again. I was so tired of the part I had to play. Why is it that the screen Chinese is always a villain? And so crude a villain—murderous, treacherous, a snake in the grass! We are not like that. How could we be, with a civilization that is so many times older than the West? We have rigid codes of behavior, of honor. Why do they never show these? Why should we always scheme, rob, kill? I got so weary of it all—of the scenarists' conception of the Chinese character. You remember Fu Manchu? *Daughter of the Dragon?* So wicked!" When they say I perpetuated those stereotypes I wonder.

But I couldn't take any more of America. So, in 1928 I sailed for Germany to make *Schmutziges Geld*. Someone tells me that means *Dirty Money*. Then I go to Paris, then London, then back to Berlin. The whole time my sister Lulu is traveling with me. A reporter writes, "Maybe Lulu is headed for pictures." I laugh. I am "the toast of Europe."

I learn to speak German and French. At least I *said* I learned those things. Perhaps I just learned how to pronounce the words before the camera. Perhaps I had no idea what I was saying. Perhaps I learned my lines by typing out my scripts. It doesn't matter, because I was a star. In 1929, I was in *A Circle of Chalk* with Laurence Olivier. At night, at the stage door, people waited for *me*. Did they wait for Olivier? Never. I would walk outside into the fog or rain and they would be there—young men in their tuxedos, young women with their bangs cut straight and blunt. Those young men lusted for me. Those young women tinted their faces ivory with ocher powder hoping to duplicate my complexion.

In 1931, Sessue Hayakawa says, "Come back to America to star in *Daughter of the Dragon*." I tell the reporters, "It is good to be home. I'm glad they want me back here to make a picture. I must confess I was discouraged when I left Hollywood. But I wasn't bitter. Everyone had been kind to me. And I'm grateful now; it wasn't easy at the start. It makes me appreciative of good fortune." The next year I'm in *Shanghai Express*.

Is China your home country? When I went to China after I lost the part in *The Good Earth*, I thought, ah, perhaps this is my home. The officials held a four-hour state dinner in Nanking. But I spoke Cantonese. They spoke Mandarin. I say to my interpreter, "Tell my everything they say. I want to know everything." So through the dinner he quietly whispers in my ear what the others say as they stand to make their toasts. "Does she know that her films are banned in our country? What of this courtesan in *Shanghai Express*? Is this how she wants the world to view Chinese women? Does she realize how she degrades our mothers and sisters and wives and daughters?" I sit there. I smile. I listen. I tell them in English, "When a person is trying to get established in a profession, he can't choose his parts. He has to take what is offered. I came to China to learn." In America, they write, "She was received like a princess."

I stayed in China for ten months. All my life I had been homesick for China even though I had never been there. A rhythm of life there harmonized with something in me that had been out of tune. I was no longer restless. It's hard to explain. Our Chinese expression—"being in harmony with heaven and earth"—is the essence of it. I went to Toishan to visit my home village. The women came out. They didn't believe I was real. They thought I was machinemade on the movie screen.

When I return to America I work hard to raise money to help the people of China. I speak everywhere. Paramount doesn't mind. They are helpful. They write press releases for me. They say, "In view of current events in the Orient, anything Japanese annoys Anna May Wong, Chinese actress." I have an apartment overlooking a Japanese garden. When I look at it I get angry. I'm not soothed. I keep a bowl of goldfish. I have fish because it is calming to watch them swim and I can forget things that bother me. But now I can't stop thinking of that garden. Paramount sends out another release: "Last night Miss Wong moved to a furnished home in another part of Hollywood, far from any landscaping suggesting Japan."

But you would say, *Is it enough not to look at a Japanese garden?* Of course not. I have one of the largest and most expensive wardrobes in Hollywood. I've bought gowns in Paris, New York, Hollywood, and China. So I auction more than two hundred gowns, ensembles, wraps, accessories—including fans, jewelry, and headdresses. All the money goes for relief funds.

You say, *Perhaps you are a woman of the world?* But I ask you, do you know how strange the world is? One day—it's 1927—I'm looking in the paper and I see this in the classifieds: "Anna May Wong, screen star, call at 908 N. State Street. Important, Mother." I don't know what to do. I go with two police detectives to the apartment to investigate. A Mrs. Waha answers the door. She saw me in a picture and thinks I am her daughter who ran away from Macao. "Are you my daughter?" she asks. I tell her no.

Here's another story. It's 1932. I have to take the train from Los Angeles to New York. I think, this is nice. Let's choose a way that will go through Canada. Why not? You have time. It will be beautiful. It will be relaxing. It will be different. In Detroit, I get off the train to chat with friends who've come to the station. But Canadian immigration officials are there and won't let me back on the train. So I spend the night in Detroit and the next day take an all-American train to New York.

This is what I know: when I kissed Jameson Thomas in *Piccadilly*, British censors cut it. When I was courted on screen in *Haitang* by a Russian duke, Hungarian officials banned the film. No film lover can ever marry me. If they get an American actress to slant her eyes and eyebrows and wear a stiff black wig and dress in Chinese costume, it would be all right. But me? I am true Chinese. I must always die in the movies, so that the white girl with the yellow hair can get the man.

I ask you, how can I be a woman of the world when no place is home to me?

My father was a laundryman. You know what this is like. Nonstop work. People treating you badly and not paying the proper amount. You know the story, *No tickee, no washee*. I go to Chinese school but I hate it. Instead, I go to the movie theater to see *The Perils of Pauline*. Do you remember, Stella, how we used to laugh about that, how you saw the same things in Waterville and wished you were *somewhere* else and I was in Los Angeles and wished I were *someone* else?

I was born Wong Lie Tsong. It means something like Frosted Yellow Willows or Frosted Willow Blossoms or Hoar-Frost of the Willow Trees. All my life I'm wishing for something different. To be someone different. I remember coming home from the serials and standing in front of the mirror and acting out all the parts. I would look Caucasian. I remember how surprised I was when I was chosen to represent China in a school pageant because I was the most "typically Chinese girl" in class.

I'm ten years old and working at a furrier company. Sometimes I'm a model. Once they dress me in a mink coat and brocaded ankle-length pantaloons and take my picture for the rotogravure section of the newspaper. My father is so impressed by my elegance that he cuts out the picture and sends it to my half-brother in China. My brother writes back, "Tsong is indeed very beautiful, but please send me the dollar watch on the other side." You know what I say to that? A fur coat doesn't tick.

One day I hear about a movie they're making about the Boxer Rebellion—*The Red Lantern*. I go to a casting agent. Was it Tom Gubbins? No. It was Reverend Wang, the Baptist minister. He says, "Well, you got big eyes, big nose, big ears and mouth. I guess you'll do." He changes my name to Anna May Wong. I'm twelve years old. I don't care. I want to be in pictures. For two more years I go after school to work on different movies as an extra. I work so hard. My brothers, my sisters, they keep it a secret. They know how mad my father will get. One day, one of my sisters say she has to tell Father to help her own conscience. He says, "If you are going to miss school, miss Chinese school. I have to pay for that."

My family is ashamed. They say people in Hollywood use harsh words. They say acting is not an honorable profession. They say all those things about white men: "They will take advantage of you. They will compromise you." My father gets so angry he tries to arrange a marriage for me. He doesn't ask me what I think. But I'll tell you. I think, I don't want a husband to boss me around. I don't want to live my life in Chinatown. I don't want to marry a cook or a laundryman. I don't want a husband who will take all my money, even if he lets me keep working. Besides, no Chinese man will marry me. I've become too American to marry one of my own race.

My father gives up and I never marry. And when I'm in *The Thief of Bagdad* my costume is so see-through that my family never forgives me. In their eyes, I am like a courtesan. Only my brother Richard is faithful to me. Still, does my father complain that I bring home money? Does he complain when I support the whole family? Does he complain when I buy one brother a typewriter and help another to learn photography? Does he complain when I put all my brothers through school? But here is the truth: I was beautiful as the slave girl.

After *The Thief of Bagdad*, the press begins to call me the "celestial maiden." They call me "sloe-eyed." They call me "exotic." They call me the "Oriental Siren," the "China Doll," the "Lotus Girl," the "Chinese Flapper." They call me the "Queen of the B-films." They say I've never cut my hair, never worn eyeglasses, never worn wool underwear, never curled my hair, never eaten lobster, never been on a bicycle, never owned a radio. They say I have the longest nails in Hollywood. They make it *news* again when I grow them back two inches and protect them with gold nail guards for *Dangerous to Know*.

Have you ever thought about what it would be like to be beautiful? In 1938, *Look* called me "The Most Beautiful Chinese Girl in the World." I remember once in London I stopped a debate in Parliament when I walked into the visitor's gallery. They stopped everything just to watch me walk, to watch me sit down. When I came back from my "Triumph Abroad," they said I was the "Toast of the Continent." They said my complexion was as a "rose blushing through old ivory," that my face shone on the screen like a Ming vase. But I ask you, did I get work? When they want a Chinese, they hire Louise Ranier, Sylvia Sydney, Dorothy Lamour, Myrna Loy, and Sigrid Gurie.

Behind my back, people talk about how lonely I was. Some say, "Didn't Anna May have tuberculosis?" Some say, "Didn't Anna May drink?" "Didn't she have sad love affairs?" "Didn't she become a virtual recluse?" "Didn't her brother have to take care of her?" Did any of them ever ask *me*?

This is what I want to ask you: What would you do if your family was ashamed of you? What would you do if you were their worst secret? This is what I did. It is the end of 1930 and I'm on Broadway doing *On the Spot* with Wilber Crane. My mother crosses the street in front of our house in Chinatown and is hit by a car. My brothers call and tell me. They leave nothing out. Fracture of the skull. Broken leg. Internal injuries. They call later to say that our mother is dead. Do you know how I feel to be so far away? Do you know how I feel when the police let the driver go free? I file a lawsuit. My father and my brothers and sisters join me. What would they do if I wasn't there?

So I say, let people gossip all they want. Does it change my life? Does it make me disappear? When I returned from China I found here restless seeking for something that couldn't be found. The Chinese found it many years ago—a sort of serenity, an inner calm that comes from the understanding of life. This is such a short life. And mine is truly short. Only fifty-four years. And when I die my brother Richard sells my clothes to our friends. To you, Stella, and you, Verna. The others? They know who they are.

People say, oh, she died of a broken heart. She died of disappointment. She died of too much bitterness. She died to pay for her sins against the Chinese people. But I say nothing matters one way or another. I have learned not to struggle but to flow along with the tide. Time adjusts all things—even fingernails.

THE FAMILY HOUR

Sheerekha Pillai

*t*here is a word for nigger in every language
It is karamban in mine.
Heads pressed close together holding hands
and breath my family and I absorb the abundant
American dream. We watch TV.
The special report says a crazed lunatic
has fired fifteen rounds of gunfire at an unarmed
crowd returning home from the city to the suburbs.
He is black.

It does not matter afterwards as a black woman says shooting is not the
    answer
no matter what the problem.

It does not matter afterwards as the story uncloses the psyche of the man,
revealing that he was undergoing paranoid delusions.

It does not matter that the sympathetic reporters telling
and retelling the tragedy are also black.

It does not matter that the mayor of New York City was black,
 or that mother's hard-working colleagues are also black.

It does not matter the history that spits against our walls.
Little Rock, Arkansas, was only ten years before my parents' marriage.

It does not matter why my closest friend feels the need to be strong
and aggressive with everyone she meets. Her grandmamma told
her before she left her home to travel the world,
always keep your head held high chile and speak loud, 'cause we all
been crying quiet with our heads held low for too long.

No stories of pain or analysis of hurt matter anymore. For my parents
and I partaking in the daily American libation
we a clustered whole
a slice of an immigrant people
only see that he is a karamban
and there is a word for nigger in our language too.

FROM "THIRTY AND FIVE BOOKS" IN *DURA*

Myung Mi Kim

*W*hen ready for use, cut into pieces of different sizes,
nearly square, but somewhat longer than they are wide.

To each note a number of officers, specially appointed,
not only subscribe their names, but affix their seals.

In this way it receives full authenticity.

Not the return of money but its continued removal further
and further from its starting point.

The situation waste and wild.

Stamped by purse. Bone soldered. Labor open.

Light and propagation. That stolen. Torment a sum of pieces prices.

Bodies in propulsion. Guatemalan, Korean, African-American
sixteen-year-olds working check-out lanes. Hard and noisy
enunciation.

A banter English gathers carriers.

What is nearest is destroyed.

Winds from all four corners blowing even while ships
crossed open seas. Fantasy of steadfastness.

Mother whose son. Shopkeeper whose shop
is burned.

Even still along routes and canals. Camel-load, hemp
drawn. Means of circulation. Concentrated in the strong rooms.

Grim and binding. Dummy laws. Lauded dummy dress.

Civil. Event.
One is hurt. One is armed.
The fourth coordinate is any measure of time.
Is a report possible.
Tracks dug into prominence then into crabgrass.
Separate yet contingent. Across banisters and encampments,
polluted.

Square towers of a city in the distance often appear round.

Largest of earth's continents discovered. Printing
press sowing knowledge.

Just as festered. Just as smelly.

Gum and balm. Pierced shade for the updrawn stream.

When days have passed. Pent.

In vain to understand the entries among the oldest
strains of eggplant. How to tie a goat with assurance.

PART 5

MOVEMENT

*passion
and
commitment*

VIOLENCE IN OUR COMMUNITIES:
"WHERE ARE THE ASIAN WOMEN?"

Helen Zia

This article is based on the discussions and position paper of a group formed in 1991 to study the nexus of violence against Asian women and hate crimes. In the course of more than a year, the group produced several drafts of the position paper; I edited the final draft, which was never distributed beyond the initial discussion group. Much of the analysis presented here is based on the year-long discussions of the study group, which I joined near the end of the process.

The core participants must be recognized for their commitment, dedication, vision, and hard work on behalf of the Asian American community and women in general, and especially for their efforts on behalf of Asian women and girls. They are: Patti Chang, Diane Chinn, Cindy Choi, Rose Fua, Inderpal Grewal, Deeana Jang, Jennifer Kanenaga, Mimi Kim, Kathy Lim Ko, Jeanette Lazam, Debbie Lee, Lata Mani, Leni Marin, Beckie Masaki, Blesilda Ocampo, Lia Shigemura, Doreena Wong, and Lily Wu. I am honored to convey their views in this piece. Commentary made without attribution to the group is my own; in any case, the responsibility for what is presented is mine alone.

$\mathcal{W}$here are the Asian women?" This was the question a group of Asian American women asked in the San Francisco Bay Area. They began meeting in 1991 to try to find an answer, to put names on the flesh-and-blood Asian American women whose lives ended in violence and invisibility.

The question arose during the San Francisco Asian Women's Shelter annual event. As one of the speakers that night, I referred to the fact that after ten years of the anti-Asian violence movement work since the Vincent Chin case, all those named on the growing list of anti-Asian violence victims were men. I wondered why, and so did several other women present.

The group that met in San Francisco to examine this question was no ordinary gathering of women. Among them were community activists, lawyers, and service providers working on anti-Asian violence issues, sexual assault and domestic violence problems, and for the rights of immigrants, lesbians, women, and people of color. They were Korean American, Chinese American, Filipina, Japanese American sansei, Southeast Asian and South Asian American. By identifying and analyzing the roots of Asian women's invisibility, they hoped to begin a dialogue within the anti-Asian violence movement that would include Asian women.

It seemed inconceivable that Asian American women would not be subject to hate violence, particularly since violence against both women and Asians was increasing. Did Asian American men come into contact with perpetrator types more often? Were Asian American men more hated by racists? A feminist analysis of the subordination and vulnerability of Asian American women, whose dominant stereotype is sexual exoticism and passivity, contradicted such reasoning. Where were the Asian women? Why wasn't there more concern about their apparent absence?

In my own research, I had found a few Asian women from random news clippings, footnotes in books, word of mouth. They were women like:

• Ly Yung Cheung, a nineteen-year-old Chinese woman, who in February 1984 was seven months pregnant when she was pushed in front of a New York City subway train and decapitated. Her attacker, a white male high school teacher, claimed that he suffered from "a phobia of Asian people" and that he was overcome with the urge to kill this woman. He successfully pleaded insanity. If this case had been investigated as a hate crime, there might have been more information about his so-called phobia and whether or not there was a pattern of racism. But the murder was not investigated as a hate crime.

• Fifty-two-year-old Japanese American Helen Fukui disappeared in Denver, Colorado on December 7, 1984. Her decomposed body was found weeks later. The fact that she disappeared on Pearl Harbor Day, when anti-Asian speech and incidents increase dramatically, was considered significant in the Asian American community. But the case was not investigated as a hate crime, and no suspects were ever apprehended.

• An eight-year-old Chinese girl named Jean Har-Kew Fewel was found raped and lynched in Chapel Hill, North Carolina in 1985, two months after *Penthouse* magazine featured pictures of Asian women in various poses of bondage and torture, including hanging bound from trees, in deathlike poses. At his trial, the killer admitted that pornography played a significant role in his attitudes. Jean's rape and murder weren't investigated as possible crimes of anti-Asian violence.

• The serial rapist who kidnapped and raped a Japanese exchange student in 1992 was convicted in Oregon, where he was a student. He had also assaulted a Japanese woman in Arizona and another in San Francisco. He was sentenced to jail for these crimes, which were not pursued as hate crimes, even though California has a hate crimes statute.

• Two Asian women were gang-raped by fraternity "brothers" at Ohio State University in two separate incidents. One of the rapes was part of a racially targeted "game" called "the Ethnic Sex Challenge," in which the fraternity men followed an ethnic checklist indicating what kind of women to gang-rape. In this case, the targets were Asian women. Because the women feared ostracism by their communities, neither woman reported the rapes. However, the attacks were known to a few campus officials, who did not take them up as hate crimes or anything else.

Any of these incidents could have been pursued as anti-Asian violence and investigated as state hate crimes and/or federal criminal civil rights cases. Had the victims been male, there might have been a hate crimes investigation, but the fact that the victims were female added the potential of a gender bias on the part of the criminal. So the attacks on these Asian women remained virtually unnoticed, through the inattention of law enforcement and the community at large.

The San Francisco Bay Area Asian American women's study group began its efforts to uncover why violence against Asian women seemed to draw less attention than other anti-Asian violence. The group found it disturbing that the predominant forms of violence that Asian women experience—domestic violence and sexual assault—never galvanized community interest the way that hate crimes did. There seemed to be greater enthusiasm to mobilize against whites who attack Asian men than to organize against the significantly more prevalent attacks on Asian women in their own homes. This suggested that part of the answer might be found in how violence against women is viewed in the Asian American community.

The group's fundamental premise was that any discussion of violence in the Asian community must also address sexual assault and domestic violence, despite current civil rights and hate crimes law, which utilizes a narrow legal framework. On the basis of their experience with and knowledge of Asian women survivors of violence, group members compared sexual assault and domestic violence issues to legally defined hate violence. Under the law, designation as a hate crime requires bias motivation by race, religion, national origin, and, under federal law and in certain states, sexual orientation. If other possible motivations exist—as in the case of a robbery-assault at an Asian-owned store, or in the case of a sexual assault against an Asian woman—the incident might not be classified as a hate crime. Prior to the Violence Against Women Act in 1994, gender was not a protected category or class, so any crime with a gender component—for example, when the attacker is male and the victim is female—would fail to receive consideration as a hate crime. The net impact of this legal framework is to exclude women from hate crimes protection.

The women activists in the discussion group concluded that this narrow legal approach to violence does not work for Asian women. So they proposed a broader look at the common links between anti-Asian violence and violence against Asian women. By rejecting the existing legal definitions and reframing the way violence is classified to take a more expansive view, they found that hate violence, whether based on race, gender, class, religion, or sexual orientation, is connected by a common root. Such violence is used as a means of exerting power, control, and domination by one group over another. And the most pervasive form of violence within the Asian American community, as throughout society, is violence against women.

This approach is a radical departure from the legalistic, more commonly accepted notions of violence and hate crimes. A new paradigm for violence emerged from the group's discussions, which accounts for the power, control, and privilege in the relation between the attacker and the victim. The new paradigm proved to be inclusive of the violence experienced by Asian women. Using this broader approach, the group reviewed several different types of violent incidents involving Asian women that had been overlooked by the criminal justice system as well as the Asian American community. This review raises some provocative issues. The following incidents of anti-Asian violence were among those they examined:

In the case of the white man who claimed that his "phobia of Asians" caused him to push Ly Yung Cheung in front of a subway train, the new paradigm examines the power relationship between the attacker and the victim. In acting on his alleged "fear" of an entire race of people, the attacker chose the most vulnerable person to kill—a nineteen-year-old pregnant woman. Using a broader paradigm of hate violence, this murder of an Asian woman by a stranger, who was a white man, would be considered a hate crime.

The group also cited the example of Kwok Ray, a Chinese woman who was found dead, stuffed into the trunk of her husband's car in Sacramento, California, in November 1991. Her husband, Kent Ray, a white man, had used domestic violence to assert his power and privilege, based on race and gender differences, over his wife, just as did the killer of Ly Yung Cheung. Using a broader paradigm of hate violence, the murder of an Asian woman by her husband, who is a white man, should be considered a hate crime.

Veena Charan, a South Asian woman, was shot to death in 1990 by her ex-husband as she was walking their son to school. The ex-husband, a South Asian man, was of the same race and ethnicity. After a police chase, he shot himself. Veena had endured violent abuse for years before she left her husband, pressing criminal charges and obtaining a divorce and a restraining order. But her ex-husband, like the killers in the two previous examples, used violence and his power and privilege as a man to control an Asian woman. Using a broader paradigm of hate violence, this murder of an Asian woman by her ex-husband, who is an Asian man, should be considered a hate crime.

Pushing the envelope even further, the group applied their paradigm to the case of Ni Win, a Chinese woman who was shot to death in a San Francisco restaurant in 1991 by her lover, also a Chinese woman. Their relationship, like relationships in other lesbian and gay battering cases, followed the pattern of heterosexual domestic violence: extreme isolation as well as threats and violence that increase over time. The conventional approach to classifying hate crimes requires some difference according to race, gender, national origin, religion, or sexual orientation between the victim and the perpetrator. This case, however, most clearly illustrates the difference between the existing legal hate crimes framework and the group's view of hate violence as a means of exerting power and control, because both victim and killer were the same race, gender, national origin, and sexual orientation. But the fact that the two women belonged to the same legally protected groupings (or "classes") does not diminish the fact that violence was the ultimate exercise of power and control used by one to dominate the other, in the same way it was used in the other hate crimes. For an Asian lesbian batterer, perceived power may be related to economics, class, or education and may include threats to "out" her lover to family or employers. Using a broader paradigm of hate violence, this particular murder of an Asian woman by her partner, who is an Asian woman, would also be considered a hate crime.

In each of these examples, an Asian woman was murdered. Whether her killer was a stranger or acquaintance, of a different race or the same race, male or female, the common link that connects these victims was that their vulnerability as Asian women was exploited through the use of violence. This is not to suggest that every incident of violence against an Asian woman would be a hate crime under the group's paradigm. Violence was used in each of these cases as a means of control; fear, intimidation, threats, and physical violence were employed to deprive these women of their human rights. It is significant that none of these cases would be deemed a hate crime under the current legal framework.

The exclusion of Asian women is what prompted the group to construct an approach that could address violence against Asian women as hate crimes. The group recognized that their view differs radically from the more conventional approach of the anti-Asian violence movement, which has adhered to prevailing legal definitions. The group also recognized that not everyone will agree with them. Indeed, they were not unanimous on every point themselves. But they hoped that dissent would help initiate a broad discussion on how to include violence against Asian women in the community's hate crimes response.

In advocating such a discussion, none of the group's analysis is intended to diminish the work and accomplishments of the anti-Asian violence movement. But the existing legal framework has limited the anti-Asian violence movement to a case-by-case legal approach, taking on only the most blatant cases of legally classified hate violence. Only crimes perpetrated with a single, clear-cut motivation, like a racial attack without robbery or rape, are defined as hate crimes. Only assaults committed by strangers—and then only whites, not other people of color—are taken up. And only individual acts of violence are addressed, not institutionalized or systemic violence. These are serious weaknesses because, unfortunately, most incidents of anti-Asian violence are more complex, particularly those against Asian American women, given that gender will always be a factor.

To facilitate a discussion of these questions in the Asian American community, the study group identified five major factors that contribute to the invisibility of Asian women and the violence they experience:

First, there is the very manner in which race and gender are constructed in mainstream society. "Women" are generically considered to be white, while "Asians" are generically considered to be male. If an incident of violence against an Asian woman is recognized at all, and sexual assault is involved, the crime will typically be viewed as a gender crime with no consideration of race. For Asian women, as for other women of color, the intersection of race and gender is a place of invisibility.

Second, violence against women has become so commonplace in the media and popular culture that it is seen as "normal." Women are depicted as passive victims who "enjoy" or even "deserve" abuse; men are viewed as aggressive, unemotional. They are more intelligent and more valued, and they solve problems by force. Such stereotypes contribute to a climate in which it is permissible to batter women. Moreover, acts of violence against women are considered private or personal crimes, sexualized crimes of passion that happen to individuals, rather than a social problem of epidemic proportions. Racist stereotypes add further distortion: Asian women are the exotic, docile prostitutes, while Asian men are "asexual" and "inscrutably evil." The sexualization of violence against Asian women can be found in popular culture, on numerous Internet sites, and in pornography, which figured significantly in the life of the rapist and murderer of eight-year-old Jean Har-Kew Fewel in North Carolina in 1985.

Third, women are often blamed for violence against themselves. Of battered women, people ask, "Why did she stay?" Sexual harassment and assault victims are thought to "invite" or "provoke" attack somehow. The background of a female victim may come under more scrutiny than the attacker's; crimes against sex workers are frequently not pursued at all. Victims of other crimes are not scrutinized in this way; the victim of a robbery is not asked why she wears nice clothing or jewelry or drives a fancy car.

Fourth, assumptions about ethnicity are used to further minimize the violence Asian women experience by rationalizing that Asian cultures accept gender violence. This has resulted in the use of "cultural defenses" of Asian immigrant men who abuse, assault, or murder their partners. Such was the case of Dong Lu Chen, a Chinese man in New York who killed his wife in 1987 by pounding her head with a claw hammer. His attorney claimed that in China if a man believes his wife has committed adultery, he will threaten to kill her; otherwise Chinse society would consider him morally weak. The judge sentenced Chen to five years' probation, the lightest sentence possible, saying that he was "driven to violence by traditional Chinese values about adultery and loss of manhood." In this case, license was given to Asian men to use patriarchal culture to excuse violence against

Asian women. By characterizing differences in the Asian community as "cultural," issues of race, gender, class, and sexual orientation become depoliticized and subsumed as "cultural."

Finally, women in general are silenced, intimidated, and often discouraged from speaking up about violence. Asian women are doubly discouraged from reporting violence. Although the tracking and monitoring of criminal incidents of domestic violence have improved over the years, there are virtually no available statistics specific to Asian Pacific Islander communities. Similarly, the Hate Crimes Statistics Act of 1990 mandated the federal tracking of hate crimes, which in accordance with federal definitions includes those against Asian Americans, but no gender data are provided. It remains to be seen how well the federal Violence Against Women Act of 1994 will address both gender and race crime statistics. Ironically, the policy of confidentiality for the protection of victims, which has been so fundamental to the domestic violence and sexual assault movements, has also limited women's ability to publicize incidents of violence.

In addition to the five major factors enumerated by the study group, another reason for the invisibility of Asian women victims has become more troubling since the group's discussion ended. This is the rise of hate crimes committed by people of color against each other, including crimes by and against Asians. Little dialogue has taken place about the complex issue of racial tension and hate crimes among communities of color. While such incidents occur against both Asian men and women, reluctance to recognize assaults by people of color as hate crimes again leads to the invisibility of violence against Asian women. For example, following the Los Angeles civil disturbances in 1992, bias-motivated rapes of Asian storekeepers by other people of color were rumored to be occurring, but they were not taken up in the community. In the San Francisco Bay Area, a Korean woman was murdered by an African American man in the store where she and her husband worked. Her face was beaten so severely that local police initially had difficulty ascertaining her race. Similarly, during the reign of hate by Latino youths against the South Asian community, Indian women were sexually assaulted in Jersey City, New Jersey. As long as this situation fails to receive serious attention in the Asian community, such violence against Asian women will remain doubly invisible.

Sadly, the result of these several factors is predictable. No Asian women appear in the documentation of anti-Asian violence. Progress can be made toward ending this invisibility and making violence against Asian women a serious and urgent issue. The San Francisco discussion group recommended specific, practical measures that can be taken up now by those in the anti-Asian violence movement and the Asian American community: support the struggles that are integral to the safety of Asian women; monitor and take on cases of violence against Asian women; discuss the links between gender violence and legally proscribed anti-Asian violence in the community and in public forums.

Violence against Asian women may also be hate violence, but it has not been recognized as such because of the biased ways in which women, particularly Asian women and other women of color, are viewed in society. Equipped with a broad vision that integrates violence against women with the hate crimes in a new paradigm, our communities will be better able to combat all forms of violence, including domestic violence and sexual assault. We must shift as a community from anti-Asian violence organizing to an Asian anti-violence movement in which we stand against all violence, including violence against women. We must work together to create a society and communities that do not permit the battering, abuse, rape, assault, torture, maiming, or killing of anyone—female or male.

The answer to the question, "Where are the Asian women?" is clear. We are everywhere. One only has to look.

AGAINST THE TIDE: REFLECTIONS ON ORGANIZING NEW YORK CITY'S SOUTH ASIAN TAXICAB DRIVERS

Anuradha G. Advani

i decided to become a community and union organizer after seeing my efforts to tutor a seventh-grade Indian student in literature and English as a Second Language (ESL) stymied by his economic situation. The son of a cook and a waiter in a popular Indian restaurant, he also worked thirty-five hours a week there for only $2.00 an hour. His circumstances focused my desire to advance my community by addressing basic needs for decent working conditions and shelter.

In 1990, I moved to New York City in search of an independent, adventuresome life that was far from home. Since New York has a more visible and neighborhood-based working-class South Asian community than the San Francisco suburb where I grew up, I foresaw rich organizing possibilities. Initially I joined the Committee Against Anti-Asian Violence (CAAAV), which had been advocating for and organizing primarily Chinese and Korean victims of hate crimes. By joining, I intended to make CAAAV more accessible and responsible to South Asians. As a parallel strategy, I formed the South Asian Alliance For Action (SAAFA), with four other Indian American recent college graduates in 1991. I hoped to bring CAAAV and SAAFA together in coalition. Though SAAFA disbanded after one year due to personal conflicts and political differences, our many discussions helped all the members clarify our particular goals for community service work. A few CAAAV members decided to investigate a former SAAFA member's proposal to work with South Asian taxicab drivers.

THE LEASE DRIVERS' COALITION: ORGANIZING WITH MULTIPLE ANCHORAGES

Taxicab driving ranks second in New York City's occupations with respect to its associated mortality rate; only owning a small business, including South Asian minimarts, gas stations, and newsstands, as well as Korean greengrocers, ranks higher.[1] Drivers in the taxi industry as a whole are ninety-nine percent male, and ninety-one percent immigrant. Forty-three percent of the drivers of Manhattan-based yellow cabs, which pick up people on the street, are South Asian, with roughly equal numbers from the Bangladeshi, Indian, and Pakistani communities, respectively. Another fourteen percent of yellow-cab drivers are Chinese.[2]

A full-scale workers' organization was far from our minds when we began to investigate what appeared to be language-based discrimination against drivers. The Taxi and Limousine Commission (TLC), the industry's regulatory body, had advised aspiring drivers to take its English course, which cost $400, in order to pass the English exam required for a cab driver's license. While exploring this issue, the Lease Drivers' Coalition (LDC)—probably the first South Asian-based labor organization in the United States[3]—was formed. Organizers of the LDC had institutional and personal ties to CAAAV and SAAFA.

The new LDC initiated a two-page survey, as much to open up contact with the drivers' community as to gather information about working conditions. We used multiple community/work spaces to reach a fraction of the roughly twenty-two thousand yellow-cab drivers: gas-station and street-corner hangouts as well as taxi garages, mosques, community fairs, and Indian/Pakistani restaurants. The survey showed that the taxi drivers' primary concern was the industry's low wages, whereby drivers, as independent contractors, survived on a daily median take-home income of $45.00, after leasing the car for $90.00 per twelve-hour shift from a cab-fleet owner. Drivers were also extremely vulnerable to being robbed of even these meager cash earnings. Despite such oppressive economic conditions, the "contradiction between being workers and having a middle-class consciousness, or aspiration"[4] remained a great hindrance in organizing the taxi drivers. Moreover, drivers also seemed more or less resigned to the physical risks inherent in this occupation—in part because they perceived taxi driving as a temporary step to a professional career.

The survey also revealed that since drivers are not legally considered employees but instead are "independent contractors," they receive no medical benefits, overtime, pension, or paid vacation.[5] In the name of protecting passengers, Taxi and Limousine Commission officers also routinely issued tickets for minor infractions of its many detailed rules, which cut deeply into the drivers' meager earnings.[6] TLC officers and city police also regularly physically abused drivers without provocation.[7] Without adequate English or knowledge of the justice system, immigrant taxi drivers were often at a loss to assert themselves against such harassment.

LDC organizers, who tried to respond to the taxi drivers' needs, included many women. As one LDC member explained, the sheer number of South Asian cab drivers was a motivating factor for her to get involved; the fact that they were of a different gender was not that important. Although South Asian cultural norms for women's roles would have made it inappropriate and uncomfortable for me to conduct outreach to drivers taking a tea-break at Indian/Pakistani restaurants in the wee hours of the morning, we had male organizers who could operate in these situations. Our being young women sometimes surprisingly created a space for organizing, as when the owner of one garage surmised from my Hindi/Urdu conversation with a driver that, far from wanting to stir up trouble, we were actually looking for husbands! As drivers are perceived as lewd in South Asia, I was pleasantly surprised to not be sexually harassed while leafleting and surveying. Perhaps this was because the drivers were too perplexed, wondering who our motley crew was and why we were bothering to be concerned about them! During one meeting a few months into the organization, I was upset at the exchange of sexual jokes in Hindi/Urdu; subsequently, we decided to make it a precondition for joining our organization that sexual, antigay, and racial harassment would not be tolerated. None of the women reported being harassed after that event; rather, we eventually came to be regarded as "sister" organizers.

Most nondriver Asian organizers were actually lesbian/bisexual women. Various factors may account for the strong lesbian/bisexual presence. One CAAAV member believes, "You have to come from a place of empowerment to be an 'out' lesbian, and the same kind of personality is required to be an organizer." Additionally, despite the general prominence of male movement leaders, the majority of grass-roots organizers continue to be women, as we are socialized to fulfill the role of caretaker. Young South Asian men raised in the United States also have pressure on them to be high-wage earners, as they are expected to support not only their future wives and children, but also their elderly parents; women have a bit more choice with respect to their avocation. Whatever the reasons, the strong lesbian/bisexual presence in the LDC created an organizational predisposition to be sensitive about issues of violence, since women, gay people, and South Asians are all groups that it is considered "safe" to beat up.

RESISTANCE: OPERATION SAFE CAB

Our first campaign, Operation Safe Cab, began in December 1992. Because the informal economy lacks regulation, its workers, including cab drivers, are continuously exposed to violence, which is often racial. Through the late 1970s, the TLC required a simple Plexiglas bullet-proof partition between driver and passengers, which has been shown to protect drivers from attack; however, such basic safety requirements became a casualty of the deregulation of the industry.[8] We sought to make the city council once again require cab owners to install the partitions. As well, we demanded that the city institute the operation of a signaling device used by Boston bus drivers. This device provides the driver with a push-button emergency radio which signals the police department of his need for help and his exact whereabouts.

The specific measures we sought to improve taxi driving safety were aimed to include cab drivers of all ethnic backgrounds, not just South Asians. LDC together with other CAAAV projects viewed racial conflicts in the contexts of the needs of the American postindustrial economy.[9] This framework, aimed at long-term solutions to racial violence, was difficult to develop and sustain, given that South Asian immigrants layer new prejudices about U.S. people of color upon all the caste and color prejudices of the homeland.[10] Having repeatedly faced attack, South Asian drivers tended to see African American and Latino prospective passengers, or "fares," as a physical threat.[11] But calling their behavior racist was not only an oversimplification, it was also a judgment more easily tenable to one who rides in the passenger's seat of a cab, and not the driver's seat.[12] Nonetheless, LDC prioritized crossing the boundaries perpetuated by racial/economic oppression. Thus our experienced taxi activists attempted to craft a coalition between LDC and the companies of for-hire vehicles, whose drivers provide door-to-door service in poorer neighborhoods of the Bronx, Brooklyn, and Queens, and face a much higher rate of assault than do yellow-cab drivers, whose orbit is generally Manhattan. We felt that these drivers, whether African, African Caribbean, Italian, or Russian, would share similar concerns about the need for increased job safety.

Trying to build support for a city-council initiative on driver safety, we turned to communities, rather than to established unions, and circulated petitions at fairs, Indian/Pakistani restaurants, and mosques. However, in focusing on safety issues, we worried that we were forcing an issue on the drivers, who had indicated that their top concern was meager wages. But for a nascent organization to change the wage structure of the entire yellow-cab industry was virtually impossible; instituting safety measures was definitely a more "winnable" goal. After one year of organizing, it also became clear that we had indeed correctly intuited the drivers' frustration with being crime victims. In October 1993, after three Pakistani drivers were murdered in a twenty-four-hour period, seven thousand drivers demonstrated in midtown Manhattan about the need for better safety measures. This speedily and well-planned mass demonstration was called by other small drivers' organizations, many of them ethnic-specific groups that, unknown to us, had active networks organized around particular CB radio channels. Parking their cabs on the side of the road, drivers carried coffins on their heads to symbolize lives lost to city neglect. LDC organizers contributed to the demonstration by leafleting, and by notifying our contacts in the mainstream, South Asian and East Asian media. Within two days, the transportation committee of the city council, whom our taxi activists had lobbied for several months, hurriedly convened a hearing on safety in the taxicab industry.

The hearings, however, reinforced lessons that I had learned about the limits of identity-politics. Much to our chagrin, we saw that one of the major ethnic-based drivers' organizations, Pak Brothers, used an oppositional style of race-based organizing to frame its safety campaign. Rather than emphasizing the need for safety devices, Pak Brothers urged the city council to pass a "right of refusal" measure, which would give the drivers the legal right to refuse to pick up any passenger by whom they felt threatened. Obviously, South Asian drivers were likely to refuse to pick up Latino and African American fares, which in the long term would incur the resentment of these communities, intensify their own isolation, and lead to later retribution. On top of this, the Latino chair of the Taxi and Limousine Commission invoked his identity as the son of a murdered cab driver to invalidate LDC's testimony about the need for safety measures.[13] This served as an acute reminder that people of color in influential positions do not necessarily effect or enact progressive policies.

ACHIEVEMENTS

Through our efforts and those of many other organizations, the city council eventually mandated safety partitions and, instead of the radio, signal lights which could flash a distress signal. This significant victory impressed upon me the drivers' hopefulness in changing their collective situation, and the excellent networks they had created on their CB radios. The most difficult part of the work had been constructing an organizing paradigm that used these existing networks.

Our subsequent successful campaign to stop a proposed fare increase, which would have led to a decrease in ridership and in drivers' tips, did not utilize the CB radio networks, however. Instead, we flooded the Taxi and Limousine Commission office with preprinted postcards from taxicab passengers.

We also began to form a working coalition with one other drivers' group, United Friends, in 1994. Jointly, we produced a newsletter, *Peela Paiya*,[14] and conducted a quintessentially American fundraising campaign by printing and selling t-shirts. As well, we built coalitions with multiethnic and South Asian activist organizations that (unlike LDC) did not utilize class as a primary anchorage of their identity. Among the organizations were the Center for Constitutional Rights, Youth Against Racism, and South Asian AIDS Action. As part of its membership drive, LDC decided to submit drivers' applications for the 1994 green card lottery.[15] One of the Indian American lawyers from Youth Against Racism volunteered to review these applications. While we assisted South Asian AIDS Action community educators to contact Pakistani drivers, they in turn volunteered to bring us contacts in the Bangladeshi drivers' community.

By the summer of 1994, LDC had 150 dues-paying members. Nondriver organizers like myself sometimes felt disconnected from the membership; however, the preponderance of U.S.-educated, nondriver organizers in the group had its advantages. Operating under the auspices of an established, progressive antiviolence organization like CAAAV, with trained advocates, office resources, and familiarity with the U.S. political system, LDC could provide direct services that both addressed drivers' individual needs and attracted new members. For instance, LDC staff regularly advocated for taxi drivers contesting unfair tickets and harassment by the Taxi and Limousine Commission and police officers. In conjunction with LDC, CAAAV also began working to bring about change in the police's treatment of our communities, by demanding reform of the police academy curriculum with input from Asian representatives, and sensitivity training for officers, as well as access to police "brass." CAAAV's experience in advocating for police brutality victims was visibly effective when an undercover cop assaulted LDC organizer Saleem Osman. Overnight, we were able to mobilize one hundred Asian American activists, cab drivers, and supporters to march to the detention center where Saleem had been held in handcuffs for over twenty-four hours after being beaten. I felt a heady feeling of victory as we accompanied him out the door of the courthouse after his arraignment.

REFLECTIONS ON BUILDING A PAN-ASIAN MOVEMENT

However, the rally and march also illustrated several divisions behind the facade of unity: the differences in organizing frameworks, the lack of diversity among South Asian drivers, and the still peripheral position of South Asians in the Asian American movement.

The majority of the thirty-odd cabdrivers at the rally for Saleem's release were affiliated not with LDC, but with Pak Brothers, with whom LDC had major differences. Not only had Pak Brothers supported the right of refusal as a safety measure, but we also inferred that they were either a front for, or were being coopted by, the pro-industry Taxi and Limousine Commission. At the demonstration, they staged a confrontation, accusing us of wanting to control the rally and the cab drivers' movement by denying them the right to speak to the crowd. Drivers in their organization were told at one point not to march with us to the detention center. Though this would have diminished our strength and shown the police that the movement was divided, LDC did deny them the right to speak, because we felt there could be no compromise between their organizing framework and ours.

Additionally, none of the drivers present at the demonstration were Bangladeshi or Indian. At that time, LDC's membership consisted of a fairly homogeneous group: Muslim, Punjabi-speaking, Pakistani drivers, who reflected our initial contacts during the 1992 outreach drive.[16] Once a South Asian group becomes identified with a particular national group, changing the group's composition is very difficult; and the perception of LDC as a Pakistani organization unfortunately circumscribed our organizing strategies.[17]

The still peripheral position of South Asians within the anti-Asian violence movement was also evident at the demonstration. On one hand, the rapid mobilization of Asians of diverse backgrounds, including those in prominent legal organizations, acknowledged Saleem as a pivotal character not just in LDC but also in CAAAV. It also showed CAAAV's affirmation of the importance of South Asian issues for the anti-Asian violence movement.[18] Nonetheless, the demographics of the demonstration showed that East Asian nondrivers numbered twice as many as the South Asian cab drivers. The South Asian cab drivers there were carrying CAAAV's anti-police brutality placards in Korean and Chinese, as there was not a single placard in Bengali or Punjabi, and a mere few in Urdu. Rather than a positive crossing of boundaries, this dynamic reflected an inability to mobilize bilingual South Asian volunteers in the day-to-day running of the organization.[19]

Such dynamics have contributed to the reluctance of South Asians working on other issues to participate in a pan-Asian community movement. Ultimately, however, I think a set dictum on whether or not South Asians should organize with East and Southeast Asians is limiting. Different modes of organizing, from specific South Asian nationality-based groups to pan-Asian groups, are appropriate depending on the issue, the organizing framework and method, and the timing of the group's formation.

STEERING AGAINST THE CONSERVATIVE TIDE

Lease Drivers' Coalition, as an ethnically/racially based progressive workers' organization, has been able to interest and involve South Asian drivers in securing their rights in a way that the official taxi drivers' union has not.[20] At the time I left the organization to move back to California, nondriver organizers were attempting to redefine their role in the struggle in light of Saleem's strong leadership and increased driver involvement. LDC was also continuing its coalition-building efforts. Given the tidal wave of antiimmigrant, antiaffirmative, and antipoor sentiment, coalitions are crucial in enforcing our hard-won measures, as well as in guarding against the resurgent attacks on poor people and immigrants.

A dramatic increase in the number of CAAAV's police brutality cases with the advent of the Rudolph Giuliani administration in 1994 is one indication of the impact of the conservative trend. The police officer who beat Saleem also verbally abused him with the words, "Why don't you guys go back to your country! There's no black mayor here any more!"[21] Her words, though xenophobic, illustrate the interesting conception that the destinies of South Asian communities in the United States are inextricably linked to those of other people of color. It is noteworthy that the officer was a Latina who may well have experienced racial harassment herself. Cases such as these challenge anti-Asian violence organizations to go beyond focusing solely on European Americans as perpetrators.[22]

Organizing with LDC and CAAAV provided me with many such insights into the complexity of the production of institutional racism.

LIVING TODAY: HIV, AIDS, AND ASIAN AND PACIFIC ISLANDER WOMEN

Elsa E'der, Que Dang, and Karen Kimura

Over the last three decades, HIV (Human Immunodeficiency Virus) and AIDS (Acquired Immunodeficiency Syndrome) education and services to underserved populations have required awareness of and sensitivity to diverse cultural beliefs concerning disease. In the United States, thousands of people of color have created community-based agencies to serve multicultural populations and have acquired professional medical and psychological expertise in response to the AIDS crisis. They link Western medicine, indigenous healing techniques, and culturally specific traditions related to death and grief. Ultimately, the survival of PWAs (People with AIDS) in underserved populations is directly related to the special skills of service providers.

Prevention efforts battle the social stigma associated with HIV/AIDS and the persistent notion that AIDS is a disease found only in gay communities. It is reported that half of all new HIV cases in the U.S. and ten million of the estimated twenty-three million adults infected with HIV worldwide are predominantly heterosexual women of color. Because of limited access to health care by APIs [Asian and Pacific Islanders], there is reason to believe that the statistics do not reflect the actual number of cases of full-blown AIDS.

Jamie (not her real name) is a heterosexual Chinese woman living with AIDS. Born and raised in Thailand, she came to the U.S. in 1966 to attend college and currently resides in Los Angeles.[1] Peou Lakhana is a first-generation Cambodian refugee who grew up in Holyoke, Massachusetts.[2] She has been a caseworker at the Gay Asian Pacific Alliance (GAPA) Community HIV Project in San Francisco[3] for four years. She is working towards a master's degree in social work and community organizing at San Francisco State University and hopes to be able to apply her experience and skills in Cambodia one day.

QUE & KAREN: *Do you know how you contracted HIV?*
JAMIE: Through a blood transfusion in 1983. I wanted to get pregnant, but my fallopian tubes were blocked. The gynecologist wanted to perform surgery so fast [that] I didn't have time to think about taking my own blood out for the transfusion.

Q & K: *When did you find out you were HIV positive?*
JAMIE: In 1991, I went to Thailand to see my family. I started to have a swollen lymph node in my neck. This doctor in Bangkok put me on antibiotics. I requested a biopsy. In Thailand, HIV testing is automatically done on preoperative patients, and that was how I discovered I was HIV positive.

LAKHANA: Generally, in Asia, services for people with HIV or AIDS are limited. In the U.S., Asians tend to get access to Western health care systems during medical crises, rather than for maintenance and preventive care. Language skills, fear of deportation (especially in the wake of the passage of California's Proposition 187), and distrust of Western medical practitioners compound the situation. For most Asians, it is not a simple matter of denial about HIV and AIDS.

The Women's Outreach and Education Programs targeting Asian and Pacific Islanders not only inform women about symptoms and available resources, they also encourage safer sex negotiation in a culturally relevant context. Many women still believe that being married protects them against AIDS. For example, Asian women tend not to discuss condom use with their partners for fear that bringing up the topic implies infidelity or promiscuity. Gender roles that limit discussion of sexual behavior have an impact on education about sexually transmitted diseases.

Also, it is difficult to convince people to test for HIV when they are not feeling sick. Positive thinking is used as a strategy to fool "bad spirits" that cause health problems. I knew a Cambodian man with a toothache who believed that seeing a dentist might invite a worsened condition. He thought that he would lose some of his life force if the tooth were pulled out. When the tooth was removed, the pain went away, but he was depressed.

Q & K: *After you found out about your HIV status, how long did you stay in Thailand?*

JAMIE: I didn't stay long. I found out that none of the private hospitals in Bangkok wanted to treat HIV patients. I was scared. I could not even get hold of information to read about AIDS except [for] a book I found myself. It said that if one contracted HIV, one would die very soon.

LAKHANA: I often meet clients after a diagnosis of PCP [pneumocystis carinii pneumonia, an opportunistic AIDS-defining infection], which is a marker for disability benefits. They arrive in our office in a state of crisis, fearing imminent death. Sometimes, this visit is their first introduction to Western medical care. After being tested for the AIDS virus, they are informed of their HIV status and/or are diagnosed with AIDS.[4] Once a disease is named, some patients fear that it acquires its own power, the power to cause devastation and death. Therefore, reluctance to discuss illness does not necessarily stem from stereotypical "Asian silence" or from denial. Instead, it may originate from deep cultural respect for things unspoken or unspeakable.

Cultural mechanisms of coping and survival are often proactive and have been passed down from ancient times. One of my clients is a refugee Vietnamese Buddhist monk. Most of his family members died during the war. His Buddhist background taught him that to stay healthy, you must chant and apply poultice and eat herbs from the earth. When he was sick, he felt that he would get better by praying and taking herbs. He chose this rather than Western medicine. I encouraged him to use Western medicine as additional therapy. But because of his limited English, he was treated badly during a medical appointment. He was scared, confused, and angry. When he dropped out of services, he said, "I feel good. Going to the hospital makes me feel sick; I don't want to feel sick when I'm not."

Q & K: *When you came back to Los Angeles, did you tell any of your friends?*
JAMIE: At that time, the very few friends [I had] were Asian, so I didn't tell them. I did not know who to turn to, so I called the AIDS hotline, which finally hooked me up with an AIDS agency in Los Angeles.

Q & K: *Were you feeling sick at this time, and did you seek any medical attention?*
JAMIE: No, I still had very good health. I was referred to an HIV clinic, but it was open [only] one afternoon a week. They had just one nurse and one doctor. I had to wait many hours. I wasn't sick, but my skin was so itchy. My legs and arms were covered with eczema caused by sensitivity to mosquito and flea bites in Thailand.

LAKHANA: Many first-generation immigrants do not tell their families about their HIV status. Few disclose that they have AIDS even when they're in the process of dying. I knew a Filipina who had two children. She struggled to stay healthy for as long as possible so that she could take care of them. This finally motivated her to use agency services. Her commitment to overcoming life's obstacles—including disease—fueled her strength. She lived for four years after diagnosis. Unfortunately, her mother, who had trouble coping with her daughter's condition, was not supportive. Her husband, who is also HIV positive, now takes care of the children.

Q & K: *Did you tell your family? What was their reaction?*
JAMIE: Yes. They didn't know anything about AIDS except that there was still no cure and that it made people die very fast. They were scared. They thought the disease could be transmitted through casual contact, through food and water. They didn't want me to eat at the same table with them. I had to have my own dishes and eat by myself. It was sad. They didn't mean to hurt me, but just because they didn't know, they started to isolate me.

Q & K: *What was your husband's reaction?*
JAMIE: He started to get scared of me. He treated me like a leper. It made me feel bad and sad. He remained in Thailand. I came back to L.A. and started treatment.

LAKHANA: One of my co-workers is working with an eleven-year-old Chinese boy who is HIV positive. Before he was hospitalized, his mother, who was his primary caregiver, treated him only with herbs. Frantic nurses called our agency when they discovered that she had removed the IV from her son's arm. These nurses may not have known that her son became HIV positive through a blood transfusion. Also, direct injection into the bloodstream is particular to Western medicine. Some Chinese believe that the integrity of the body's *chi* [essential energy] remains intact only when the skin is not broken.[5] When we arrived at the hospital, our Cantonese-speaking case manager was able to explain to her why the IV was necessary, but she also validated the use of herbs. In this situation, we worked to empower the woman as a mother, so that she could administer Western as well as traditional Chinese medicines. She learned how to administer intravenous infusions. We created a chart incorporating all the medications and treatments. Thus she continued to be the primary caregiver for her son.

Q & K: *Where do you find your strength?*
JAMIE: I understand the nature of this disease. I have survived it for thirteen years, during which I had good health. Knowledge and understanding take away some of the fear. I know that in order to survive, I have to be determined to fight this illness to the end. I stopped working and attending school. I have to make taking care of my health my primary goal in life. I also find strength through God, through Chinese herbs, through support groups, and through my love for my family. I don't want to die before my parents, it would break their hearts.

LAKHANA: I find my strength from the process of connecting with people. The experience that really affected me was working with a forty-five-year-old Thai man who passed away two years ago. I met Prayot when he had KS [Karposi sarcoma], reddish purple lesions, all over his body.[6] We worked together until his last breath. He basically taught me about life, the joyous parts and the cruelest. I witnessed him crave life and suffer death. To this day, I talk about my relationship with him as if I had lost my father, or my brother, or my grandfather.

Our services work because we treat people like family, *ohana*.[7] We try not to be cold or sterile. Among Pacific Islander populations, however, the predominance of non-Pacific Islander providers in the field complicates outreach. The 1995 National AIDS Conference in Hawai'i illustrated the continuing need for involvement and resources earmarked for Pacific Islander populations. Of the more than five hundred conference participants, the dominant groups were Asian and Caucasian.

It is true though, that once Pacific Islanders come into services provided by APIs, they are at least less inhibited about communicating their fears. A client of mine once thought that he contracted HIV by drinking raw duck's blood, which was part of his normal diet. Because he told me this, I was able to dispel misinformation about his condition.

Q & K: *How do you feel about AIDS research being done?*
JAMIE: I would like to see more research on traditional Chinese medicine, herbs, and Chi Gong [an Asian movement therapy that helps build *chi* energy], but I know it's difficult for people in this country to do so because the doctors here are only trained in Western medicine. Also, the big pharmaceutical companies here more or less control the medical system and medical research in this country. Like the doctors, they know about herbs, but they don't believe in them and therefore are not interested in doing research on them.

Q & K: *What would you say to other API women who are HIV positive?*
JAMIE: I would tell them to come out . . . and try to get connected with other Asian women. I would let them know that one cannot and should not try to face this illness alone. AIDS affects not only the physical, but also the mental, emotional, and social aspects of the infected person.

LAKHANA: At the agency, we give people a safe place to voice concerns, fears, hopes, and anger. Sometimes they just can't talk to their own family members. We provide a safe medium, not too close to home and yet not so distant that they might feel like a burden or imposition.

Most Asians, whatever their religion, believe in an afterlife that eases their dying process. What they are most afraid of is pain and suffering before death. Many come to a compromise where they give up a part of who they are by taking morphine-based painkillers. These medications and/or HIV in the brain cause serious dementia. Family members, caretakers, and service providers become less able to rely on previous ways of relating. It's really hard when you don't recognize them and they don't recognize you.

Q & K: *What motivates you to talk about your experience?*
JAMIE: All the ignorance, the fear, discrimination, and negative stigma about AIDS and people with AIDS in the whole Asian community. It makes me sick and mad. Like the doctor who was scared to treat me. I think it's time to make these people know something about AIDS. It's a common disease. It just happens to not have a cure yet, and a lot of people die from it.

There are a lot of people who have and can survive this disease for many years. [People should] show love, compassion, and support for people with AIDS, instead of condemning them.

ESSENTIAL FACTS ABOUT HIV TRANSMISSION

There are three requirements for HIV transmission:

1. HIV has to be present.
2. There has to be contact with blood, semen, vaginal fluids, or breast milk carrying HIV. Not all bodily fluids (tears, sweat, urine) contain sufficient amounts of the virus to infect a person.
3. HIV has to have a way to enter the body, i.e., through cuts, sores, or mucous membranes.

GUIDELINES FOR SAFER SEX AND NEEDLE USE

*   Always use a condom for anal and vaginal intercourse and fellatio.
*   Use a barrier for oral sex on women.
*   Clean needles 3 times for 30 seconds with bleach before each use. Never share needles during intravenous drug use, tattooing, or piercing!

Editors' note: On January 13, 1997, "Jamie" passed away due to AIDS-related illnesses. She is survived by her husband and family in Thailand. "Jamie" will be remembered for her strength and courage in speaking out about how AIDS has affected Asian and Pacific Islander women.

SPEAKING OUT: MEMORIES OF A NISEI ACTIVIST

Chizu Iiyama and Lisa S. Hirai Tsuchitani

Forcibly imprisoned in World War II detention camps a semester before they were due to graduate, a group of roughly one hundred and fifty seniors of Japanese ancestry at the University of California at Berkeley were not allowed to attend their college graduation ceremony. Those who had completed the requirements for their degrees prior to their incarceration eventually received their diplomas in the mail while in camp. Others never finished their degrees.

Fifty years later, at the request of Japanese American community members, twenty Japanese Americans of the Cal Class of 1942 were finally honored as graduates at the University's annual convocation held on September 16, 1992. Robed in caps and gowns and leis of blue and gold cranes, standing on the stage of a full-to-capacity Zellerbach Hall amidst thunderous applause and silent tears, these graduates were welcomed back to U.C. Berkeley with a standing ovation by family members, friends, and well-wishers. It was an auspicious homecoming, although fifty years late.

Among these graduates who had received their college diplomas from Cal by mail in 1942 was Chizu Kitano Iiyama. "As if a hand was stretching out from the beauty of the Berkeley campus to the grime and isolation of the camps," this piece of paper delivered hope to her while she was living in a horse stall at the temporary detention center in Santa Anita. It also came to symbolize a significant turning point in her life, commemorating the beginning of her lifelong career as a passionate advocate of economic, political, and social justice for all people.

I first met Chizu during my first year in college. In an attempt to address the importance of community studies research and the use of oral history as a vital methodological tool for such research, I wrote my first college term paper in Asian American Studies on her life experiences. The following article is woven from this paper and the many unforgettable discussions Chizu and I have shared since then during car rides to and from fund-raising events and meetings, "mailing parties," and home-cooked meals in the warmth of her kitchen. Although the sequence of her stories is mine, the words are hers—words which convey important lessons in idealism and integrity, in endless hope for the future and selfless love for one's community, for all of us struggling to combat the dehumanizing forces of a racist patriarchy that seeks to fragment and destroy us.

"SPEAKING OUT WAS NOT ENCOURAGED WHILE I WAS GROWING UP."

From a very young age, Chizu was already developing and honing the skills that she would rely on throughout her lifetime career as an activist. Despite the disapproval of her parents, she continually articulated her insights and perspectives on anything of interest to her, outspokenness for which she would be

punished often. Her hopes of continuing on to college and pursuing a career in
teaching were not necessarily encouraged, either; they were perceived by many at
the time to be "futile." By supporting herself through school, however, Chizu
obtained her degree in Psychology. These early experiences of challenging the
expected gender roles of women by "not following the traditional Japanese mode of
being quiet and subservient" proved especially invaluable to her later on as a social
worker in the Topaz Detention Camp.

*M*y mother was very unhappy that I did speak out, and I was probably punished more than anybody else in my family because I would ask, "Why?" They'd tell me to be quiet. You know, looking back at it now, if I had just kept quiet then I wouldn't have gotten any punishment, but I insisted on saying something. So I guess from the time I was little I was difficult for my parents.

My mother didn't think I should go to school. Though my parents did not encourage me to go on to college, my sister did—my sister Kiyo. I did want to be a teacher, but when I asked about being a teacher at Cal they [faculty members] said, "No, you won't get a job as a teacher because you're Japanese American."

I worked several years as a school girl [a form of domestic work]—$10 a month to wash clothes and cook meals. Just enough for carfare. They were nice people who I worked for, but I always felt the class difference as a servant. What I resented most of all, which I didn't show and didn't say, was when I would be eating in the kitchen and they'd be eating in the dining room and they would ring a bell whenever they needed anything. I would have to jump up and go over there to see what they wanted. . . . I resented it so much that I swore that when I had children, they would never have to do that.

When I was going to Cal, the young men would ask, "What are you majoring in?" and I would say, "Well, I'm majoring in Psychology." They'd say, "Oh, go on! You're really majoring in a MRS. Degree!" and in a sense they were right, because women went to Cal and got married and that was it. You stuck onto the profession that your husband had, and your role was to stay home and take care of the children . . . to be a nice wife. That was basically what all of us were brought up to be.

"AN EXHILARATING INTRODUCTON TO MASS MOVEMENTS AND HOW THEY CAN CHANGE THINKING."

Chizu was "formally initiated" into her life of activism while imprisoned at the
Topaz Detention Camp in Utah. "Fresh out of U.C. Berkeley," she described herself
at the time as "naive and optimistic with the glow of youth, trying to

make sense of the rapid course of events which led us from the freedom of a
university campus to a desolate desert camp surrounded by barbed wire." By
serving as a social worker, however, she "learned firsthand the problems that
these crowded, Spartan living conditions posed for individuals and families" and
"felt the anguish of people who lost their homes and businesses, [and were] fearful
of their future."

During this time, she also met Ernest Iiyama, her future husband, who
introduced her to a group of former Nisei Young Democrats from the Bay Area.
A left-wing branch of the Democratic Party during the 1930s, the group's
discussions on national and international labor organizing and politics at first
felt intimidating. Challenging the beliefs about the American economic, political,
and social system that she had been taught in school, the Nisei Democrats opened
Chizu's eyes to a "new world." Her introduction to such authors as Karl Marx
and Carey McWilliams served as an ideological base from which she would
draw additional inspiration for her later involvement in civil rights issues for
people of color and the working class in New York City, Chicago, and the
Bay Area.

I define "political" to mean being aware of what is happening throughout
the world and being willing to do something on an organized basis about
what you consider to be injustice or inequality. I learned about American institutions in school and it all sounded so glorious. We were the most democratic country in the world because we had such a wonderful system of
"checks and balances." But I didn't know the real workings of the political
system.

When I was in Topaz and hit twenty-one, I registered as Republican.
The man had said, "Why don't you be a Republican?" and I said, "O.K. It
doesn't matter. Either one." So I registered as Republican and later I
changed to Independent. Most Japanese Americans were like that—they
didn't know the difference between Republicans and Democrats.

[Being a member of the Nisei Democrats] gave me a feeling that you
can do something, that you can make change, that it's possible for a group of
people who are dedicated to be able to make change in the current structure. For the first time I met communists. In fact, the first meeting I went to
I was just shocked. I had to think through, "Do I want to be in this group?"
You open the door—now this is in the barracks, the bachelors' barracks—
and there is this big sign that says, "Workers of the World Unite!" I thought,
"Oh my God! What are they talking about?" I was just intrigued by these
knowledgeable people.

They always had good food! And we were always hungry in camp for
something good to eat. I used to say to my sister when she asked me why I
went [to the meetings], "They serve good food!" Good food for the mind
and body.

*The intense controversy over the distribution of a loyalty questionnaire in
detention camps provided Chizu with the opportunity to articulate the political
awareness and consciousness that she was developing through her social work and
participation in the discussion groups with the Nisei Democrats. Posing two
questions requiring declarations of complete loyalty to the United States, this
questionnaire "provided an effective point of protest and organization against the
government, from which more and more evacuees felt alienated."[1] Such feelings of
alienation came to be expressed in numerous ways, especially at block meetings
held throughout the camps. The emotional intensity of one of these meetings in
particular created a context for Chizu to successfully challenge the patriarchal
code of conduct for women to merely "be seen and not heard," a code that she
would continue to challenge throughout her life.*

It was a cold February evening, but the atmosphere at the camp was hot and
turbulent with the announcement of a block meeting. For this was 1943, inside the Topaz Center—a concentration camp for Japanese Americans removed from the San Francisco area during World War II. At issue was the
response to a government questionnaire supposed to expedite clearance to
leave Topaz for areas outside of the West Coast, and to offer inmates an opportunity to serve in the U.S. Armed Forces.

The anger and frustration of being incarcerated in these dismal camps
exploded at that meeting. Most of the Nisei [second-generation Japanese
Americans] in our block were young; the meeting was dominated by vocal
opponents of the questionnaire—Question 27, to serve in the U.S. Armed
Forces, and Question 28, a loyalty oath to swear allegiance to the U.S. and
forswear allegiance to Japan. Issei men [first-generation immigrants] asked
us what our citizenship meant; I had no answer. On the other hand, I knew
that Japan was an imperialist nation which invaded other countries in Asia
and committed terrible crimes. I grew up in San Francisco, had never visited Japan, and had never questioned that I was an American. So how was I
to answer the questions?

I listened to the remarks of some of the "pro-Japan" people. No Nisei
spoke up. Our future depended on how we voted, and I didn't feel comfortable with the tremendous emotional sweep in the meeting. I kept waiting
and waiting for someone to say something, but nobody said anything. I
therefore raised my hand to speak, and with shaking knees and a quavering
voice I asked that people in the audience think carefully about their response to the questionnaire, that they not be pressured into making a decision. Their answers could determine their future.

There was this silence after I spoke at that meeting. There was a moment of quiet disbelief that a woman would express an opinion. A few angry remarks were directed at me, and the meeting ended. But then I was afraid to walk through the gauntlet of people who were angry.

The next day my parents were castigated for sending me to university. I was threatened to be beaten up. We took this threat seriously enough that I ate at my sister's mess hall for a period of time. I was told later that for about half a year my parents were isolated except for a few friends, and that the waitresses refused to serve them tea.

I had to think hard. "Do I want to do this or not?" The meeting was going so excitedly, and people were screaming and all. Then when I felt that nobody was going to say anything, I did. I'm sure my voice was pretty catchy. I did not speak boldly. Since then, I think I have learned to speak much more boldly on the things that I believe in.

Looking back on that incident, would I have spoken out if I knew it would affect my parents? I am so sorry I caused them grief. But I guess that's when my life of activism started.

"THERE WAS A KIND OF VIGOR THAT WAS EXCITING."

Shortly thereafter, "to the relief of my parents," Chizu left Topaz for Chicago, where she married Ernie. The newlyweds then decided to move on to New York City, where they quickly became immersed in the excitement and freedom that "city life" had to offer. Although instructed by officials upon leaving Topaz to "not gather with other Nisei, nor speak Japanese, nor call attention to [themselves]," the Iiyamas became active members of the Japanese American Committee for Democracy. Here Chizu also became involved in the American Labor Party movement, continuing to study and practice the ideas she had been introduced to by the Nisei Democrats while in camp.

In 1948, the Iiyamas moved back to Chicago. In the "windy city," Chizu relentlessly continued her activism in the Japanese American community, helping to organize a political group, "Nisei for Wallace," to support the Progressive Party's presidential candidate in 1948, Henry Wallace. Although the specter of McCarthyism discouraged many Japanese Americans from joining their efforts, the Iiyamas continued to canvas their neighborhood to support Wallace, campaigning for "Peace, Freedom, and Democracy." Despite the presidential victory of Harry S. Truman, this slogan continued to be their "mantra" as they helped Issei and Nisei rebuild their lives after the war through the Chicago Resettlers Committee.

The city of Chicago also provided Chizu with the opportunity to work with other communities of color in their fight for economic, political, and social justice. Her involvement in these early struggles of the civil rights movement affirmed her belief in the beauty and power of building coalitions across racial lines. These experiences served as poignant reminders to her of the possibilities for creating a better future for the next generation of children after she and her family returned to the West Coast.

New York, New York . . . what a wonderful place! On its crowded subway I heard many different languages and accents. People were so colorfully dressed. I felt I could talk to myself in Japanese, wear a kimono, and walk down Fifth Avenue, and no one would bat an eyelash!

And such a diverse and fascinating group of Japanese people. Here I met Issei who were so different from my parents and their friends. They were progressive in their politics—artists, writers, cabinetmakers, newspaper reporters, and restaurant workers. Some were refugees from Japan who were employed by the Office of War Information. They were very vocal in their opposition to Japanese militarism.

They regaled us with stories about their activities. For example, when the Japanese training ships came to New York before World War II, these enterprising men hired a tugboat, drew up long banners with slogans like "Down with Militarism and the Emperor System!" and sailed around the training ships. What a shock it must have been to the Japanese sailors who had not been exposed to a contrary viewpoint in Japan.

Others worked with the Chinese resistance movements [against Japanese militarism in China]. We also reacted to racist remarks made by public officials, held dances and social events for nisei servicemen before they shipped overseas, and worked on the relocation of people from the camps.

And at that time in New York City we had a very strong left wing movement. It was just incredible to me to go to Madison Square Garden [for a demonstration] . . . twenty-five thousand people there and everyone really trying to make a change in the American system so that working people could be represented. You really felt like you were part of a positive group of people to make a more democratic country . . . by getting people into city councils, into Congress, with the idea that they could advocate for civil rights for everybody.

We lived near the University of Chicago on the South Side. So many Japanese Americans also lived there in sunny apartment houses. I loved the sound of birds nesting in trees, the proximity of the beaches, the creak of the swing on the porch as we sang in the dusk . . . our family of one, then two children. My husband worked in an assembly plant as an industrial worker, and then as a machinist and a union steward.

We organized a political group, "Nisei for Wallace," for the 1948 elections. We had over sixty Japanese Americans who signed up with us, but redbaiting took its toll and we ended up with about twenty. I could remember one of my Japanese American friends was working for the Republican Party and when he saw the energy we had, he offered me a paid job with the Republican Party! He said, "Why don't you come over and we could work something out?" And I said, "No, I'm doing this because I believe in something." There was a lot of energy and enthusiasm. We were so idealistic, we thought we might even win.

I learned something about politics—about the force of McCarthyism and how it could devastate movements. And I think that even today we have not gotten over the effects of McCarthyism when you look at the union movement and the lack of a progressive left in this country. It was smashed—just smashed in the fifties and never really recovered.

I worked for the Chicago Resettlers Committee. We helped people find housing and jobs and offered counseling. We set up recreational and educational activities for Issei and Nisei and served as a liaison with various social service agencies in the city. We became a community center, to engender a sense of community which had been lost by the wartime dispersal.

I believe that one of the groups most hurt by the detention camps were Issei men, many in their fifties and sixties. Without a good knowledge of English, considered too old for new career or jobs, and often displaced as the family wage earner by their younger wives, they would come to the Resettlers Committee to meet their friends. They would grumble to me, "Now that they are making the money, our wives are turning sassy!" with a glint in their eyes, but masking some of their feelings about the turnabout in their families.

In Chicago, I also worked as a group social worker in the heart of a black working-class district of the city. I visited the homes of some of my children, and learned about the spirit of black people under awful conditions of poverty—of such overcrowding that people slept on blankets in the kitchen, of walls covered with newspapers to cover holes. I had children who could not come to classes because they didn't have shoes. And yet the mothers were friendly, offering me coffee whenever I visited.

In those days, before Martin Luther King, there was an active civil rights movement. We joined the Young Progressives, which was a multiracial organization, in their demonstration to open up the beaches to blacks. We brought our blankets, our children, and food to effect a "sleep-in." We received lots of publicity, and we think we encouraged the eventual opening of the beaches due to our efforts.

It's hard to remember that in those days employment was very limited for minorities, especially for blacks. I joined the Urban League and the National Association for the Advancement of Colored People in picketing Carson Pirie Scott [a department store], which did not hire blacks. One of my relatives related his astonishment and embarrassment at seeing me with a placard, shouting out slogans. I was glad that my mother did not live in Chicago.

The experience that left the deepest impression on me happened in the early fifties. My husband, my six-year-old daughter, and I were on a petition campaign to stop atomic testing and to call for a worldwide ban on the development of nuclear weapons. This was the beginning of the McCarthy period, when charges of communism were attached to any activity not condoned by the government.

We stood at the corner of one of the streets close to the black community. A short, heavy white man glared at us through "slitted" eyes. He made growling sounds as people stopped to speak to us or sign our petition. Finally, he dashed across the street to grab my petition. My daughter was so frightened that she screamed. Immediately, the doors of the houses close by opened, and about ten black men and women bounded out, asking, "Did he hurt you?" and clutching the white man's collar. We explained to our black friends what we were doing, and they all signed our petition. We freed the white man, who scuttled out of sight. It was a demonstration to me of the bonds that we have with other people of color.

"THE WAY OF LIFE I REMEMBERED SO FONDLY."

The Iiyamas' fond memories of their prewar life on the West Coast eventually compelled them to move back to California. After having encountered much discrimination while trying to buy a home in the working-class suburbs of Chicago, the Iiyamas decided to "try their luck" in the Bay Area. Here, they established their permanent "roots," surrounded by family members and friends who continued to support them in their commitment to issues of social justice for years to come.

By this time the mother of three children, Chizu felt especially compelled to become active in her community, continuing the work she had begun in New York City and Chicago with West Coast members of the Japanese American community and other communities of color. Her involvement included participation in such organizations as the Richmond Human Relations Commission, Bay Area Asians for Nuclear Disarmament (BAAND), the Friends of Hibakusha (FOH), the Japanese American Citizens League (JACL), and the National Coalition for Redress and Reparations (NCRR), organizations in which she continues to remain active to this day. Through such involvement, she has been able to persistently pursue her ideals of democracy, equality, and justice.

It was one of those February days when the snow on the streets of Chicago had accumulated for weeks and was shades of black and gray. My lovely sister in Berkeley had sent me a letter, and enclosed a twig with a plum blossom, asking if we were planning to return to California. How could we resist?

Living in Berkeley, then in Richmond, I plunged into all kinds of activities. My family of three children attending school meant Parent-Teacher Association meetings, Cub Scouts, and Campfire Girls. In addition, I joined the Richmond Neighborhood Councils to develop a sense of community. I was appointed to the first Richmond Human Relations Commission, and how well I remember our first meeting. It was held on the night of a huge march on Washington, and we watched the magnificent speech by Martin Luther King. We marched in parades for civil rights and supported local efforts to integrate our schools.

It was during the war in Vietnam that we again took to the streets. Our whole family participated in the first protest march against the war—not many people, and amidst some hostility and charges of being unpatriotic. . . . We were booed as we marched down Market Street. People called us "commies" and told us to go back where we came from. I just felt that there was a real need for educating people. We helped to organize the Bay Area Asians for Nuclear Disarmament, and marched under their banner. Every year we were gratified to see opposition grow to this devastating war.

In 1969 we visited Ernie's family in Hiroshima for the first time. We spent several nights talking to his mother about the atomic bombing of Hiroshima. She related in her quiet yet bitter voice the destruction of the city and the painful and often lingering deaths of her friends. She recounted the fate of many of Ernie's schoolmates, often in graphic detail. It was a sobering experience for us. We got more involved in campaigns for peace.

We joined Friends of Hibakusha[2] and helped with the visits of the Japanese doctors to examine victims of the bomb who are living in the States. We also participated in demonstrations against nuclear proliferation. And in 1986 I spoke at the World Peace Conference in Hiroshima.

I was asked to speak as an American, and I think that was the first time I spoke to an international audience. The first thing I said was, "As an American, I apologize for dropping the bomb on Hiroshima. It was a terrible act." And I got all these Japanese people coming up to me afterwards saying, "You're the first American to ever apologize for the act of bombing Hiroshima." I was just shocked because they had been having these peace rallies over and over again. But no American peace groups had ever apologized. I often wonder what the world would be like today if we had been able to stop the headlong development of nuclear weapons.

I had been active in the Japanese American Citizens League in Chicago and supported efforts to get citizenship rights for our parents. [The Naturalization Law of 1790, which granted naturalized citizenship only to "white" immigrants, was not nullified until 1952 with the passage of the McCarran-Walter Act.] We worked on many legislative issues. From 1968 to the signing of the bill in 1971, we worked on the repeal of Title II of the Internal Security Act of 1950. This bill authorized the president in case of war, invasion, or insurrection to order detention without trial, in effect codifying the imprisonment of Japanese Americans during World War II. [Later on] we were told by knowledgeable politicians that a Redress Bill, asking for an apology and a token sum of $20,000 for people incarcerated in camps during World War II would never pass. And to have it signed by President Reagan? Pipe dreams . . .

But we did it! It was such a group effort—the JACL, the NCRR, the National Council for Japanese American Redress (NCJAR), and many thousands of individuals all over the country. We reached [out to] local city councils, veterans' groups, civic organizations, other minorities, unions, churches . . . any place where there were people. And with the tremendous help of our Nisei politicos and veterans.

I worked especially with the NCRR on a grass-roots campaign. We held meetings and our annual "Days of Remembrance," fanned out for signatures on petition campaigns, spoke to innumerable schools and community groups, and lobbied members of Congress. I testified before the Senate Appropriations Committee with a number of other NCRR members. It was the first time I met the group around Lillian Baker (who was against redress) and could not believe the kinds of words which issued from their lips. It was like a backward trip in time to 1942, with its misinformation and charges against Japanese Americans. But they [the opposition and their charges] were so effectively answered by our delegation. When they stated that "Japanese Americans had a good time in camp," our witness followed by talking about the loss of her baby in camp. When they charged that we were "unpatriotic and dangerous," we followed up with a veteran of the 442nd [the all-nisei 100th/442nd was the most decorated unit of its size during World War II], who described the feats of the 100th/442nd combat units. We knew we made an impact on the Senate Committee.[3]

"MAINTAIN YOUR IDEALISM BY DOING SOMETHING."

At the age of seventy-three, Chizu seems to be more active than ever. Whether organizing and chairing meetings for the Northern California JACL Women's Concerns Committee, writing exhibition narratives and coordinating public programs for the National Japanese American Historical Society, or developing curriculum materials for public schools on ways to teach students about peace for the Hiroshima and Nagasaki Fiftieth Anniversary Commemoration Committee, she remains highly enthusiastic and optimistic. In the midst of her many community activities and projects, she has also found time to pursue a career in teaching, working at Contra Costa College as head of the Early Childhood Education Department for the past eighteen years.

A captivating and compelling storyteller, Chizu has taught me many invaluable lessons on how to "destroy the stereotype of the passive, quiet Asian American woman"—lessons on the importance of "speaking out." As one of few Asian Pacific American women in the graduate school of education at U.C. Berkeley, I have found strength in her words to confront the humiliating and isolating remarks and stares I have received from fellow students and professors in my field. I am greatly indebted to the powerful legacy of activism that women like Chizo have left for the women of my generation. By remembering and telling such stories of our grandmothers, mothers, and daughters, may their spirits continue to guide and inspire us.

I loved working at Contra Costa College with its diverse student body, including many foreign students. I taught Head Start teachers, foster parents, day-care providers, parents, and prospective elementary school teachers. I learned so much from my students!

Children intrigue me, and we realized the need for training people who work with children. I helped to organize a Therapeutic Nursery School and a West County Children's Council, and spent time serving on their boards and getting funding. I have continued my interest in the welfare of children and am serving now as Treasurer of the Early Childhood Mental Health Program.

1995 is a very important year—the fiftieth anniversary of the dropping of the atomic bomb on Hiroshima and Nagasaki, the end of the war between Japan and the United States, and the creation of the United Nations. The bomb has totally changed for all time the future of the world. We hope to focus on peace, and are preparing a year of activities to include discussions by survivors, a children's art exhibit, dance and media programs, an art and history exhibit, a peace curriculum for schools, library presentations, etc.

And although most of my energy at this point is directed towards education, there are political issues that are still on my agenda. With the El Cerrito Human Relations Commission, we are trying to get a minority judge for our area. We are concerned about hate crimes and anti-immigrant forces in California. I just walked on a picket line before the Federal Building protesting American policy in Cuba.

People have asked me why I spend so much of my time on so many different activities. They don't realize that I also play—my husband and I take Tai Chi, yoga, and line-dancing when possible; go to concerts, the theater, the movies. After each assignment, we visit another country.

I guess looking back I see peaks and depressions, peaks and depressions in terms of political process. Being realistic with your idealism is what I had to learn. Every time you stick your neck out a little you get more strength, even if you get squashed down. But you also need supportive people—you need to find like-minded people who can help you and support you. People like this give you a lot of faith.

[Looking back,] I think I cherish the friendships we have made, the stimulation of interacting with different people, the challenge of completing a task that I believe in. . . . I would like to thank my family and especially my husband Ernie, who has worked with me and been so supportive.

A STRAIGHT SEX ASIAN LOVE/PILIPINA (P)UCKING POEM

celine salazar parreñas

for dan shimizu in san francisko, kalipornya, usa

*i*magine world war 2
here, between our hips.

even tho the apartment where we fuck
50 years from (pili) pinas & the imperial army
or yr internment camp ancestry
my irrelevant geography
manila jus a memory as we make home
here these hips.

still,
i am in guerra: me a guerrilla/puta
u the invader masaker &
i scream kill in my kuming

pero, later
in the night i recognize home
yr chest/ in the rough of the stains,
the quiet & still/ the aftermath of
blood on the sheets/ the bed spent:
whatever is war, here, we work thru

where there is no napalm,
no ten cameras shooting,
no helicopters no white guy directing
but the *apokaflips now*
in my memory insisting

i am this body filmed so much in fucking
so much enuf 2 think of it here.
nothing here! no vietnam nothing!
the only evidence of explosions or implosions
r jus my hips, swelling, wells
of our shifting heavy in sleep
despite complicated epics before us
& the generations & nations & movies

IT WENT BY ME

Trinh T. Minh-ha

Something very beautiful
just went by me
something not to tell
in words in feelings
so fragile so wild
something yet to tell
is no longer
why and when it left
i can't tell

NO NAME

Trinh T. Minh-ha

Sick
I must be
to go on asking
why
when it hurts so badly

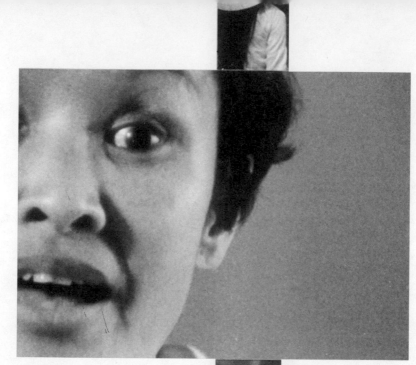

FOR A SHOW

Trinh T. Minh-ha

*W*ord over word
helpless and uneasy
you performed what you called
a striptease
as for me
if I were caught in my nakedness
I would, as you said,
do no more
than flash-ing

WORDWARRING

Trinh T. Minh-ha

*W*ordcaresses
you always point with
your eyes
wordarrows
you react with
markers mines missiles
while laughing
in spite of myself
I take them in
stinging
burning
bleeding
at a loss

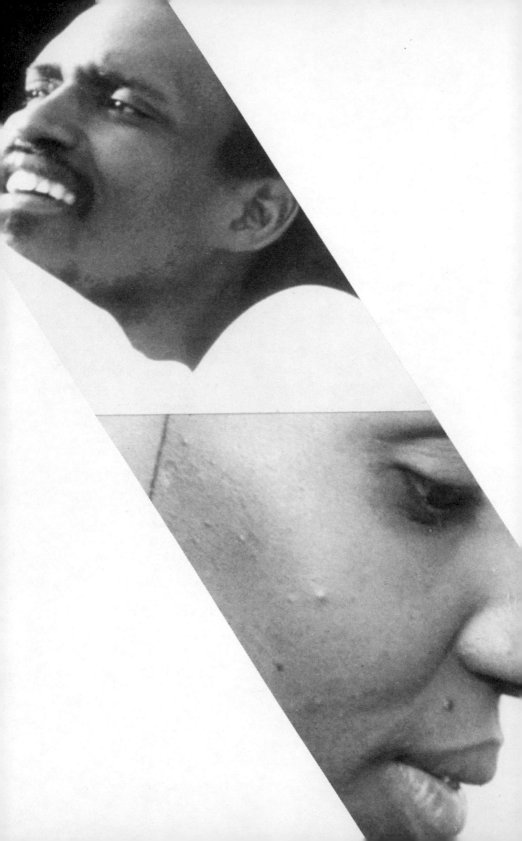

MONOTONE

Trinh T. Minh-ha

*t*he day I thought
I, she won
sole retainer of
what I so desired
even momentarily,
even if
taking all in
meant giving all back
that day perhaps
I, she were already
losing

hours then
days go by
the names of joy
sub-side
unwanted
doubts settle in
grow growing in-
to certain-ties
the tuning
the timing
never match
a promise made
a voice awaited
a call from afar
lingers in absence
makes longing a
banality a
self
inflicted agony a
slave
of hallucination

losing
sight of pro-
                portion
now I wane
now you win
now she retains
                you in-
                            sensate
as the silence
                stretches on
as I now feel
                trampled
                exposed
in all small feelings
impatience
pity, leniency
anger, hatred
shame
and sense- less
affliction

what
if differ-ence
is mere
in-difference
what
wretched feeling
led me
to such curses
as "win" and "lose"?

MOON TIDE

Trinh T. Minh-ha

g low
intoxicated
in that state
of intense
exaltation
so blind
so full
so clear
as to love
love for itself

the moon
I lay restless
another flood tide

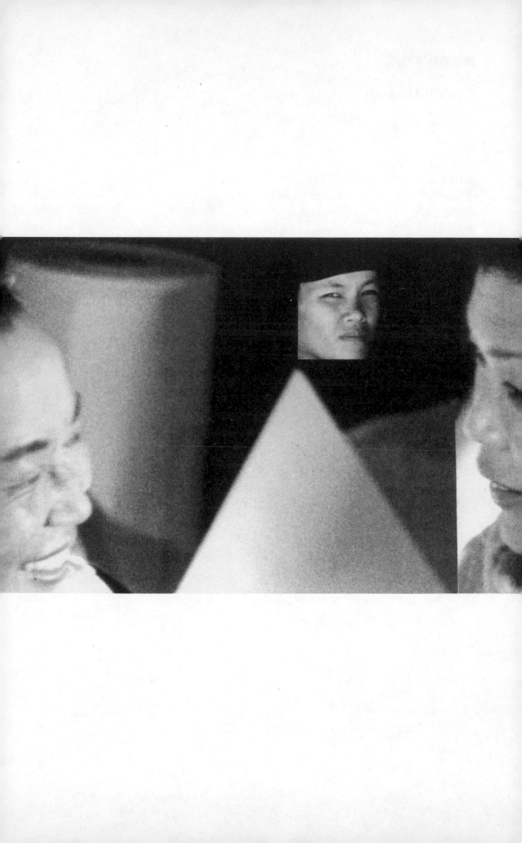

NO TO NO

Trinh T. Minh-ha

Stop damaging
such a fragrance of words
for I can't bear the lie
of that lesser intensity

no passion
no demands
no problem
no

space left undone
for fear of naming
too early too far
or perhaps too close
too familiar

fragile
to the point of rupture
time and again prey
to extreme joy
with sudden fluxes
of irrational
sadness

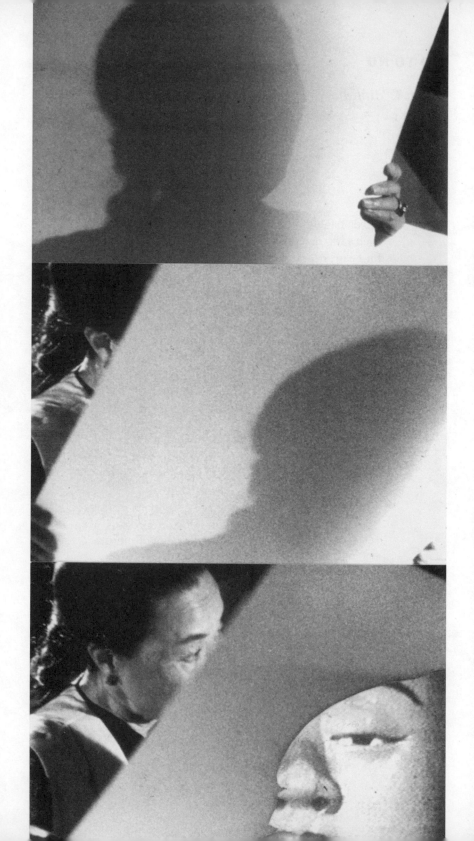

MAKING PEACE

Trinh T. Minh-ha

ick
  also i must be
  to go on making peace
  with passion
  while the world wars on
  dispassionately

PASSION AND COMMITMENT:
ASIAN AMERICAN WOMEN AND HOLLYWOOD

Sandra Liu

> Passion and commitment are words that are used a lot,
> but they really amount to something, because everything
> [about filmmaking] is so difficult on a purely logistical
> level. Without those factors, why do it—why get up in the
> morning to face the battles? *One must believe.*
> JANET YANG

*W*hat do you believe? Whether consciously or unconsciously, actively or passively, our actions and beliefs are a reflection and shaping of what we want our lives to be, as individuals living in a community, as citizens or residents of a country, as humans sharing a planet. What you have for breakfast, what you choose to wear, what movie you see on Friday night—these are not merely personal choices, but have significance for the social, political, and economic systems in which we live. For example, beginning in the late 1960s, Asian Americans protested the inhuman and subhuman, insulting, and dismissive depictions of Asians and Asian Americans in mainstream American media. In public demonstrations, we cried out, "No more Charlie Chan!" "No more Suzie Wong!" We cultivated and embraced artists from our own communities, often taking advantage of funds that were made available through affirmative action programs, and funds for multicultural or minority programs. Through the 1970s and 1980s, an independent Asian American media arts field blossomed, and Asian American film and videomakers showed their works in festivals, on public television, and on college campuses. They made suppressed histories more visible, documented significant contemporary political events and social issues, and created dignified, human characters at the same time that they honed their technical and production skills. There also were notable theatrically released feature-length movies that were directed by Asian American filmmakers. Great strides have been made in the ways in which Asian Americans are portrayed and perceived, both in our own communities and outside them, partially due to the media activism that Asian Americans have undertaken. Asian Americans are participating in all aspects of filmmaking in greater numbers than ever before. However, as audiences, critics, and filmmakers, we must ask ourselves, where are we headed? What do we want to see happen with our filmmaking efforts? What roles do films play in the lives of Asian Americans, socially and politically? In short, *what do we believe?*

The range of representations of Asians and Asian Americans has increased, and there are more opportunities available for Asian Americans working behind the scenes in film production. However, in the media arts, as is true in most prestigious professional fields, though women have made significant contributions, works directed by men—regardless of their race—continue to dominate, both in terms of the numbers of works that are released and those that gain popular and critical attention from the American mainstream.[1] In recent years, for example, Wayne Wang became distinguished as the director of *The Joy Luck Club* (1993), which recorded the highest box office sales, over $30 million, of any Asian American themed film. Of course, Wang had already achieved a modicum of fame with *Chan Is Missing* (1981), the first Asian American feature-length film to receive widespread critical acclaim. Ang Lee directed *The Wedding Banquet* (1993), which was nominated for an Academy Award for Best Film. Steven Okazaki directed *Days of Waiting* (1991), which won an Academy Award for Best Documentary, Short Subject.

With the release of *The Joy Luck Club*, Asian American women seem to have leapt onto the scene of the mainstream filmmaking and television industries. The film showcased a cast of talented and accomplished Asian and Asian American actresses, and was produced by Janet Yang, an Asian American woman working for Ixtlan, Oliver Stone's production company. Two years before the release of *The Joy Luck Club*, Mira Nair received critical acclaim for *Mississippi Masala*. During the 1994–95 television season, Margaret Cho played the central character on *All American Girl*, the first (albeit short-lived) sitcom on network television with Asian Americans as the main cast members. Cho also had some decision-making power as a writer and consultant for the show. *Maya Lin: A Strong Clear Vision*, coproduced by Freida Lee Mock, won the Oscar for Best Documentary in 1995. *Picture Bride*, by Kayo Hatta, won the Audience Award at the Sundance Film Festival in 1995 and was distributed theatrically by Miramax. *Double Happiness*, by Chinese Canadian filmmaker Mina Shum, also received numerous international awards and was picked up for distribution by Fine Line.

Though it is tempting to conclude from this veritable storm of awards and theatrical exposure that Asian American women have been wholeheartedly accepted by the media-making industries, critics, and audiences, our full participation and continued presence is by no means assured or uncontested. After one season, *All American Girl* was canceled. Connie Chung, the model of the publicly successful Asian American woman, was dismissed as Dan Rather's co-anchor on the *CBS Evening News* in May 1995. Furthermore, the awards won by *Picture Bride* and *Maya Lin* were met with incredulity. Kayo Hatta summed up some of the obstacles still facing Asian American women in the film industry:

The response to Picture Bride *getting the audience award [at Sundance] was overwhelmingly supportive and positive, so it was shocking when some critics in the* NY Times *who had not even seen the film tried to discredit us by suggesting that there must have been a voting discrepancy. They seemed unable to accept that a woman, that an Asian American film, won this prestigious audience award. They thought there must be some mistake. I think critics have this arrogance, assuming they know what kind of film audiences like. Around the same time, Frieda Mock received an Academy Award nomination for the Maya Lin project. Critics who hadn't even seen the film said, "this film probably got the nomination and* Hoop Dreams *did not because Freida Mock was once on the Board of the Academy." It was sadly uncanny how similar our experiences were . . .*

The fact that these two films were made by Asian American women was not mentioned in relation to the critics' complaints about the awards. However, taken together, the question of why the process for giving these awards was being scrutinized at this particular time and with these particular films begs to be answered. While I don't deny the possibility of coincidence or the need for a review of the awards procedures, the incidents also suggest two things. First, that Asian American women's cultural productions are viewed with suspicion by cultural gatekeepers whose job it is to monitor and defend American culture. Thus, the fact that the films actually won prestigious awards cannot mean that they deserved the awards, but rather, that the procedures are corrupt. Second, that Asian Americans are safe targets of criticism: not only has most of the non-Asian population in the United States bought the model minority myth, but Asian Americans supposedly have accepted their role as the model minority as well. Asian American women are doubly stigmatized by their race and gender. In the eyes of the critics, we are not a real market or political force, and we can be counted on not to embarrass or inconvenience mainstream institutions by protesting, demonstrating, boycotting, or pointing out racist and sexist policies. Thus, if the awards procedures did need review, then this appeared to be an opportune time to initiate it because the critics thought they could make their remarks with impunity.

The complaints against *Picture Bride* and *Maya Lin* are a reminder that not only do we still need to press for more dignified and diverse representations of Asian Americans on screen, but that the institutions—not only the filmmakers, production companies, and studios, but also the network of supporting structures such as print and television media critics, advertisers, investors, and audiences—that have continued to propagate stereotypical portrayals should receive an equal measure of Asian American political scrutiny and attention.

When Kayo Hatta, Mina Shum, and Janet Yang appeared together as part of a panel called "Moving into the Mainstream: Asian Americans and Hollywood" at the International Asian American Film Festival in San Francisco in March 1995, I took the opportunity to arrange interviews with them. In three separate conversations, we talked about their experiences as Asian American women directing and producing films. Their comments revealed a range of approaches that each woman had for defining her relationship to Hollywood.[2] Throughout my conversations with Shum, Hatta, and Yang, several intertwining themes emerged. First, the difficult reality of working in a profit-driven industry defined by a hypothetical mass market that, for the most part, does not include Asian Americans or women. Second, the ongoing pursuit of artistic freedom of expression and social ideals. And third, the persistence of race and gender issues in their work and in the responses to their work. Kayo Hatta remarked:

> Both my gender and my ethnicity inform my work. Until filmmaking is more democratic, less elitist, and diversity is the norm among films that get made, such labels [being referred to as an Asian American woman filmmaker] show other people that I am not about business as usual. If a label can help serve as a way of letting people know that there are other types of works and there are alternative voices out there, all the better. The downside of such labels is that it can pigeonhole you—I'd like to be able to pick and choose my projects just like anyone else and feel free to explore all sides, all colors of the human experience.

All three interviewees acknowledged that being an Asian American woman influenced their work and how their work is perceived. However, others' perceptions of their personal identities did not dictate what projects they pursued, and whether or how their identities would be reflected in the content of their films. Each, in her own way, responded to contemporary social attitudes as an outgrowth of, expansion of, or reaction to the civil rights gains made by people of color and white women's political movements. A comment by Janet Yang illustrates an unfortunate paradox:

> The sixties were a truly revolutionary time for this country. It was at that time that a lot of awareness was brought to the surface [about] minority issues: affirmative action, women, ideological change—essentially turning over the establishment. I think what's happening [now] politically is a backlash to that. I find that we are often overly politically correct about certain things to the point where we have to mute our own impulses or feelings or instincts, because we're afraid of saying something that may sound wrong. So it's a difficult time—I think we're just trying to find a balance.

The civil rights movements and activism of the 1960s and 1970s to increase the presence of minorities in the public life of the U.S. resulted in the creation of organizations and fostered an awareness that, in part, created a more open atmosphere in which people of color and white women were able to take advantage of opportunities to become artists and filmmakers. As the aspiring filmmakers became relatively successful or established, funding and public support began to be attacked and slowly cut back throughout the 1980s. Now, in the mid-1990s, the continuation of federally or publicly funded art and filmmaking is seriously at risk of being "zeroed out." Thus, sustaining our current level of participation in the field of cultural production will be difficult, and further gains are hard to imagine. Filmmakers face difficult and sparse choices for how to break into filmmaking and, once there, how to survive with their integrity intact. In Kayo Hatta's view,

> The studios are conservative because they will only do what has been tried before. They are very scared to take any risks. That's where the independent world has been influencing Hollywood in a positive way. Hollywood has basically hit up against a dead end in terms of finding new ideas, and the independent world is a source of new blood. Of course, the challenge, once nabbed by the studios, is whether or not an independent filmmaker can stay true to her vision. . . . What does it do to you once [the studios] get you? In exchange for financial gain, one then has to play ball, to try to work within studio limitations. It's such an irony — in the worst scenario, studios take the best of the independents and appropriate them to become studio clones. In the best situation, one maintains her vision and makes the studio system work for her . . . but it's a constant battle, balancing art and commerce.

THIS DANCE OF ART AND COMMERCE . . .

Mina Shum explains,

> Why would I do this dance of art and commerce? Because ultimately, it means that with money comes the power to get my visions across. My visions being microcosms [of] larger social issues. I'm trying to help people. I'm trying to change the way people treat each other. I'm trying to make people see things differently for the first time. And those are very noble efforts. They're very honorable. They're ambitious, and that kind of ambition has to be fueled with power, and so I will do that dance.

Most Asian American media activists, filmmakers, and critics agree that institutional change is necessary to ensure fair representation and participation of a broad range of people from diverse backgrounds, and in cultural production in general. However, how change should be accomplished and what the changes should be have been debated since the emergence of the Asian American movement. The issue is usually expressed in simple binary terms. On the one hand, according to independents, filmmakers working in the mainstream represent the vilest sort of assimilationists, selling out Asian American histories and experiences as exotic or spicy variations on the melting-pot theme. They are out of touch with reality. Their work is empty of political relevance or imperatives, whereas independent film and videomakers stand on the moral high ground by virtuously refusing to dirty their hands, aesthetic sensibilities, and politics with the taint of capitalist enterprise. Works by independent artists portray issues relevant to the Asian American community and seek to challenge the status quo representations of Asian Americans, as well as filmmaking as a consumer product.

On the other hand, from the perspective of mainstream filmmakers, artists working in the independent circuit have such limited resources and access to venues that they are, in effect, preaching to the converted, or only reaching an elite clique of highly trained and educated film viewers. Mainstream producers often view the work by independents as generally low in quality and poorly executed, or too opaque for mass audiences to identify with or understand. They are out of touch with reality. Working within mainstream institutions provides access to the largest audience and provides the greatest opportunity to change American society from within existing structures.

There is truth in both these positions. Compromises are made by many artists, both independent and mainstream. Actually, the choice presented to work exclusively in one sphere or the other is a false one. The boundary between the independent and mainstream feature film industries in the United States has become increasingly porous, especially compared with the period when the studio system was practically the only form of filmmaking in the U.S. because of its monopoly on all aspects of production, distribution, and screening venues. Nowadays, the distinctions between mainstream and independent are often arbitrary and inconclusive, often defined by subjective measures such as the size of a production budget; the expectation—or not—for a positive return on the investment; attitude towards cultural politics in a film; the mass appeal and narrative structure of a film; and the types of venues at which a film is screened.

Holding rigidly to the idea that only one approach to filmmaking can bring about meaningful social and political change also overlooks the choices balancing activism and acquiescence that a filmmaker might find necessary to make over the course of her or his career. Filmmakers can work independently or through the studios, either in successive projects or by mixing approaches within one project. Hatta, Shum, and Yang have all created strategies that they hope will allow them to balance economic necessity, political objectives, and artistic vision. In effect, they bring a strategically activist outlook to their mainstream oriented projects. Both Yang and Hatta articulated visions of the future in which race, ethnicity, gender, and other social categories of difference were not indicators of inequality but springboards to exploring the many facets of human experience. Filmgoers remarked to Yang that though *The Joy Luck Club* was about Chinese Americans, it could just as well have been about European American ethnic groups such as Greek, Italian, or Jewish Americans. According to Yang, the movie showed "the similarities between people, and not the differences." In a parallel vein, Kayo Hatta said:

> So many of my peers feel like, if you call yourself an Asian American film-maker, you're pigeonholing yourself. You're ghettoizing yourself and you're not going to be universal enough. Like you're just going to appeal to an Asian audience. That may be true on one level, but I don't want this concern to dilute my voice, my point of view. My take on it is the more specific you are, the more universal your work is. Your ethnicity, your gender, your sexual orientation — is what gives your work a unique viewpoint, it's what makes a work interesting. Bringing out the common threads of the human experience in these stories is what ultimately makes it universal. Universality is not about becoming white.

Furthermore, both Shum and Hatta emphasized the fact that a pool of well-qualified production people who also happen to be Asian American or women does exist, and that they made efforts to work with them; however, race and gender could not be their foremost consideration because, as Shum put it, "You know what? If I made a lousy film and I had [an all] Asian woman crew that wasn't ready for it, no one's going to say, 'Yeah, it was a really awful film, but did she employ fifteen people!'" Similarly, Hatta stated: "My criteria will always be not only to hire the best qualified people, but the people that I get along best with. Filmmaking is like creating a family, and you work very intensively together. If you don't get along, it's a nightmare. I want to work with both women and men who are open, sensitive, and committed, and can respect a woman director." Their strategies for survival as filmmakers balance social realities and social ideals. Being an Asian American woman plays a role in what they envision for the future, but doesn't bind them to a narrowly defined sense of cultural politics.

While the discourses about and mobilization against mainstream representations have created a needed sense of unity among Asian Americans, there also needs to be room for alternative readings and different visions. The representations offered by Asian American filmmakers reflect the heterogeneity of Asian American communities, which encompass all political proclivities, education levels, classes, ages, genders, sexual orientations, social priorities and loyalties, expectations about "going to the movies," and levels of awareness and concern about the implications of being an American of Asian descent. If one of the enduring criticisms of the mainstream film industry is that it has homogenized and flattened Asian American humanity, then the goal of Asian American media activism should be to support many voices and many visions of Asian America. Our responses can be both reformist and radical, acknowledging the shifts and improvements in the media industry as it is, and also always keeping in mind long-range goals of radically chancing the media industry, and society in general, to be democratic, inclusive, and humane. Coalitions between and support for both independent and mainstream filmmakers are necessary to articulate and enact changes for the future.

A CINEMA OF RESPONSIBILITY . . .

Films produced within the Hollywood system, and those produced independently but receiving theatrical release through mainstream distributors (such as *The Joy Luck Club*, *Picture Bride*, and *Double Happiness*) do have access to larger audiences, and, as such, they have a greater potential for affecting the public perception of Asian Americans. However, working within the mainstream system also has pitfalls which must be guarded against. Primary among the dangers of working within the studio system is the possibility of turning Asian American experiences, culture, and history into another commodity item for the consuming pleasure of mass audiences. Hollywood has conventionally avoided subjects that might be considered controversial or political in any way. As a result, mainstream feature films emphasize nostalgic sentimentality and support dominant discourses on sexuality, race, class, gender roles, and liberal consumer capitalism. Within mainstream films, socially and politically sensitive issues are usually unsatisfactorily resolved through the coming together of an isolated romantic couple rather than through any deep interrogation of and change in larger social structures. Individuals, rather than communities, are in the spotlight. Nonetheless, mainstream movies are important because they can offer opportunities for Asian Americans to be portrayed as complex, three-dimensional characters. They help to raise consciousness and increase awareness of Asian American experiences and people; however, the significance and impact of racism and sexism in the United States is often suppressed. Also, ultimately, the mainstream filmmaking industry as exemplified by Hollywood is elitist and highly competitive. By setting our eyes on this prize, we risk reinforcing and replicating a system in which the integrity and vision of very few filmmakers ever have a chance of surviving.

The filmmakers I interviewed affirmed that they are extremely aware of the implied responsibility in being a successful Asian American woman in the industry. The responsibilities are manifold: to represent Asian American communities, to present positive images of Asian Americans, to help other aspiring filmmakers. Janet Yang stated,

If every character in every movie is going to be seen as the definitive characterization of that category of person, then there's nothing we can do.

That is overly politically correct. I can sympathize and empathize with [those] concerns: There are so few movies with Asian Americans, the expectations for each one is so high because everybody wants it to speak to their own particular situation, and not every movie can do that. You can't think too much about the pressure to speak to everyone or about being a spokesperson for the community. It's just not a creative or effective way to go about one's work in this field. That's the job of politicians. There's a difference between artists and politicians by their very nature. Politicians try to speak for everybody; we cannot speak for everybody.

The problem with the expectations often expressed by members of the Asian American community is that "community needs" and "positive representations" are difficult to pinpoint. Positive representations can be as limiting as the negative stereotypes that we have tried to combat, and are subject to endless refinements. Communities are continuously changing, especially in Asian America, which is one of the fastest growing racial groups in the U.S. What Asian Americans want to see in films depicting our experiences will be similarly complex, specific, and diverse. Kayo Hatta observed, "There's so many Asian American stories that have yet to be told. We have [had so] many years of American cinema sorely lacking in any meaningful stories of Asian American life, or other communities, that we can go on for a long time, and we still won't reach into the complexity and diversity of our communities and the stories that we have to tell."

As federal funds from such sources as the National Endowment for the Arts are cut back and eliminated, the pressures on the few filmmakers who have had some success in the mainstream movie industry will increase. My hope is that artists will continue to be responsible and responsive to Asian American communities and audiences in the ways that they can: hiring and supporting talent on screen and behind it, portraying complex social situations and characters, exploring new narrative techniques that subvert or deconstruct dominant hierarchies and ideologies. We also need to create infrastructures to support cinematic productions by and about Asian Americans. Hatta offered her vision:

Rather than relying on the powers that be, my dream is to do it on our own. We're going to have to find ways to create our own production companies and to get it together in terms of people in the executive level. We have to form our own means by which we can do our work. We're going to have to be more savvy about knowing how to get money for funding films and then also producing work that will encourage people to invest in Asian American projects.

Audiences and critics, for their part, must support the artists and filmmakers, and acknowledge the particular difficulties of creating films, whether as independent directors or producers, or in the studio system. They must extend sympathetic support to the filmmakers for surviving in a financially precarious field, at the same time that they are critical of the representations that are produced. Needless to say, being an Asian American woman does not guarantee insight, sensitivity, knowledge, talent, or political vision.

Hatta, Shum, and Yang pointed out that they do not make movies for the sole purpose of representing the Asian American community. Giving priority solely to race suppresses other aspects of Asian American identities and suggests that there is only one Asian American experience. It suppresses historical, ethnic, and national specificities, and can lead to an uncritical acceptance of other social categories that have been marked by unequal power relationships. Both Shum and Yang emphasized that while their ethnicity and gender informed their work, their artistic vision was not limited to those identities. As Shum put it: "I want to have what Scorsese and Coppola and all those guys have because I deserve it. It's as simple as that." Just as European American men have had the freedom to produce or direct almost any movie that interests them, so should Asian American women.

The goal for Asian American women media artists cannot simply be to gain equity in numbers behind the screen in executive and high-level production jobs—though, of course, this would be a start. Critics, audiences, and filmmakers are well aware of the need to challenge demeaning and dismissive portrayals not only of Asian Americans, but of all types. Mina Shum summarized her objective:

> All I want to do is make more room for more individuals' voices out there, because the more people are with me, the more chances I have to survive, the more chances we'll survive as a community. And I'm not talking about just Chinese, I'm talking about a community of dissidents. There's a lot of us out there who don't fit into the mainstream. Whether it's sexual orientation, class, philosophical, or religious, there's a group of us who are displaced people.

Simultaneously, we need to become more educated about the media industry so that our criticisms and suggestions will be appropriate to the particular situations media artists confront when working in various sectors of the industry. Social change achieved in this manner is not glamorous or instantaneous, but it is based on social, political, and economic realities in the United States. Media artists working in the mainstream and independently are both important contributors to social change. Rather than accepting conventional wisdom about their supposed opposition, we need to parlay advantages in all fields into permanent and wide-reaching benefits for everyone, and that is to have the freedom and access to resources to participate responsibly in an egalitarian and democratic society as our passions dictate.

In the face of the sobering reality that Asian American women still have a long road to travel before achieving credibility, power, and acceptance as filmmakers, Janet Yang, Mina Shum, and Kayo Hatta are role models for the passion and commitment filmmakers require to survive with integrity and to make a difference. Thus, I end this essay with their words of encouragement.

> My film [Double Happiness] is about finding the courage to dream: when we have grown up with generational [and] cultural conflicts, when we have to come of age within two communities, and bridge both worlds, there are so many elements within that fight that tell us "no," "you can't," and "you shouldn't." And what I want to say with my film and my career and my life is that anyone can if you want, and if you have the courage and the talent and the energy to pursue your dreams, don't let anyone say no. I've had millions of people say no, but I keep coming back, I just keep getting up again. (Mina Shum)

> I made a lot of my key decisions in those crucial years following college and in the beginning of my career, and I made decisions that seemed highly impractical in some ways, but I did so because I was following my heart—and my nose. You have to follow your instincts. You may fail, you may not be able to make a viable career of it, but at least you're doing what you like! (Janet Yang)

> Don't ever underestimate yourself. You would amaze yourself at what you're able to do if you push yourself and challenge yourself and put yourself into really difficult situations, because that's exactly what we did . . . We were driven by a relentless passion to make this film. That's one thing I would tell aspiring women directors, but the other thing is to lighten up, to remember to enjoy the process, to have fun! (Kayo Hatta)

WORK, IMMIGRATION, GENDER: ASIAN "AMERICAN" WOMEN

Lisa Lowe

for Lydia

Hello, my name is Fu Lee. I am forty-one years old, married, and I have a nine-year-old daughter. I have been living in Oakland Chinatown since I left Hong Kong twelve years ago. . . .

I worked as a seamstress at Lucky Sewing Co. for two years. Before that, I worked as a seamstress at other similar sweatshops. All of the workers worked long hours, ten to twelve hours a day and six to seven days a week. We were paid by the piece, which sometimes was below the minimum wage. Overtime pay was unheard of. You may think sewing is an easy job, but it requires a lot of skill. For fancy dresses, with laces, tiny buttons, and tricky fabric patterns, you really have to concentrate so you don't make any mistakes. My wage was never enough money for our family to live on. We always worried about our daughter getting sick because we had no health insurance.

My eyes hurt from straining under poor lighting; my throat hurt because of the chemical fumes from the fabric dye. Sometimes, I would wear surgical masks so I don't have to breathe in all the dust from the fabric. My back never stopped hurting from bending over the sewing machine all day. Our boss was like a dictator. He was always pushing us to work faster. There was a sign in the shop that said, "No loud talking. You cannot go to the bathroom." When we did talk loudly or laugh during work, he would throw empty boxes at us and tell us to go back to work. When there was a rush order, we had to eat lunch at our work station.

Last year, my employer closed his shop and left us holding bad paychecks. We found out that he had filed for bankruptcy and had no intention of paying us our meager wages. The twelve Chinese seamstresses including myself were so mad. After working so hard under such horrendous working conditions, we should at least get our pay.

With the help of Asian Immigrant Women Advocates, we began searching for ways to get our pay.

$m$rs. Fu Lee's testimony,[1] at a community hearing initiated by Asian Immigrant Women Advocates (AIWA) in Oakland, California, describes the conditions of many Asian immigrant women in the San Francisco Bay Area garment industry: low-waged or unpaid labor, forced increases in productivity through long workdays or speedups, repetitive manual labor, occupational hazards and environmental toxins, poor lighting and ventilation, and no union or collective bargaining protections. Before the Lucky Sewing Co. closed shop and left the sewing women with bad paychecks, Mrs. Lee and the other seamstresses were to have been paid $5 a dress; the subcontractor was paid $10 a dress, yet each dress was sold by Jessica McClintock, Inc. for $175.

In the Bay Area garment industry, women sew clothing that their meager wages (if they receive them) will not permit them to buy as commodities. The women work under physical conditions that are unsafe, unhealthy, and fatiguing. Furthermore, the policy of paying the worker by the piece exploits the immigrant women in ways that extend beyond the extraction of surplus value from hourly low-waged factory labor. The incentive to complete as many pieces as possible makes certain that the sewing women will work overtime without compensation and will intensify her productivity even if it results in exhaustion or personal injury. Because many of the women speak little or no English and consider that their employment options are limited, because eight out of ten Chinatown immigrant families with multiple wage earners say they would "barely get by" if there were but one breadwinner in the family, they are forced to accept the payment terms dictated by the employer.[2] Many also bring work home and solicit the help of children and relatives, making the domestic space of the home an additional site of labor.

Mrs. Lee's testimony gives a vivid picture of the working lives of many Asian women in the U.S. But when viewed in all its complexity, it also reveals the necessary relations between Asian American women, Asian, and Asian immigrant women, and suggests the important roles that Asian American women can play within the broader coalition of U.S. women of color.

~~~

Asian American and Asian immigrant women represent a linked group emerging out of colonialism and war in Asia as well as immigrant displacement to the United States. Along with other racial and ethnic women workers, these women constitute an important low-paid workforce within the U.S., "occupationally ghettoized" in particular sectors: menial, domestic, and reproductive labor, textile and garment industries, hotel and restaurant work, and a current mix of mass production, subcontracting, and family-type firms. Asian immigrant women are at once determined by the histories of Western expansionism in Asia and the racialization of working populations of color in the U.S.[3] In light of post-1965 Asian immigration to the United States, Asian women in America are a complex and changing group composed of different generations and populations. The recent immigrants from South Korea, the Philippines, and South Vietnam leave behind societies greatly disrupted by colonialism, U.S. war, and partition, in the case of Korea and Vietnam. Their countries of origin continue to be disadvantaged economically in relation to the U.S., making Asian immigrants to the U.S. vulnerable to exploitation. As Lucie Cheng and Edna Bonacich have argued, not only does the underdevelopment associated with U.S. imperialism lay the groundwork for labor emigration, but U.S. industries have special control over laborers who are at the mercy of immigration laws, and who, owing to language, training, culture, and the type of jobs they perform, are outside of unions and the labor movement and often without access to other kinds of support.[4] For example, there is no union protection for the large workforce of Asian immigrant women in the microchip and semiconductor industries in Silicon Valley, California (although important work is being done by activist groups to protect workers from unhealthy environmental conditions such as inadequately tested toxic chemicals, unsafe lighting, injurious repetitive manual motions, and poor ventilation).[5] There are also no legal protections for "mail-order brides" and domestic workers from the Philippines, who are dependent upon their "husbands" and "employers" for visas and green cards; their isolation from other women and the Filipino community leaves them with little support to resist the exploitation of their unpaid domestic and sexual labor.[6] This "trafficking" of Filipinas to the U.S. as "mail-order brides" is continuous with the long history of U.S. militarism and exploitation of sex workers in the Philippines.[7]

Once in the U.S., Asians are asked not only to become fluent in U.S. American language and culture, but to conform to a citizenship narrative in which the immigrant gives up ties to the former homeland to take up membership in the new society. In this narrative, the model citizen transcends their "particular" embeddedness in the concrete conditions of the immigrant and attains the universal perspective of the national collectivity. But at the same time Asian women are working under conditions that prevent them from enjoying the protection and privilege of other U.S. citizens. As she encounters the difference and disparity between her working conditions and the opportunities of the normative U.S. citizen publicized around her, the working Asian immigrant woman may be less likely to *identify* with the model of the citizen than to *disidentify* with it. Her horizon is constituted by the material conditions of her female immigrant "lifeworld": low wages for menial, repetitive labor, poor environmental health conditions in the workplace, capitalist penetration of the immigrant "home," gender discrimination, and racism exclude her from the equal citizenship promised by democratic inclusion.

American liberal society depends upon the notion that representative democracy is a system to which all individuals have equal access and in which all are represented. Yet the conditions of Asian immigrant women laborers reveal how the myth of equal citizenship is inherently contradictory, to the degree that it holds out the state as an inclusive unity, but asks for the suppression of difference (of race, ethnicity, class, gender, and locality) as a requirement for representation by that state.

~~~~

Many experiences of Asian immigrant and Asian American women workers are shared by other women of color in the U.S. labor force, particularly Latina immigrants. Latina women also emigrate from nations in which colonialism and neocolonialism have disfigured "native" societies, nations which continue to be economically subordinated to the U.S. In the final section of my discussion, I want to draw out the rich theoretical and practical force of Asian immigrant women workers in relation to existing oppositional social movements in the United States, and in relation to the work already accomplished by U.S. women of color.[8]

Asian immigrant women and other racialized women are formed through the intersecting processes of racial formation, labor exploitation, and gender subordination, and are therefore differentially situated in relation to existing or historical social movements organized around a single form of domination: for example, the liberal feminist critique of patriarchy, the critique of capitalism from the standpoint of class exploitation and class struggle, and the critique of racism and internal colonialism from the standpoint of racialized ethnic minority subjects. The isolation of one axis of power, such as the exploitation of labor under capitalism, underestimates the degree to which capitalism in the U.S. is conjoined with and made more efficient by other systems of discrimination and subordination—patriarchy, racism, colonialism, and heterosexism. U.S. women of color theorists such as Chela Sandoval, Angela Davis, and Evelyn Nakano Glenn have criticized single-axis political organization, pointing out that an exclusive gender politics may obscure class hierarchy and racism, while an exclusive class politics may fail to address gender stratification, race labor, and homophobia.[9] Moreover, many women of color have argued that the hierarchization of forms of oppression, as well as the false unification of women of color, are impediments to theorizing and organizing movements for social change. In this sense, Asian American and Asian immigrant women are currently a powerful example of the politics of women of color. As a result of being in a dialectical relationship to existing social movements, Asian American and

Asian immigrant women offer a paradigm of struggle and cohesion for cross-ethnic, cross-race, cross-national, multiple-issue politics.

~~~~~

Ultimately, Asian "American" women (I use quotation marks here to signal the ambivalent and multidirectional sets of identifications that both U.S.-born Asian and Asian immigrant women have to the nationalist construction "American") must be situated in a dialogue with women working in colonized, neocolonized, or economically subordinated regions, as well as with women workers migrating to the U.S. from these areas. Given the transnational context of women's oppression in the U.S. and the global nature of the garment and electronics industries, this linkage seems crucial to Asian American feminist and women of color politics.

From the early post-World War II years through the 1960s, the U.S. political economy was dominated by the notion of development—the capital, technological, and educational development of the U.S., as well as neocolonial development and the appropriation by the U.S. of surplus profits in Asia and Latin America. In that period, opposition to these forms of capitalist and imperialist development was primarily articulated in terms of class issues.[10] The late 1960s marked the beginning of a period in which the expression of opposition to oppression became increasingly mediated by analyses of other forms of domination, not only capitalism and imperialism, but also patriarchy and racism.[11] Following the 1970s, "free-trade zones" were established in various sites of the "Third World," in which tax-free privileges in trade were combined with new incentives, such as the provision of buildings and utilities by local governments and the ease of profit repatriation. By the 1970s, networks of industrial zones throughout Southeast Asia and Latin America opened up these regions to investment by Japanese and U.S. transnational companies. Trade policies like GATT and NAFTA have accelerated the flow of capital, goods, and services across national boundaries while undermining the few existing laws protecting workers, consumers, and the environment. With U.S. capitalism's shift of production globally, the use of nonwhite women's labor worldwide has led to a reorganization of the categories and relations of national, racial, and gender differences that were characteristic of the earlier mode of capitalism that had once concentrated production within the U.S.

U.S. oppositional social movements of the 1970s—feminist, labor, civil rights, and ethno-nationalist—produced particular narratives of political development for people resisting domination. According to these narratives, the "woman," "worker," and "racial or ethnic minority" were to develop from a pre-class-identified position to that of politicized participants who become "conscious" of their exploitation under patriarchy, capitalism, and racism. Asian American women, like other U.S. women of color, had a different political formation than that prescribed by *either* the narratives of liberal capitalist development and citizenship or the narratives proposed by these oppositional movements of the 1970s. The experience of Asian American women and U.S. women of color of the 1970s was more complex than that of the "woman" posited by feminist discourse, or the "proletariat" described by Marxism, or the "ethnic" subject projected by civil rights and ethno-nationalist movements. A different social history, a different narrative of politicization, and a different logic of political organization distinguish women of color from the subjects of these oppositional movements. It is in encountering these "differences," and in encountering the practical obstacles of "differences" among women of color, that women of color politics has historically articulated its necessity, and its predicament.[12]

Since the political subject woman of color does not "develop" solely as a "woman," a "worker," or an "ethnic" subject, women of color may be said to be politically "anti-identitarian" in representation and practice. Norma Alarcón has argued that the association of "identity politics" with the women of color movement is a false one, that the concept of women of color has always been predicated upon differences—of class, sexuality, race, geography, national origin, religion, and generation.[13]

Narratives of consciousness aim at developing a subject position or perspective from which totalization becomes possible, whereas women of color have tended to locate themselves in relationship to intersecting dominations, often translating these locations into powerful critical positions. In the 1980s, work by Audre Lorde, Cherríe Moraga, and the collective Asian Women United of California, for example, exemplify "situated" nontotalizing perspectives on conjoined dominations, as well as the emergence of politicized critiques of those conjunctions.[14]

While Marxism proposes that the classical contradiction exists between capital and labor, the situation of working women of color makes it apparent that we must always speak of more than one contradiction. We may speak of a racial contradiction by which the state claims to be a democratic body in which all subjects are granted membership, yet racial, ethnic, and immigrant subjects continue to be disenfranchised and excluded from political participation in that state. And we may speak of gender contradictions: that the economic concept of abstract labor (that work is equivalent to pay) fails to account for unwaged female domestic labor in the home and unequal pay for women in the workplace; or that the discourse of formal legal equality is contradicted when a woman's choice to conceive or bear a child may still be contested by husband, father, or state. Throughout lived social relations, it is apparent that labor is gendered, sexuality is racialized, and race is class-associated. A multiplicity of social contradictions with different origins converge at different sites within any social formation—the family, education, religion, communications media, sites of capitalist production. Each set of contradictions is uneven and incommensurable, with certain contradictions taking priority over others in response to the material conditions of a given historical moment. Nowhere is this more in evidence than in the "life-world" of women of color, who are situated within multiple sets of social relations.

The necessary alliances between women of color within, outside, and across the border of the U.S. grow out of the contemporary conditions of global capitalism. Immigrant women working in the garment industries of Los Angeles are virtually part of the same labor force as those employed in Asia or Latin America. The sweatshops of the garment industry located in San Francisco and Los Angeles, for example, employ immigrant women from Mexico, El Salvador, Guatemala, China, South Korea, Thailand, and the Philippines, while in these countries of origin, U.S. transnational corporations are also conducting garment assembly work.[15] Third World women migrate from countries of origin already "colonized" and distorted by U.S. corporate capital and come to labor as racialized "women of color" in the U.S. In this sense, despite the obstacles of national, cultural, and linguistic differences, there are material continuities between the conditions of Chicanas and Latinas working in the U.S., the women working in maquilas and low-cost manufacturing zones in Latin America, and the Asian women occupationally segregated both within the U.S. and in Asian zones of assembly and manufacturing.

While the determinations of class, race, and gender make possible the continuation of labor exploitation for women of color, it may also precisely constitute the ground from which the cross-generational, cross-national, cross-class, anti-racist, and feminist struggles against those dominations emerge. The important work of organizations like AIWA (Asian Immigrant Women Advocates) in the San Francisco Bay Area, in which second- and third-generation Asian American women work for the empowerment of immigrant Asian women workers in the garment, hotel, and electronics industries, or the Garment Workers' Justice Center in Los Angeles and La Mujer Obrera in El Paso, suggests some ways of thinking about the mutual processes of politicization that occur between "U.S. women of color" and "Third World women." AIWA is an inspiring example of a kind of organization whose practices combine the forces, ideas, and labors of diverse Asian American and Asian immigrant women. The cross-generational women in AIWA are from different national origins, classes, and language backgrounds. While AIWA organizes Asian immigrant women around the more traditional labor issue of workers' rights—as in the campaign to secure pay for the seamstresses in the shop contracted by manufacturer Jessica McClintock—it also focuses on bringing Asian American and Asian immigrant women together as members of Asian communities, and addresses issues that are of concern "outside" of the workplace, such as childcare, healthcare, language, and literacy. In this way, AIWA and other groups are able to address the specific issues confronting immigrant women who do not easily "fit" into mainstream unions. AIWA does not organize itself in a traditional hierarchy that would place "organizers" above "workers" or Asian American women above immigrant women; instead, AIWA's structure encourages reciprocally transformative relationships between Asian American organizers and Asian immigrant working women.[16] Miriam Ching Louie writes: "The challenge to AIWA organizers is to use the classes (in English) so that workers can reflect on their own lives, determine what is fair, visualize alternatives to oppressive conditions, and practice demanding their rights. . . . Organizers must also transform themselves in the process."[17]

Other projects create and maintain solidarity across racial and ethnic groups, and across national boundaries: groups like the Border Workers Regional Support Committee (CAFOR) and the Coalition for Justice in the Maquiladoras (CJM) have helped Mexican maquiladora workers organize against U.S.- and Japanese-owned parent companies. The Support Committee for the Maquiladora Workers in San Diego, some of whom are Asian immigrant women, helps document the exploitative, unsafe working conditions of the maquiladoras and provides various support services for the mostly female Mexican workers.[18] Recently, the Support Committee helped retrieve back wages for workers formerly employed at Exportadora de Mano de Obra in Tijuana, Mexico, through bringing suit in U.S. courts against the parent company, National O-Ring, a division of American United Global Corporation. One hundred and eighty workers had lost their wages when National O-Ring suddenly closed the Exportadora plant in Tijuana, precipitated by the women workers having brought charges of sexual harassment against the company president. "Solidarity among workers should cross the border as easily as companies move production," says Mary Tong, the director of the Support Committee for Maquiladora Workers. Asian "American" projects are changing in response to the changes in immigration and immigrant communities over the last two decades, and shifting to take on the difficult work of forging understanding and political solidarity between Asian and non-Asian groups across racial and national boundaries.

Chandra Mohanty has written about the movements *between* cultures, languages, and complex configurations of meanings and power that "experience must be historically interpreted and theorized if it is to become the basis of feminist solidarity and struggle, and it is at this moment that an understanding of the politics of location proves crucial."[19] As Asian "American" women, we must struggle to understand not only the process of our various "minoritizations" as racialized women, but also the different processes of newly immigrant women who may already be a proletarianized, gendered labor force in their "home" countries. The experiences of women in sites as different as South Korea, Sri Lanka, or Egypt are determined by their specific national histories of colonialism, decolonization, nationalist struggles, postindepenence capitalist development, and multinational incursions.[20] Asian American women of color must be as vigilant as we have always had to be to avoid universalizing nationalist notions of "womanhood" or struggle. Audre Lorde wrote in 1979, "Community must not mean a shedding of our differences . . . [but] learning how to take our differences and make them strengths."[21] This attention to "difference" is still, and all the more, crucial for Asian American women today.

SILENCE OF FORM

Mong Lan

*t*he wind has little to do with this city, or this time
or this world,
        or this bridge
these rocks, this place
ravaged divested
of human form
or the fire that created this lesion
charred wood, trunks thinned, dulled, ashen

the wind has to do with the soil
sculpting it into bodies that walk in the realm
of dreams
the wind has to do with the sea
angering it
pulling its threads, gnawing at the drowned
bodies, ankles and false teeth
bad teeth and roaming tongues
sometimes spitting out live bodies
with shiny black backs and blind webbed feet

fog walks around the ocean
as the surf swells and mist deafens

2

one shore, two shores overlapping
like long necks
        or long thighs

        or the form of sex

mist of forearms
hands floating, feet unsure of gravity
fingers unsure of their physical matter,
death swooping down but thrust beyond attention
uvular, angular with limbs
(hair caught in mouths, cheek against smooth stomachs,)
uteral, elliptical

like a mango carved in half
slippery as seaweed
treading skin in the dark to the rhythm
of the salsa, and it keeps on raining
against the windows, and it doesn't matter
that the idle women next door are looking in
through the mist of sultry sweat
one after the other
and it doesn't matter
that sweat pours like rain
and tastes like the sea
and sometimes it doesn't matter
that there isn't love.

3

you there, the woman who doesn't want to be fucked
by his bloody penis
'sangra, pero funciona' so he says
the ugly condomless thing
what is one to do with it
you ask, what is one to do with it

and he walks out of his window
onto the roof and urinates
into the bushes

and comes back in carrying the night's nakedness
with him
a black cold to the touch
Guanajuato's 3 A.M. mountain-murmuring
in his eyes
the town's echo of solitary lights
the coyote's howl under his nails
like the howl of the wind

4

the boy who hung himself
        was a mandolin player

and that was all, and he survived
only his twenty-second birthday

and they said of him that he loved
to play the mandolin daily
and that was all
olive skinned, he played as no one
should've flirting with inviolate eternity

and he hung himself
and that was all

5

what do people hear when
they see you?

they hear angels.

6

the phosphorescence of the sea
changes, becomes hollow like a shell
then clear, full as a voice,
dusk curving, twilight unfolding
the clouds like silver stones cast
la luna llena touching thatched roofs and
sand bodies love-entwined
the calm linearity of the withdrawing horizon, the persistent
chant of salty foam
satin wind
and coral waters gouging deep
lines into border rocks

sea anemones
the mimicry of fish
the gush of snails clinging for their lives

along the coast like unwashed underarm matter
the tide pools waiting
for the stone-eating sea

I had a dream
of you
you diving against pastel skies
pear-perfect
smooth as a well-oiled crane
(as when you nude arise from slumber
in a centrifugal swing
legs tucked toes pointed
pulling you forward)
tense then relaxed outstretched
hands dipping to pointed toes
your body opening out like a pocket knife
falling

we are at the edge where ocean
laps land
on a cliff a silver house as if painted there

I imagine you posing for me
your nude arms outstretched ready to plunge
into another dimension
camera in hand I ask nothing of you
I take only this mental picture of reluctance
and the austere silence of horizon
and rocks

7

you are asleep your breathing cut short
then released, motionless as if your breathing
controlled the movement in the room
the metal chair, the wicker basket made in Mexico, your socks, your clothes
the September slant of the light thrown against the walls

you will leave me tomorrow
and not tell me

words no longer contain it
your breath cannot, your blood refuses
your nocturnal hand is gestureless
as cold ash,
your clothes strewn on the floor
like trampled banana peel
your breath cut short, then prolonged
like a long shadow, resonating
slanted silence,
charred bones, and dark
sand

8

skin and odorous flesh
body that would fail after time
hands dried by salt that have worked the sea
hands unknown to the sea
madness-soused hands

death was there, but you didn't see it
swelling, breaking, incessantly
brewing, glass birds and black
birds, and the murmuring earthworms
and silver stones in the sky
in the sand carried by the burning
silent wind

Notes

Preface

1. Our first books and videotapes were supported by grants from the U.S. Department of Education's Women's Educational Equity Act Program. They were made for Asian American girls and young women. The books for high school students included *With Silk Wings: Asian American Women At Work* (1983), by Elaine H. Kim and Janice Otani, *Dear Diane: Questions and Answers for Asian American Women* and *Dear Diane: Letters From Our Daughters* (1983) in Chinese/English and Korean/English. The videos were *Four Women* (1982), *On New Ground* (1983), and *Frankly Speaking* (1983), directed by Loni Ding. In the mid-1980s, we produced three other videos, a thirty-minute documentary profiling women of five Asian heritages called *Talking History* (1984), directed by Spencer Nakasako; *Dust and Threads* (1986), a thirty-minute training video for Asian immigrant women working as hotel maids and garment workers, directed by Louise Lo; and *Slaying the Dragon: Asian Women in U.S. Television and Film*, a sixty-minute documentary video directed by Deborah Gee (1987–88) with matching funds from KQED-TV.

Isabelle Thuy Pelaud, *Three Women and a Master*

Thanks to all the members of my family mentioned in this paper for trusting me with their representations. Also thanks to Bob Bartz, Ethne Luibhcid, Ulla Reinitzer, Khatarya Um, and the editors of *Making More Waves* for their support and critical comments.

1. The Supreme Master Ching Hai (Ching Hai Wu Shang Shih), *The Key of Immediate Enlightenment*, vol. 1. Formosa: The Meditation Association in China, 1990.

2. Newsletter, "The Supreme Master Ching Hai," no. 36 (June 1994). Formosa: The International Supreme Master Ching Hai Meditation Association.

3. Ibid.

4. The Supreme Master Ching Hai (Ching Hai Wu Shang Shih), *The Key of Immediate Enlightenment*, vol. 2. Taiwan: The Meditation Association in China, 1991.

5. The Supreme Master Ching Hai (Ching Hai Wu Shang Shih), *The Key of Immediate Enlightenment*, vol. 3. Taiwan: Infinite Light Publishing Co., 1992.

6. "The Supreme Master Ching Hai," no. 33 (March 1994). Formosa: The International Supreme Master Ching Hai Meditation Association.

7. "The Supreme Master Ching Hai," no. 32 (February 1994). Formosa: The International Supreme Master Ching Hai Meditation Association.

8. "The Supreme Master Ching Hai," no. 40 (November 1994). Formosa: The International Supreme Master Ching Hai Meditation Association.

9. Master Ching Hai, *The Key of Immediate Enlighhtenment* (Sample booklet). Taiwan: Infinite Light Publishing Co., 1993.

Yen Le Espiritu, *Race, Class, and Gender in Asian America*

1. Mary Romero, *Maid in the U.S.A.* (New York: Routledge, 1992), 17.

2. Kimberlee Crenshaw, "Demarginalizing the Intersection of Race and Sex: A Black Feminist Critique of Antidiscrimination Doctrine, Feminist Theory

and Antiracist Politics," in *University of Chicago Legal Forum: Feminism in the Law: Theory, Practice, and Criticism*, 139–167. In this analysis of the crosscurrents of racism and sexism, Crenshaw argues that racism denies black men and women access to established gender norms: black men are not viewed as powerful, and black women are not seen as passive.

3. Angela Davis, *Women, Race, and Class* (New York: Random House, 1981).

4. Davis, *Women, Race, and Class*; Crenshaw, "Demarginalizing the Intersection."

5. King-Kok Cheung, "The Woman Warrior Versus the Chinaman Pacific: Must a Chinese American Critic Choose Between Feminism and Heroism?" in *Conflicts in Feminism*, ed. Marianne Hirsch and Evelyn Fox Keller (New York: Routledge), 235. In this analysis of Chinese American literature, Cheung argues that many Chinese American male writers and critics who have challenged white racism nonetheless remain in thrall to the norms and arguments of the dominant patriarchal culture. She calls on Asian American men and women to work toward notions of gender and ethnicity that are "nonhierarchical, nonbinary, and nonprescriptive" (246).

7. Crenshaw, "Demarginalizing the Intersection," 185–189. See also George Lipsitz, *A Life in the Struggle: Ivory Perry and the Culture of Opposition* (Philadelphia: Temple University Press, 1988), 204–205. In this portrait of Ivory Perry, a rank and file leader of the black movement, Lipsitz recounts that while Perry was sensitive to hierarchies of race and class, his episodes of domestic violence indicate that he was inattentive to gender as a category of domination.

7. Nancy D. Donnelly, *Changing Lives of Refugee Hmong Women* (Seattle: University of Washington Press, 1994), 74–75.

9. Sucheng Chan, "The Asian American Movement, 1960s–1980s," in *Peoples of Color in the American West*, ed. Sucheng Chan, Douglas Henry Daniels, Mario T. Garcia, and Terry P. Wilson (Lexington, Mass.: D.C. Heath and Company, 1994), 528.

9. Pierrette Hondagneu-Sotelo, *Gendered Transition: Mexican Experiences in Immigration* (Berkeley: University of California Press, 1994), 193–194.

10. Hondagneu-Sotelo, *Gendered Transition*, 194.

11. Chandra Talpade Mohanty, "Cartographies of Struggle: Third World Women and the Politics of Feminism," in *Third World Women and the Politics of Struggle*, ed. Chandra Talpade Mohanty, Ann Russo, and Lourdes Torres (Bloomington: University of Indiana Press, 1991), 13.

12. Cheung, "The Woman Warrior," 245–246; Robyn Wiegman, "Black Bodies/American Commodities: Gender, Race, and the Bourgeois Ideal in Contemporary Film," in *Unspeakable Images: Ethnicity and the American Media*, ed. Lester D. Friedman (Urbana and Chicago: University of Illinois Press, 1991), 311.

13. Karen J. Hossfeld, "Hiring Immigrant Women: Silicon Valley's 'Simple Formula,'" in *Women of Color in U.S. Society*, ed. Maxine Baca Zinn and Bonnie Thornton (Philadelphia: Temple University Press, 1994), 74. In this study of women's labor in California's famed high-tech industrial region, Silicon Valley, Hossfeld finds that workers who are "small, foreign and female" are confined to the lowest-paid jobs in manufacturing assembly work.

14. Linda Y. C. Lim, "Capitalism, Imperialism, and Patriarchy: The Dilemma of Third-World Women in Multinational Factories," in *Women, Men,*

and the International Division of Labor, ed. June Nash and Maria Patricia Fernandez-Kelly (Albany: State University of New York, 1983), 83.

15. Marcelle Williams, "Ladies on the Line: Punjabi Cannery Workers in Central California," in *Making Waves: An Anthology of Writings by and about Asian American Women*, ed. Asian Women United of California (Boston: Beacon Press, 1989), 157.

16. Gary Okihiro, *Margins and Mainstream: Asians in American History and Culture* (Seattle: University of Washington Press), 91.

17. Lim, "Capitalism, Imperialism, and Patriarchy," 88.

18. Edna Bonacich, "Asian Labor in the Development of Hawaii and California," in *Labor Immigration Under Capitalism: Asian Workers in the United States Before World War II*, ed. Lucie Cheng and Edna Bonacich (Berkeley: University of California Press, 1984), 165–166.

19. Hossfeld, "Hiring Immigrant Women," 75.

20. Ibid, 65.

21. Judy Yung, *Chinese Women of America: A Pictorial Essay* (Seattle: University of Washington Press, 1986), 107.

22. Evelyn Nakano Glenn, *Issei, Nisei, War Bride: Three Generations of Japanese American Women at Domestic Service* (Philadelphia: Temple University Press, 1986); Nazli Kibria, *Family Tightrope: The Changing Lives of Vietnamese Americans* (Princeton: Princeton University Press, 1990).

23. Glenn, *Issei, Nisei, War Bride*, 218.

24. Wiegman, "Black Bodies," 311.

25. Ibid, 331.

26. Mohanty, "Cartographies of Struggle," 4.

Dana Y. Takagi, *Maiden Voyage*

My special thanks to Russell Leong for his encouragement and commentary on this essay.

1. See Donna Haraway, "Situated Knowledges: The Science Question in Feminism and the Privilege of Partial Perspective," *Feminist Studies* 14, 3 (1988): 575–599.

2. See Teresa de Lauretis, "Feminist Studies/Critical Studies: Issues, Terms, and Contexts," in *Feminist Studies/Critical Studies*, ed. Teresa de Lauretis (Bloomington: Indiana University Press, 1986), 1–19; bell hooks, *Yearning: Race, Gender and Cultural Politics* (Boston: South End Press, 1990); Trinh T. Minh-ha, *Woman, Native, Other* (Bloomington: Indiana University Press, 1989); Chandra Talpade Mohanty, "Under Western Eyes: Feminist and Colonialist Discourses," in *Third World Women and the Politics of Feminism*, ed. Chandra Talpade Mohanty, Ann Russo, and Lourdes Torres (Bloomington: Indiana University Press, 1991), 52–80; Linda Alcoff, "Cultural Feminism versus Post-Structuralism: The Identity Crisis in Feminist Theory," *Signs* 13, 3 (1988): 405–437.

3. Trinh T. Minh-ha, *Woman, Native, Other*, 28.

4. Steven Epstein, "Gay Politics and Ethnic Identity: The Limits of Social Constructionism," *Socialist Review* 17, nos. 3/4 (May/August 1987): 9–54. Jeffrey Escoffier, editor of *Outlook* magazine, made this point in a speech at the American Educational Research Association meeting in San Francisco, April 24, 1992.

5. Of course there are exceptions, for example, blacks that "pass." Perhaps this is where homosexuality and racial identity come closest to one another, amongst those minorities who "pass" and gays who can also "pass."

6. I do not mean to suggest that there is only one presentation of self as lesbian. For example, one development recently featured in the *Los Angeles Times* is the evolution of "lipstick lesbians" (Van Gelder, 1991). The fashion issue has also been discussed in gay/lesbian publications. For example, Stein (1988), writing for *Outlook*, has commented on the lack of correspondence between fashion and sexual identity, "For many, you can dress as femme one day and a butch the next."

7. See Judith Butler, *Gender Trouble* (New York: Routledge, 1990); Michel Foucault, *The History of Sexuality, Volume 1: An Introduction*, trans. Robert Hurley (New York: Vintage, 1980); Monique Wittig, *The Straight Mind and Other Essays* (Boston: Beacon Press, 1992); David Greenberg, *The Construction of Homosexuality* (Chicago: University of Chicago Press, 1988).

8. Compare for example the histories: Ronald Takaki's *Strangers from a Different Shore*, Sucheng Chan's *Asian Americans*, and Roger Daniels' *Chinese and Japanese in America* with Jonathan Katz's *Gay American History*, Jeffrey Week's *The History of Sexuality*, Michel Foucault's *History of Sexuality*, and David Greenberg's *The Construction of Homosexuality*.

9. See Steffi San Buenaventura, "The Master and the Federation: A Filipino American Social Movement in California and Hawaii," *Social Process in Hawaii* 33 (1991): 169–193.

10. Wynn Young, "Poor Butterfly," *Amerasia Journal* 17, 2 (1991): 118.

11. See Asian Women United, *Making Waves* (Boston: Beacon Press, 1989).

12. All too often we conceptualize different identities as separate, discrete, and given (as opposed to continually constructed and shifting). For an example of how "identity" might be conceptualized as contradictory and shifting moments rather than discrete and warring "homes" see Minnie Bruce Pratt, "Identity: Skin Blood Heart" in *Yours in Struggle: Three Feminist Perspectives on Anti-Semitism and Anti-Racism*, ed. Elly Bulkin, Minnie Bruce Pratt, and Barbara Smith (Ithaca, N.Y.: Firebrand Books, 1984), 11–63, and commentary by Biddy Martin and Chandra Talpade Mohanty, "Feminist Politics: What's Home Got to Do with It?," in *Feminist Studies, Clinical Studies*, ed. Teresa de Lauretis (Bloomington: Indiana University Press, 1986), 191–212.

13. See Jeff Nunokawa, "All the Sad Young Men: AIDS and the Work of Mourning," in *inside/out*, ed. Diana Fuss (New York: Routledge, 1991), 311–323.

14. Haraway, "Situated Knowledges: The Science Question in Feminism and the Privilege of Partial Perspective," in *Simians, Cyborgs, and Women* (New York: Routledge, 1991), 188.

Sumi K. Cho, *Asian Pacific American Women and Racialized Sexual Harassment*

This article is dedicated to the spirit of resistance displayed by Professor Rosalie Tung, Dr. Jean Jew, attorney Carolyn Chalmers, and the students at the unnamed university who organized for justice for Asian Pacific women fighting racialized sexual harassment. My dissertation advisor, Ronald Takaki, and graduate mentors in Ethnic Studies at U.C. Berkeley, Elaine Kim, Ling-chi Wang, and Michael Omi, provided invaluable training and support for this interdisciplinary research and writing. I would like to thank the Asian Pacific American Law Students Association at the University of Michigan for inviting me to present this article in April 1996 and the Center for the Study of Women in Society in Eugene, Oregon, for funding assistance. A longer version of this article was published in Adrien Wing, ed., *Critical Race Feminism* (New York: New York University Press, 1997).

1. This letter and other materials cited for this case are on file with the author. I am not at liberty to disclose publicly the sources related to this case.

2. Formal complaint of Japanese female student to university Affirmative Action Office (on file with author) (hereinafter "formal complaint").

3. Transcript of conversation with former vice-president of Japanese student organization (on file with author).

4. As in many such cases involving an abuse of power in a sexual relationship, the woman was reluctant to come forward to file a complaint. When she learned that the professor had initiated and ended relationships with at least two other Japanese students, she decided to report him to campus officials so that other women could be warned of his pattern of racial stalking. Her requests were modest and would have preserved his anonymity. She merely suggested in her formal complaint that the professor undergo counseling so that he no longer "acts in a predatory manner toward Japanese women, and no longer needs to subordinate women sexually." She also recommended that he undergo HIV counseling.

5. The administrative body in charge of reviewing such complaints decided not to pursue the claim. In a letter to the complainant, the affirmative action officer concluded that the professor was not acting as an "agent" of the university and that such actions fell within the sphere of "private" behavior outside the reach of the university's administrative regulations. This defensive, liability-conscious response reflects an unnecessarily legalistic interpretation of standards that must be met simply to investigate a complaint of wrongdoing. The denial of the university's liability as a basis for dismissing the complaint reflects the general conflict of interest of administrative offices ostensibly created to hear such discrimination or harassment complaints whose staff are paid by the university. This central conflict of interest poses a catch-22 for a complainant: If a grievant establishes an agency relationship and corresponding legally actionable injury, then the university fears litigation and assumes an adversarial position against the grievant and is naturally unhelpful in providing a remedy. If a grievant cannot articulate the required agency relationship between the offender and the university to invoke legal liability, then the university assumes no responsibility to address or investigate the existing internal complaint. Hence, there is only an appearance of an internal administrative remedy, when in reality, legal standards of liability absent legal protections and procedures for the grievant control the internal process. In this case, the conflict between the purpose of the Affirmative Action Office and the university's interest is also suggested by the removal of two previous African American officers for doing their job too effectively. Following the departure of the second African American, the current officer (who rejected the student's complaint) was hired for the job

through an internal promotion, absent a search, itself a violation of the university's affirmative action policy that he was hired to safeguard. The current officer is white. Letter from affirmative action officer (on file with author).

6. Following the Affirmative Action Office's decision not to investigate, frustrated and concerned Asian Pacific American and Japanese student organizations attempted to warn incoming students of the possible targeting of Japanese women by the professor. Even this small, cautionary effort would not be allowed. An attorney retained by the professor wrote the student organizations threatening them with legal action for defamation and invasion of privacy. The attorney claimed the relationship was consensual and that because the student was not in the faculty member's class, there was no harassment. The lawyer did not deny the relationship. "[Y]ou can be held liable for dissemination of 'true' facts as well as false ones in some instances." The irony of the legal intimidation is that the lawyer defending the sexual predator had recently formed a "feminist" law firm to address issues of discrimination against women. The lawyer closed her letter to the students advising them "to seek legal counsel immediately." "I expect a written apology, if appropriate," she continued, "and written confirmation of your intention to abide by the requirements of the law within ten days of the date of this letter." Letter from feminist lawyer (on file with author).

7. Within days of the attorney's letter, the university counsel also emphasized the "possible legal liability for invasion of privacy or defamation" should the organization alert their members. "Your own endeavors, if more narrowly focused, should have the benefit of careful legal review for your own protection." Letter from university counsel (on file with author).

8. Colleen Fong provides a notable exception to this usual blindspot in model minority literature. In her dissertation on model minority images of Chinese in popular magazines, she focuses specifically on Chinese women. Colleen Valerie Jin Fong, "Tracing the Origins of a 'Model Minority': A Study of the Depictions of Chinese Americans in Popular Magazines" (unpublished Ph.D. dissertation, University of Oregon, 1989).

9. I refer to this popular depiction of Asian Pacific women as servile as the "Mrs. Livingston syndrome" after the loyal, soft-spoken maid attending to the needs of the bachelor father and son in *The Courtship of Eddie's Father*, a television sitcom that ran from 1969 to 1972. Mrs. Livingston, a likely war bride, never complained and never appeared to have any social life or concerns other than dutifully and contentedly providing for her boss's needs. The actress portraying Mrs. Livingston, Miyoshi Umeki, epitomized the stereotypical passive, traditional Asian woman in major Hollywood films such as *Sayonara* (1957) and *Flower Drum Song* (1961). See Darrell Hamamoto, "Monitored Peril" 11–12 (1994); see also Gina Marchetti, "Romance and the 'Yellow Peril'" 126 (1993).

10. Catharine MacKinnon discussed the psychological function of sexual harassment: "How many men find it unbearable that a woman out-qualifies them in an even competition? Perhaps they assuage their egos by propagating rumors that the woman used her sexuality—something presumptively unavailable to men—to outdistance them. These stories may exemplify a well-documented inability of both sexes to see women in anything but sexual terms. Willingness to believe the stories may illustrate the pervasive assumption that, since a career is so intrinsically inappropriate for a woman, her sexuality must define her role in

this context, as well as in all others." Catharine MacKinnon, *Sexual Harassment of Working Women* (New Haven: Yale University Press, 1979), 39. See also Morrison Torrey, "We Get the Message: Pornography in the Workplace," 22 *S.W. U.L. Rev.* 53, 75–77 (1992) (discussing how competent, attractive women, in contrast to competent, attractive men, are disliked by coworkers and "are often believed to have exploited reasons other than skill and talent to achieve their position").

11. Torrey, "We Get the Message," 44 (discussing sexual harassment as a condition of work for which there is an economic connection between harassment "compliance" and material job benefits).

12. Tony Rivers, "Oriental Girls," *Gentleman's Quarterly* (British ed.), October 1990, 161, 163. I thank Margaret Lin for bringing this article to my attention, and for her activism organizing protest against the article. See letter from The Coalition Against Negative Media Portrayal of Women to Condé Nast Publications Re: "Oriental Girls: The Ultimate Accessory" (undated, on file with author).

There is a booming subgenre in pornography of Asian Pacific women, but I was unable to stomach this research after one attempt to document some of the offerings. The subgenre is replete with the submissive stereotype and frequently uses Asian Pacific women in particularly masochistic and demeaning forms of pornography. Researchers who have investigated this subgenre report titles of videos such as *Asian Anal Girls, Asian Ass, Asian Slut, Asian Suck Mistress, Banzai Ass, China deSade, Oriental Encounters, Oriental Sexpress, Oriental Lust, Oriental Callgirls, Oriental Sexpot, Oriental Squeeze, Oriental Taboo,* and *Oriental Techniques of Pain and Pleasure,* Final Report of the Attorney General's Commission on Pornography, 388–433 (1986), cited in James Moy, *Marginal Sights: Staging the Chinese in America* (Ames: Univ. of Iowa Press, 1993), 136–137. See also Diana Russell, *Against Pornography* (Berkeley, Calif.: Russell Publications, 1993), 53–55, 61–62, 64, 65, 102–105, observing that pornographic portrayals of Asian Pacific women reveal "common racist stereotypes about Asian women as extremely submissive and knowledgeable about how to serve and 'please a man'" and documenting the considerable reliance upon bondage and torture in this subgenre that caters to male arousal through the domination; Michael Stein, *The Ethnography of an Adult Bookstore: Private Scenes, Public Spaces* (Lewiston, N.Y.: Mellen Press, 1990), 60–61, cited in Eddy Meng, "Mail Order Brides: Gilded Prostitution and the Legal Response," 28 *U. Mich. J.L. Rev.* 197 n. 204 (1994) (citing magazines such as *Oriental Pussy* and *Hong Kong Hookers,* in addition to pornographic video titles). Meng also uncovered an Internet service entitled, "Oriental Fetish," that encourages users to "[l]earn the secrets of Oriental Sexuality" (230 n. 206).

In addition to the seamy industry of pornography, there are semipornographic portrayals of Asian Pacific women in other more "respectable" outlets. Sweeps week often features sensational "exposés" of sex tourism industries in Bangkok, Thailand or in the Philippines for talk shows and local news stations. Teaser ads for such "news" segments typically expose as much skin of young Asian Pacific girls as is allowed on television. The advertising industry has bestowed its highest Clio award on the Singapore Girl commercials, whose soft-focus, smiling flight attendants in traditional dress comprised the entire campaign along with the tag line, "Singapore Girl, You're a great way to fly." A recent

CD cover for New York recording artist John Zorn displays sadomasochistic images of Japanese women "bound and suspended by ropes taken from Japanese pornographic films," Elisa Lee, "Uprooting the Garden of Torture," *Third Force* Nov./Dec. 1994, 18. Mail-order bride industries posing as matchmaking businesses with names such as "Cherry Blossoms" or "Lotus Blossoms" also exploit stereotypical images of willing, pliant, and impoverished Asian Pacific sex partners for middle-aged American males disenchanted by "liberated" American women. See Venny Villapando, "The Business of Selling Mail-Order Brides," in *Making Waves*, 318, 320.

13. As the article continues, "The stereotype of the Oriental girl is the greatest sexual shared fantasy among Western men, and like all the best fantasies it is based on virtual ignorance and uncorrupted by actuality." Rivers, "Oriental Girls," 163. Post-World War II Hollywood churned out a number of films which chronicled the interracial sexual relationships between white American military men and Japanese women as a metaphor for U.S. military victory and dominance over Japan. Gina Marchetti analyzes the Geisha genre, in films such as *Teahouse of the August Moon* (1956), *The Barbarian and the Geisha* (1958), *Cry for Happy* (1961) and *My Geisha* (1961), which metaphorically represent "a bellicose Japan, through the figure of the geisha," as a "yielding and dependent nation," 179. Marchetti analyzes postwar Hollywood films set in Hong Kong such as *Love Is a Many Splendored Thing* (1955) and *The World of Suzie Wong* (1960) as cold war narratives that allow "America to assert and legitimize its presence in Asia as an 'enlightened' Western power opposed to British colonialism and promising a neocolonial prosperity in the face of socialist leveling" (110).

14. See, e.g., Michael Small, "For Men Who Want an Old-Fashioned Girl, The Latest Wedding March is Here Comes the Asian Mail-Order Bride," *People*, Sept. 16, 1985, 127–129; see also Marchetti, "Romance and the 'Yellow Peril,'" 158 (stating that Hollywood films in the 1950s and early 1960s such as *Three Stripes in the Sun*, *Teahouse of the August Moon*, *Sayonara*, *The Barbarian and the Geisha*, *The Crimson Kimono*, and *Cry for Happy*, among others, portrayed interracial love affairs between Japanese and Americans by using the "myth of the subservient Japanese woman to shore up a threatened masculinity in light of American women's growing independence during World War II").

15. For more information on these interconnected power relationships and their impact on the international transfer of stereotypes, see Eddy Meng, "Mail Order Brides," 200–209 ("Gender and ethnic stereotypes of Asian Pacific women as submissive, exotic, and erotic run rampant in marketing materials which hawk Asian Pacific brides as sex partners who double as domestic servants."); Elaine Kim, "Sex Tourism in Asia," in *Critical Perspectives of Third World America* 2 (1984), 214 (volume on file at the Asian American Studies Library at U.C. Berkeley) (analyzing the links between colonial domination, U.S. military presence, and sex tourism in Asia); Elisa Lee, "Ordering Women," *Third Force*, July/August 1995, 22 (Lee notes the link between the stereotype of Asian Pacific women as "submissive sexpots" and the history of U.S. militarization in Asian countries. "The Philippines and Thailand were often considered prime 'R & R' stops for American military men, and the prostitution industries that serviced the U.S. military exploded there during the Vietnam and Korean wars.") See, generally, Thanh-Dam Truong, *Sex, Money, and Morality: Prostitution and Tourism in Southeast Asia* (London: Zed Books, 1990) (exploring the

vast sex tourism industry in Thailand); Elizabeth Uy Eviota, *The Political Economy of Gender: Women and the Sexual Division of Labour in the Philippines* (London: Zed Books, 1992) (discussing the lucrative sex tourism industry in the Philippines); Saundra Pollock Sturdevant and Brenda Stolzfus, *Let the Good Times Roll: Prostitution and the U.S. Military in Asia* (New York: The New Press, 1992) (examining the connection between U.S. military presence in Asia and the development of sex tourism industries).

16. Rivers, "Oriental Girls," 163. Suzie Wong is the Hollywood prototype of the masochistic eroticism of Asian Pacific American women. In *The World of Suzie Wong* (1960), a classic for such stereotypes, Nancy Kwan portrays "Suzie Wong," a prostitute who falls in love with a struggling American artist self-exiled in Hong Kong, played by William Holden. The Hong Kong hooker invites Holden to beat her so she can show her injuries to her Chinese girlfriends as a measure of his affection. In the final "love scene," Suzie pledges to stay with her American man until he says, "Suzie, go away."

17. There are two legally recognized forms of sexual harassment. Quid pro quo involves harassment that is implicitly or explicitly linked to the conferral or denial of economic benefits as a condition of employment. See *Meritor Sav. Bank, FSB v. Vinson*, 477 U.S. 57 (1986); 29 C.F.R. § 1604.11(a)(1), (2)(1993). Hostile environment consists of harassment that is so intimidating or offensive that it unreasonably interferes with one's work performance. See *Harris v. Forklift Systems*, 114 S. Ct. 369 (1993); 29 C.F.R. § 1604.11(a)(3) (1993). See generally MacKinnon, "Sexual Harassment."

18. Out of three hundred faculty, for example, she was selected by her dean to represent the school at Harvard Business School's seventy-fifth anniversary in 1983. Speech by Rosalie Tung, "Asian Americans Fighting Back," University of California, Berkeley, April 1990 [hereinafter, Tung speech], reprinted in "Rosalie Tung Case Pries Open Secret Tenure Review," *The Berkeley Graduate*, April 1991, 12–13, 30–31 (copy and videotape of speech on file with author).

19. Tung speech.

20. Tenure is the grant of lifetime employment for faculty at institutions of higher education. Once tenure is granted, one can be fired only for cause, financial crisis, or programmatic, institutional changes. Historically, tenure was offered to guarantee one's academic freedom to express even unpopular ideas without threat of dismissal. See B.N. Shaw, *Academic Tenure in American Higher Education* (Chicago: Adams Press, 1971).

21. According to Tung, the thirty letters were collected in batches. After an initial attempt to procure negative letters in the first set of letters, he mailed a second set, and then a third. Tung speech.

22. *University of Pennsylvania v. Equal Employment Opportunity Commission*, 493 U.S. 182, 185 (1990). Tung's research focused on bilateral U.S.-China and Pacific Rim trade relations.

23. Tung speech. See also Maria Ontiveros, "Three Perspectives on Workplace Harassment of Women of Color," 23 *Golden Gate, U.L. Rev.* 817, 818 (1993) (observing that some women of color, particularly Asian Pacific American women and Latinas, are perceived to be "less powerful, less likely to complain, and the embodiment of particular notions of sexuality").

24. Ontiveros, "Three Perspectives" (citing comments quoted in January 26, 1990 issue of *Newsday*).

25. *University of Pennsylvania*, 493 U.S. 182 (1990).

26. At the same time, the Court suggested two loopholes for violators to exploit: the elimination of "smoking gun" evidence, and the redaction of tenure files. "Although it is possible that some evaluators may become less candid as the possibility of disclosure increases, others may simply ground their evaluations in specific examples and illustrations in order to deflect potential claims of bias or unfairness." *University of Pennsylvania*, 493 at 200–201. Writing for the unanimous Court, Blackmun further emphasized that "[n]othing we say today should be understood as a retreat from [the Court's] principle of respect for legitimate academic decision making." Id. at 199. These passages can be interpreted as a telegraphing of a legally permissible way to discriminate. Gil Gott, "Court Limits Tenure Review Secrecy," *The Berkeley Graduate*, February 1990, 5 (commenting that faculty may interpret the opinion to mean they can continue to discriminate as long as they "beef up their 'academic' arguments to better conceal their real motivations in order 'to deflect potential claims of bias or unfairness'"). The Court failed to discuss the issue of redaction, a process that removes attributions of comments from evaluations to preserve anonymity. Redactions can create a jigsaw puzzle which subverts the purpose of gaining access to peer review files in order to root out discrimination. See generally Tim Yeung, "Comment, Discovery of Confidential Peer Review Materials in Title VII Actions for Unlawful Denial of Tenure: A Case Against Redaction," 29 *U.C. Davis L. Rev.* 167 (1995).

27. Plaintiff's Memorandum in Opposition to Defendant's Motion for Summary Judgment at 20, *Jew v. University of Iowa et al.*, 749 *F.Supp.* 946 (1990) (No. 86-169-D-2) (hereinafter, Plaintiff's memo) (on file with author).

28. *Jew v. University of Iowa*, 749 *F.Supp.* 946, 949 (S.D. Iowa 1990).

29. The federal trial record reveals the depth of this academic jealousy toward Jew. During her promotion deliberations one faculty member voting against Dr. Jew commented that "women and blacks have it made." Another "no" vote stated that Dr. Jew had received many more advantages than he had received. Soon after deliberations, another opponent asserted that "women and blacks don't have any trouble getting jobs." Id. at 953.

30. According to Jew: "the image white men still have of Asian women is the Singapore Girl. In [*Traveler*] magazine, the top twenty travel items are listed. Singapore Airlines is again the number one airline. The most cited reason is the Singapore Girl. Despite the strides we've made in overcoming sex stereotypes, even the most enlightened of travelers admit they enjoy this very much." Interview with Dr. Jean Jew, October 15 1991, cited in Sumi Cho, "The Struggle for Asian American Civil Rights" (Unpublished dissertation, University of California, Berkeley, 1992). The article Dr. Jew is referring to appeared in the October 1991 issue of Condé Nast's *Traveler* magazine reporting the Readers' Choice Awards for the 100 top travel experiences. Under "Top 10 Airlines," Singapore Airlines finished first under the article headline, "The Singapore Girls aim to please—and always do." The article recognized the calming and contradictory nature of the stereotype of the Asian Pacific female stereotype for allegedly "enlightened" U.S. travelers: "Yet how curious that the American traveler, having absorbed two decades of feminism, feels so sanguine about an airline that trades without hesitation on the image and allure of the 'Singapore Girl.' This young and lissome creature, a vision of Asian beauty, attentiveness, and grace in a sa-

rong kebaya . . . earn[s] just $1,200 a month and can't do more than fifteen years of basic cabin service. But this clearly bothers their passengers not at all." *Traveler*, October 1991, 223.

31. Interview with Dr. Jean Jew, in Cho, "The Struggle." See also Martha Chamallas, "Jean Jew's Case: Resisting Sexual Harassment in the Academy," 6 *Yale J. L. and Feminism* 71, 84 (1994). Chamallas agrees that stereotypes played a key role in shaping the primary injury: "The false narrative constructed about Jew was believable in part because of its familiarity. Jew was portrayed as a cold, conniving woman whose success was due to her sexual relationship with a man in power rather than her achievements as a teacher and researcher. The narrative drew on both sexual and racial stereotypes. It supported the stereotype that women sleep their way to the top; that women are not really good at science and if they achieve in that area, it must be due to the talent of men; that women of color are promiscuous; and that Asians overachieve in their jobs but are not truly talented or creative."

32. Plaintiff's memo, p. 19 of timeline addendum.

33. Plaintiff's memo, p. 6 of timeline addendum.

34. Jew, 749 *F. Supp.* at 949.

35. Plaintiff's memo, p. 7 of timeline addendum.

36. Chris Osher, "U. of I. to Promote Professor in Bias Case," *Des Moines Register*, August 29, 1990.

37. Andy Brownstein and Diana Wallace, "UI, Regents Liable in Sexual Harassment Case," *The Daily Iowan*, August 29, 1990.

38. Linda Hartmann, "UI Faculty Say Appeal Sends Bad Message," *Iowa City Press-Citizen*, Oct. 13, 1990.

39. Andy Brownstein, "Regents: First Amendment Behind Appeal," *The Daily Iowan*, Oct. 15, 1990.

40. Ibid.

41. Peter Shane, "Harassment is Not Privileged Speech," *The Daily Iowan*, Sept. 28, 1990, 8A.

42. Chamallas, "Jean Jew's Case," 81–90 (providing a detailed description of the Jean Jew Justice Committee's successful organizing efforts to convince the university not to appeal the case to the Eighth Circuit Court of Appeals).

43. Ibid, 84.

44. Catharine MacKinnon laid the groundwork for a legal definition and theory of sexual harassment. Critical race feminists must continue to build upon this work to theorize more comprehensively the racial, ethnic, and class dimensions of sexual harassment. See, e.g., Elvia Arriola, "'What's the Big Deal?': Women in the New York City Construction Industry and Sexual Harassment Law, 1970–1985," 22 *Col. Hum. Rts. L. Rev.* 21, 59–60 (1991) (contending that the "swift merging of racial and sexual harassment" is a functional aspect of defending traditional working conditions and exclusionary practices that perpetuate the dominant white male [power] structure; Ontiveros, "Three Perspectives," 818 (suggesting a complex understanding of the interwoven racial and sexual harassment injuries in the workplace as well as a method for analyzing differential risk that subgroups of women of color encounter in experiencing and redressing what she refers to as "workplace harassment"); Kimberlé Crenshaw, "Race, Gender, and Sexual Harassment," 65 *S. Cal. L. Rev.* 1467, 1473 (1992) (arguing that the organized women's movement must "go beyond the

usual practice of incorporating only those aspects of women's lives that appear to be familiar as 'gender' while marginalizing those issues that seem to relate solely to class or to race").

45. For a related concept, see Crenshaw, "Race, Gender," 1467–1468 (referring to the dynamics of racism and sexism in the workplace as the "dual vulnerability" confronting women of color).

Elaine H. Kim, *"Bad Women"*

I am grateful to Eungie Joo, Eithne Luibheid, and Moira Roth for reading and commenting on early drafts of this manuscript.

1. Yuji Ichioka, "Ameyuki-san: Japanese Prostitutes in Nineteenth-Century America," *Amerasia Journal* 4, 1 (1977): 1–21.

2. Rose Hum Lee, *The Chinese in the United States of America* (Hong Kong University Press and Oxford University Press, 1960), 187–200.

3. Artist's statement, *Along the Street of Knives*, 1985.

4. Unpublished interview with Margo Machida, May 1992.

5. Unpublished interview with Margo Machida, November 1992.

6. Erica L. H. Lee, "[Re]Present Asian/A Representation: Politics of Being an Asian American Woman Artist" (Unpublished paper, Scripps College, 1994), 43.

7. Lee, "[Re]Present Asian/A Representation," 37.

8. Hanh Thi Pham, with Tyger-Womon, "Transsexualism" (Unpublished paper, 1993), 1–2.

9. Ibid.

10. Lee, "[Re]Present Asian/A Representation," 57.

11. September 1991 interview.

12. Xiarong Li, "Painting the Pain," *Human Rights Tribune* 3, 1 (Spring 1992): 10.

13. Artist's statement, 1990.

14. Gary Gach, "Monumental Fragments of Identity," *Asian Week*, November 26, 1993.

15. John Dorsey, *Baltimore Sun*, March 26, 1995.

16. Lisa G. Corrin, "In Search of Miss Sallie Chu: Hung Liu's Can-ton: *The Baltimore Series*," brochure for The Contemporary exhibit, Canton National Bank, Baltimore, 1995.

17. May 1992 interview.

18. See Yong Soon Min, "Territorial Waters: Mapping Asian American Cultural Identity," *New Asia: The Portable Lower East Side* 7, 2 (1990): 1–10.

19. Min has said, "Korean American is one of the identities I assume; Third World is another" (May 1992 interview).

Anuradha G. Advani, *Against the Tide*

1. OSHA.

2. This information was provided by the Taxi and Limousine Commission, 1992.

3. Filmmaker Anand Patwardhan has documented the organizing efforts of Indian Canadian farm workers. ftp://.stats.bls.gov/pub/news.release/cfoi.txt

4. The phrase is from Tanya Dasgupta, about her efforts to organize Toronto's South Asian domestic workers, at the Panel on Organizing, Desh Pardesh: A

Conference on South Asian Cultures in the West, Toronto, Canada, May 6, 1994.

5. See "Clinton's Healthcare Plan: What's in It for Cab Drivers," *Lease Drivers' Bulletin* 1, Lease Drivers' Coalition, New York, 1992, 2. Under the commission driving system where drivers earn a percentage of their receipts, the employer paid for health benefits, pension, and vacation. See Sheryl Fragin, "Taxi!" *Atlantic Monthly*, New York, May 1994, 30–34, 42.

6. Fragin, "Taxi!" 33–34.

7. "Advocacy for Victims of Police Brutality and Racial Violence," *Peela Paiya*, Lease Drivers' Coalition, New York, August 1994, 2–3.

8. See Martin Douglas, "Cabbies Angrily Debate Partitions," *New York Times*, December 3, 1993, B3.

9. See Mini Liu, "Asians and Afro-Americans," *New York Amsterdam News*, October 29, 1988; Monona Yin, "No Winners," *Los Angeles Times*, May 25, 1990, B7.

10. Harsha Ram, during a discussion at the Conference on Homophobia and Racism in the South Asian Activist Community, New York City, December 7, 1991. See also Sucheta Mazumdar, "Race and Racism: South Asians in the United States," in *Frontiers of Asian American Studies: Writing, Research, and Commentary*, ed. Gail M. Nomura et al. (Washington: Pullman, 1989), 25–38.

11. Cornel West details a personal experience of not being able to get a cab in *Race Matters* (Boston: Beacon Press, 1993).

12. This is paraphrased from the narrative of LDC organizer Vivek Renjen Bald's video *Taxi/vala, Auto/biography*.

13. *New York Times*, December 3, 1993, B3.

14. This Hindi/Urdu title translates into English as "Yellow Wheel."

15. Bangladeshis and Pakistanis were eligible to apply for the lottery, but Indians were not.

16. LDC's plans to modify *Peela Paiya* to include articles in Bengali, Punjabi, and Urdu, as well as in English represents part of the search for an effective mechanism to bring in Bangladeshi and Indian drivers from the periphery to the center, and to mobilize anchorages based on culture, religion, and language. LDC represents the vision of a truly pan-South Asian organization that has yet to be realized.

17. On the other hand, I have also found that due to the complex cultural, religious, and ethnolinguistic diversity of South Asia, the crossing of boundaries can sometimes be easier than with non-South Asians, since people's multiple anchorages do facilitate community-building.

18. CAAAV's receptivity has given South Asians access to established networks of other Asian American organizations, liberals in city government, and financial resources.

19. The open-mindedness of East and Southeast Asian CAAAV members notwithstanding, I have found it continually necessary to explain the extent of ethnolinguistic, religious, and cultural diversity in South Asian communities, so that the differences contained in the term "South Asian" do not get erased. One example of such an erasure was our own use of a green background on our "Taxi Power" t-shirts; to many South Asians, green signifies a Muslim identity. The presentation of LDC as a Muslim organization was thus unknowingly facilitated by Pakistani-identified driver-organizers and culturally unfamiliar second-

generation South Asians and East Asians. See Saloni Mathur, "Broadcasting Different," *SAMAR: South Asian Magazine for Action and Reflection* (Winter 1992): 5; and Naheed Islam, "In the Belly of the Beast I Am Named South Asian," in *Our Feet Walk The Sky*, ed. Women of South Asian Descent Collective (San Francisco: Aunt Lute Press, 1993), 242–245.

20. Steve Selter, interviewed by Anuradha G. Advani, New York City, August 30, 1994.

21. Esther Kaplan, "Cops to Cabbie: Dinkins Not Mayor," *Village Voice*, June 7, 1994, 15.

22. See Elaine Kim, "Between Black and White: An Interview With Bong Hwan Kim," in *The State of Asian America: Activism and Resistance in the 1990s*, ed. Karin Aguilar-San Juan (Boston: South End Press, 1994), 71–100.

Elsa E'der, Que Dang, and Karen Kimura, *Living Today*

Thanks to Jeannie Lee for specific language regarding safer-sex guidelines.

1. Jamie's comments are excerpted from an interview conducted by Que Dang and Karen Kimura of the Asian Pacific AIDS Intervention Team (APAIT) of Los Angeles, July 28, 1995.

2. Lakhana's comments were made in a conversation with Elsa E'der, August 5, 1995.

3. Renamed the Living Well Project of San Francisco in 1995.

4. A person is diagnosed with AIDS when HIV causes the number of main cells (T-cells) of the immune system to fall below 200, or when the immune system is so weak that infections occur.

5. *Chi* is believed to exist inside the skin and aids healing by enhancing the immune system. Balancing *chi* is based on balancing *yin* and *yang*, hot and cold energies. The primary goal of Chinese medicine, including acupuncture, is to ensure this balance, as well as the flow of *chi* in the body.

6. Karposi sarcoma is a form of cancer that can exist inside and outside of the body.

7. From the Hawai'ian language.

Chizu Iiyama and Lisa S. Hirai Tsuchitani, *Speaking Out*

1. Report of the Commission on Wartime Relocation and Internment of Civilians, p. 14.

2. The Friends of Hibakusha is a nonprofit, San Francisco-based organization dedicated to providing legal, medical, and social support to U.S. residents who are survivors of the Hiroshima and Nagasaki atomic bombings.

3. For a further discussion of the redress movement, please refer to *Japanese Americans: From Relocation to Redress*, ed. Roger Daniels, Sandra C. Taylor, and Harry Kitano (Seattle: University of Washington Press, 1991).

Sandra Liu, *Passion and Commitment*

1. In contrast, in independent film circles and academic milieus, films, and videos by Asian American women have been acknowledged as deeply innovative and politically significant. Take, for example, film- and videomakers such as Christine Choy, Loni Ding, Valerie Soe, Janice Tanaka, Rea Tajiri, and Trinh Minh-ha.

2. Yang, Hatta, and Shum do not represent the views of all Asian American

women filmmakers. For this essay, I was interested in exploring Asian American women's participation in feature film production, and thus, filmmakers working in other genres or formats, such as documentary, experimental, or short narrative films, to name a few, were not included. I interviewed Mina Shum in San Francisco on March 6, 1995; Kayo Hatta in Los Angeles on March 14, 1995; and Janet Yang in Santa Monica on March 14, 1995.

Lisa Lowe, *Work, Immigration, Gender*

1. From *Immigrant Women Speak Out on Garment Industry Abuse: A Community Hearing Initiated by Asian Immigrant Women Advocates*, May 1, 1993, Oakland, California, AIWA, 310 8th Street, Suite 301, Oakland CA 94607. Mrs. Fu Lee is one of twelve women who were not paid by a sweatshop contracted by manufacturer Jessica McClintock, Inc. AIWA has organized a long-term campaign to secure pay for these women and to reveal garment industry abuse of immigrant women workers.

2. See Chalsa Loo, *Chinatown: Most Time, Hard Time* (New York: Praeger, 1991).

3. See Michael Omi and Howard Winant, *Racial Formation in the United States, From the 1960s to the 1990s* (New York: Routledge, 1994).

4. Lucie Cheng and Edna Bonacich, *Labor Immigration Under Capitalism: Asian Workers in the United States Before World War II* (Berkeley: University of California Press, 1984).

5. The Santa Clara Center for Occupational Safety and Health (SCCOSH) is a community organization that works to reduce the exposure of workers to hazardous materials in the electronic, janitorial, agricultural, and other industries. SCCOSH, 760 N. First St., San Jose, CA 95112.

6. The Gabriela Network USA has launched a campaign to address the "trafficking" of Filipinas to the U.S. Gabriela Network, P.O. Box 403, Times Square Station, New York, NY 10036.

7. For a study of the connections between militarism and sexual exploitation of prostitutes in the Philippines, see Saundra Pollock Sturdevant and Brenda Stoltzfus, *Let the Good Times Roll: Prostitution and the U.S. Military in Asia* (New York: The New Press, 1992).

8. I have benefited from conversations with Norma Alarcón.

9. Chela Sandoval, "US Third World Women: The Theory and Method of Oppositional Consciousness in the Postmodern World," *Genders* (Spring 1991): 1–24; Angela Davis, *Women, Race, and Class* (New York: Random House, 1981); Evelyn Nakano Glenn, "Racial Ethnic Women's Labor: The Intersection of Race, Gender, Class Oppression," *Review of Radical Political Economics* 17, 3 (1983): 86–109.

10. See Arturo Escobar's "Imagining a Post-Development Era? Critical Thought, Development and Social Movements," *Social Text* 31/32 (1992): 20–56.

11. See Michelle Rosaldo and Louise Lamphere, eds., *Woman, Culture, and Society* (Palo Alto: Stanford University Press: 1974); Heidi Hartmann, "The Unhappy Marriage of Marxism and Feminism: Towards a More Progressive Union," *Capital and Class* (Summer 1979); Nancy Hartsock, "The Feminist Standpoint: Toward a Specifically Feminist Historical Materialism," *Money, Sex, and Power* (Northeastern, 1985); Catherine MacKinnon, "Feminism,

Marxism, Method, and the State: An Agenda for Theory," *Signs* 7 (1982): 515–544; Robert Blauner, *Racial Oppression in America* (New York: Harper, 1972); Mario Barrera, *Race and Class in the Southwest* (S. Bend, Ind.: Notre Dame University Press, 1979); Rodolfo Acuna, *Occupied America: A History of Chicanos* (New York: Harper, 1981); Michael Omi and Howard Winant, *Racial Formation in the United States, 1960s to the 1990s* (New York: Routledge, 1994).

12. See, for example, the moving account of the struggles of working across difference in Virginia R. Harris and Trinity A. Ordoña, "Developing Unity Among Women of Color: Crossing the Barriers of Internalized Racism and Cross-Racial Hostility," *Making Face, Making Soul/Haciendo Caras: Creative and Critical Perspectives by Women of Color*, ed. Gloria Anzaldúa (San Francisco: Aunt Lute Press, 1990).

13. For Norma Alarcón's discussion of the critical relationship of women of color to Anglo-American feminism and Chicano and Mexican nationalist discourses, see "Traddutora, Traditora: A Paradigmatic Figure of Chicana Feminism," *Cultural Critique* 13 (Fall 1989): 57–87; "The Theoretical Subject(s) of 'This Bridge Called My Back' and Anglo-American Feminism," in Gloria Anzaldúa, ed., *Making Face, Making Soul/Haciendo Caras*.

14. See Audre Lorde, "The Master's Tools Will Never Dismantle the Master's House," in Cherríe Moraga and Gloria Anzaldúa, eds., *This Bridge Called My Back: Writings By Radical Women of Color* (Persephone Press, 1981); ibid; Asian Women United of California, *Making Waves: An Anthology of Writings By and About Asian American Women* (Boston: Beacon Press, 1989).

15. For discussions of the global garment and electronics industries and the use of women's labor for assembly, see June Nash and Maria Patricia Fernandez-Kelly, eds., *Women in the International Division of Labor* (Albany: SUNY Press, 1983); Maria Patricia Fernandez-Kelly, *For We Are Sold, I and My People: Women and Industry on Mexico's Frontier* (Albany: SUNY Press, 1983); Norma Chinchilla and Edna Bonacich, "Potentials for Collective and Feminist Consciousness Among Women Working in Global Industries at Home and Abroad," paper presented at "The Feminist Future: A Transnational Perspective from California," Lake Arrowhead, November 1993. For resources on organizing cross-national labor coalitions, see Committee for Asian Women, *Many Paths, One Goal: Organizing Women Workers in Asia* (Hong Kong: Committee for Asian Women, 1991); *Beyond Borders: A Forum for Labor in Action around the Globe*, ed. Mary E. Tong, 3909 Center Street, #210, San Diego, CA 92103.

16. See Elaine Kim, paper presented at "Emerging Majorities, Warring Minorities" Conference, U.C. Santa Cruz, 1994; Lydia Lowe, "Paving the way: Chinese Immigrant Workers and Community-based Labor Organizing in Boston," *Amerasia Journal* 18, 1 (1992). See also Glenn Omatsu's important essay "The 'Four Prisons' and the Movements of Liberation: Asian American Activism from the 1960s to the 1990s," *State of Asian America: Activism and Resistance in the 1990s*, ed. Karin Aguilar-San Juan (South End Press, 1994).

17. Miriam Ching Louie, "Immigrant Asian Women in Bay Area Garment Sweatshops: 'After Sewing, Laundry, Cleaning and Cooking, I Have No Breath To Sing,'" *Amerasia Journal* 18 (1992): 14. For other discussions of Asian women's labor in the garment industry, see Chalsa Loo and Paul Ong, "Slaying Demons with a Sewing Needle: Feminist Issues for Chinatown's Women" in Loo, *Chinatown: Most Time, Hard Time*; and Diane Yen-Mei Wong and Dennis

Hayashi, "Behind Unmarked Doors: Developments in the Garment Industry," in Asian Women United of California, eds., *Making Waves*. See also *Through Strength and Struggle*, a video documentary that tells the story of Chinese immigrant women workers and the P & L and Beverly Rose Sportwear shutdowns; by Chinese Progressive Association Workers Center, 164 Lincoln Street, 2nd floor, Boston, MA 02111.

18. Support Committee for Maquiladora Workers, 3909 Center Street, Suite 210, San Diego, CA 92103; Mary Tong, Director.

19. Chandra Talpade Mohanty, "Feminist Encounters: Locating the Politics of Experience," in *Destabilizing Theory*, ed. Michelle Barrett and Anne Philips, (Palo Alto: Stanford University Press, 1992).

20. See for example, Kumari Jayawardena's *Feminism and Nationalism in the Third World* (London: Zed Books, 1986), a social history of women's work, and women's activities in feminist, nationalist, and labor movements, in Turkey, Egypt, India, Sri Lanka, Indonesia, the Philippines, China, Korea, Vietnam, and Japan. For excellent analyses of segmented labor and occupational segregation of women within different "Third World" national locations, see *Working Women: International Perspectives on Labour and Gender Ideology*, ed. Nanneke Redclift and M. Thea Sinclair (New York: Routledge, 1991). *Third World Women and the Politics of Feminism*, ed. Chandra Talpade Mohanty, Ann Russo, and Lourdes Torres (Bloomington: Indiana University Press, 1991) contains important accounts of different "Third World" feminisms in the context of the specific upheavals of decolonization, national liberation struggles, and transnational capitalism.

21. Lorde, "The Master's Tools."

CONTRIBUTORS AND EDITORIAL BOARD MEMBERS

ANURADHA G. ADVANI majored in ethnic studies at U.C. Berkeley. She participated in organizing New York City's Asian American communities through the Lease Drivers' Coalition of the Committee Against Anti-Asian Violence and the Asian & Pacific Islander Coalition on HIV/AIDS. Having returned to her California roots, she is working towards a career in teaching high school students about social justice issues.

HERSHINI BHANA is an educator and writer, born of black and indian ancestors in Durban, South Africa. "I write to honor the power of dying birds and the fire of Chango."

CATALINA "CATIE" CARIAGA is a contributing editor to *Poetry Flash*. She earned her M.A. in poetry at San Francisco State University. Her work has appeared in ZYZZYVA, *Onthebus, Dissident Song: A Contemporary Asian American Anthology, Fourteen Hills Review, Looking For Home: Women Writing About Exile*, and *Returning a Borrowed Tongue: An Anthology of Filipino and Filipino American Poetry*.

ELIZA Y. CHAN is a public affairs professional specializing in crisis communications. She coordinates media affairs, congressional relations, and community outreach programs after natural disasters, such as earthquakes and floods, and civil crises, such as the 1992 Los Angeles riots. In 1995, Chan represented Asian Women United of California at the United Nations World Conference on Women in China in Beijing, China.

CHING-FEI CHANG is a "Taiwanese Taurus turned U.C. San Diego Medical Student/Aspiring Wong Fei Hong in melon-colored scrubs/Chocolate-Covered Raisins fueling Formaldehyde Dreams/Nostalgia Addict/Queen of Similar/ Hapkido-kicking, wok-stirring, poetry-spouting gym Rat=ANALYZER OF EVERYTHING."

Born in Hong Kong, raised in Oregon, and now living in San Diego, California, MARILYN CHIN is the author of *The Phoenix Gone, the Terrace Empty*, which won P.E.N.'s Josephine Miles Award for the best book of 1994, and *Dwarf Bamboo*, which was nominated for the Bay Area Book Reviewers' Award in 1987. She co-edited *Dissident Song: A Contemporary Asian American Anthology* and co-translated *The Selected Poems of Ai Qing*. Her poetry has appeared in *Ms.*, *The Kenyon Review, The Iowa Review, Parnassus*, and ZYZZYVA. It is also anthologized in *The Open Boat*. Chin is featured in *The Language of Life*, an eight-part PBS series on American poetry.

SUMI K. CHO has a law degree and a Ph.D. in ethnic studies from U.C. Berkeley. She teaches Race, Racism, and U.S. Law, Remedies, and Employment Discrimination at De Paul University College of Law in Chicago. She writes on critical race feminism, affirmative action, sexual harassment, and praxis-oriented theory.

PASSION CUMMINGS was born and raised in Hawai'i and now resides in Southern California. Her work has appeared in the twentieth anniversary edition of *Gidra*. She is a member of Pacific Asian American Women Writers-West.

QUE DANG is a health educator working to provide culturally appropriate health services for Asian and Pacific Islander women through advocacy, education, and community activism. A 1.5-generation Vietnamese American, she lives in Los Angeles.

Born in Calcutta, CHITRA DIVAKARUNI came to the U.S. twenty years ago. She now resides in Sunnyvale, California. She teaches creative writing and is the president of MAITRI, a help line for South Asian women. She has published three volumes of poetry, *Dark Like the River, The Reason for Nasturtiums*, and *Black Candle*, and she has won many awards, including the Pushcart Prize and the Allen Ginsberg Poetry Prize. Divakaruni's collection of short stories, *Arranged Marriage*, won the American Book Award in 1996. Her first novel, *The Mistress of Spices*, will be published in 1997.

ELSA E'DER resides in San Francisco and divides her time between creative writing, cultural sensitivity training, and distributing film and video work by Asian Americans to educational institutions, public television, and cable broadcasters. She is currently at work on a documentary on women and drumming.

Originally from Vietnam, YEN LE ESPIRITU is married to a Filipino American and is the proud mother of two "pan-Asian" daughters. She chairs the Ethnic Studies Department at U.C. San Diego and is the president of the Association of Asian American Studies. Espiritu is the author of *Asian American Panethnicity* (1991), *Filipino American Lives* (1995), and *Asian American Women and Men: Labor, Laws, and Love* (1996).

NANETTE FOK, an AWU board member, currently works as a development director of the National Asian American Telecommunications Association, a national nonprofit media arts organization. She has also unintentionally amassed what is believed to be the largest wind-up toy collection South of Market Street in San Francisco, though this claim remains officially unverified.

ANU GUPTA was born and raised in New York. A graduate of Brown University, she currently attends the Yale School of Medicine. Her short stories and essays have appeared in *Living in America: Poetry and Fiction by South Asian American Writers; Becoming Doctors; Closing the Gap: South Asians as Asian Americans;* and *Diya*. She received the 1994 Marguerite Rush Lerner Award for Creative Writing.

KIMIKO HAHN is the author of three volumes of poetry, *Air Pocket, Earshot*, and *The Unbearable Heart*, which won the 1996 American Book Award. Her work appears in *Charlie Chan is Dead, Aloud, The Best American Poetry of 1996*, and *The Best American Poetry of 1995*.

LISA S. HIRAI TSUCHITANI was born and raised in San Jose, California. Her life work is inspired by the legacies of immigration and internment of her ancestors. The pioneering spirit of her Issei father, Masatoshi "Jack" Hirai, has been an especially powerful guiding force in her life.

JOSELYN TORRES IGNACIO: "I am neither this nor that nor did I thunk this up. Just Jos."

CHIZU IIYAMA is a nisei septuagenarian who received her college diploma fifty years after completing her requirements because she was incarcerated in an internment camp with tens of thousands of other Japanese Americans in 1942, the year she was to have received it. From the 1940s to the present, she has been active in numerous progressive movements to end race discrimination and war.

SUSAN ITO lives in Oakland, California. She is a hapa sansei whose fiction and poetry have appeared in numerous journals and anthologies, including the *Asian Pacific American Journal, Two Worlds Walking, The Very Inside*, and *Growing Up Asian American*. She edited a literary anthology on adoption titled *A Ghost At Heart's Edge* and is working on her first novel.

EUNGIE JOO was born in Pennsylvania and raised in upstate New York and Minnesota. A graduate student in ethnic studies at U.C. Berkeley, she plans to write her dissertation on contemporary visual art. She is a recipient of the Lila Wallace/Reader's Digest Curatorial Internship for Diversity in the Arts at the Walker Art Center in Minneapolis.

NORA OKJA KELLER was born in Seoul, Korea, and now lives in Waipahu, Hawaii. She is the author of the novel *Comfort Woman* (1997).

ELAINE H. KIM chairs the ethnic studies department at U.C. Berkeley, where she is a professor of Asian American studies. She has written, edited, and co-edited numerous articles and books, the latest of which are *Writing Self/Writing Nation* (1994), *East To America: Korean American Life Stories* (1996), and *Dangerous Women: Gender and Korean Nationalism* (1997). Kim co-founded Asian Women United of California, Asian Immigrant Women Advocates, and the Korean Community Center of the East Bay in Oakland, California.

A Korean-born American, Washington D.C.-based DAI SIL KIM-GIBSON is currently an independent filmmaker and writer. In 1993, she directed *Sa-i-ku: From Korean Women's Perspectives*, a documentary video about Korean immigrant women and the 1992 Los Angeles uprisings. Her latest film is a 60-minute documentary about the Koreans taken to Sakhalin by the Japanese as forced laborers during World War II and then abandoned in the Soviet Union. Her forth-coming book is tentatively titled *Japanese Military Supplies: Korean Comfort Women*.

MYUNG MI KIM'S books of poetry include *Under Flag* (1991), *The Bounty* (1996), and *Dura* (forthcoming). Her poems have appeared in such journals as *Conjunctions, Sulfur, Avec, Hambone,* and *positions: east asia cultures critique*. Her work has been anthologized in *Premonitions* and *Primary Trouble* as well as other collections. Kim is on the faculty of the San Francisco State University Creative Writing Program.

KAREN KIMURA is a Los Angeles native, sansei or third-generation Japanese American, and a visual artist. She works for the Asian Pacific AIDS Intervention Team as the Director of Community Services, developing media campaigns to promote AIDS awareness in the Asian and Pacific Islander communities.

BRENDA KWON is a doctoral candidate in English at U.C.L.A., writing her dissertation on Korean American writers from Hawai'i. She would like to say mahalo to the people who have encouraged her to keep writing, especially her Mom, who didn't kick her out of the house upon discovering that she wanted to be a writer.

Fluent in Spanish, French, and Vietnamese, MONG LAN was born in Saigon in 1970 and emigrated with her family to the U.S. in 1975. Educated at the University of Houston, she is a San Francisco-based writer and artist. Presently, she is developing work based on recent travels in Vietnam.

CAROLYN LEI-LANILAU was born in Hawai'i. Her writing refers to William Blake, medieval Chinese literature and philosophy as well as what it is to be Hawai'ian, Hakka, Chinese, and a woman. She is the author of *Wode Shuofa (My Way of Speaking)*, which won an American Book Award in 1987. She founded *Hale o Hawai'i Nei* and directs *Ha'ina Mai Ana Ka Puana (Tell the Story)*, an oral history project that documents the historic relationship between *Kanaka* (native Hawai'ians) and native Californians.

MARIE G. LEE is the author of *Necessary Roughness, Saying Goodbye, If It Hadn't Been for Yoon Jun,* and *Finding My Voice*, which won the Friends of American Writers Award. Her short fiction has appeared in *The Kenyon Review* and *American Voice*. Lee's essays have appeared in *New Worlds of Literature* and the *New York Times*. She is president of the board and a founder of the Asian American Writers' Workshop in New York.

PRISCILLA LEE is "an Aries-Firehorse of the type they used to drown in China, and I was raised by my unemployed Buddhist fortuneteller Grandma. My poetry has appeared in *The Kenyon Review, Mid-American Review, ZYZZYVA, Phoebe,* and *The Cream City Review*. I work as a technical writer."

SANDRA LIU is doing doctorate work in ethnic studies at U.C. Berkeley. Her current research interests include Asian Americans in film and video, Chinese

American history, ethical pedagogy, and classroom technologies. A daughter of the Chinese diaspora, Sandra is a descendant of two generations of Guangdong settlers in Indonesia. She was born in Brazil and grew up in New York City.

SOPHRONIA LIU came to the U.S. from Hong Kong in 1973, when she was twenty years old. She studied at the University of South Dakota and the University of Minnesota. Liu is a founding member of the Asian American Renaissance, a Twin Cities grass-roots organization committed to building community through the arts. As an actor and playwright, she works with the Renaissance's Theater Mu, appearing in such productions as *Yellow Fever* and *Paper Angels*. Her writing has appeared in *The Minnesota Daily*, *Hurricane Alice*, and *The Circle*. She teaches Tai Chi and chants at the local Buddhist temple. In 1992, Liu received the Governor's Award for Leadership and Contributions to the State of Minnesota.

LISA LOWE is professor in the department of literature at U.C. San Diego, where she teaches courses in ethnic studies and women's studies. She is the author of *Immigrant Acts: On Asian American Cultural Politics*. Lowe serves on the board of directors of the San Diego Foundation for Change and on the Advisory Board of the Support Committee for Maquiladora Workers in San Diego.

LI MIN MO was born in China and educated at Goddard and Emerson Colleges. She has lived and worked in Cambridge, Massachusetts, for over two decades. Mo has worked extensively as a storyteller, receiving awards and grants from the Boston Arts Lottery, the Cambridge Arts Council, the Cultural Education Collaborative, and Channel 4's *You Gotta Have Art*.

CHANDRA TALPADE MOHANTY is associate professor of women's studies at Hamilton College and member of the core part-time faculty of the Union Institute Graduate School. Her intellectual and political interests include the transnational dimensions of feminist theory, feminist and antiracist pedagogy in the U.S. academy, and the intersections among gender, race, and international development in education. She is co-editor of *Third World Women and the Politics of Feminism* (1991) and co-editor of *Feminist Genealogies, Colonial Legacies, Democratic Futures* (1996).

LINDA NISHIOKA lives and teaches in Mililani Town, Hawai'i. She is sansei, her grandparents having immigrated from Okinawa in the late 1800s to work on Hawai'i's sugar plantations. Her poems have appeared in *Bamboo Ridge, the Hawai'i Writers Quarterly*.

JESSICA OLIVER was eleven years old and a student at Francisco Middle School when she won first prize in the San Francisco Bay Area "Growing Up Asian in America" contest in 1996 for her essay, which was chosen from among 1,500 entries by a panel of professional writers, educators, and journalists. The contest is a program of the Asian Pacific American Community Fund, a nonprofit organization based in San Francisco.

LISA PARK (pseudonym) is a twenty-something, mixed-heritage, second-generation Asian American raised in the Sun Belt and interested in issues of racialization and coloniality in the U.S.

CELINE SALAZAR PARREÑAS is an award-winning multimedia producer. The 1991 winner of the Eisner Prize in poetry at U.C. Berkeley, she has published work in *Premonitions, Liwanag,* and *Asian America.* Parreñas has edited *smell this: women of color anthology* and is currently working on a new anthology of nonfiction writing by Asian Pacific Americans, *generasian x.*

Sixteen-year-old JUNO SALAZAR PARREÑAS wishes she could spend all her time writing and performing. In reality, she's just a high school kid currently applying to college. A finalist for America's Best in Screenwriting as well as a contributing writer to *The Lesbian News*, she wants to have a double major in communications and ethnic studies, hopefully at U.C. Berkeley.

RHACEL SALAZAR PARREÑAS is a Ph.D. candidate in ethnic studies at U.C. Berkeley. Her areas of interest include immigration, theories of race, class, and gender, and women, work, and family. She is currently at work on her dissertation, tentatively titled *Global Servants: Filipina (Im)migrant Domestic Workers in Rome and Los Angeles.*

ISABELLE THUY PELAUD is a graduate student in ethnic studies at U.C. Berkeley. Her interests include Southeast Asian refugees in the U.S., gender issues, and Asian American literature. She is involved in community organizing and in promoting the work of Vietnamese writers and artists through a group called *Ink and Blood*.

SHEEREKHA PILLAI graduated from the University of Michigan with honors in English and creative writing. She participated in the Teach for America program as a high school English teacher in Baltimore, Maryland, and is currently pursuing her MFA degree in creative writing at Syracuse University. Outside school, she has served as a counselor at various domestic violence and AIDS services programs, as a performer and script writer in an Asian American theatre troupe, and as an editor of an Asian American women's journal.

LISA SEE of Pacific Palisades, California, has been the West Coast correspondent for *Publisher's Weekly* since 1983. Her book, *On Gold Mountain*, which was published in 1995, is the story of the one-hundred-year odyssey of her Chinese American family.

MARIA SARITA ECHAVEZ SEE lives and writes in New York City. She hangs out with her cousins in Stuyvesant Town, Manhattan, and then retreats to Brooklyn. A graduate student in English and comparative literature at Columbia University, she works hard for her money.

JANE SINGH is currently a lecturer in the Asian American studies program at U.C. Berkeley. Her areas of writing and research include nationalism and identity in diaspora communities, globalization and migration, South Asian history in the United States, and gender differentials in the immigration and ethnic experience.

GRANATE SOSNOFF calls herself "Hapa, Korean, and Russian-Jewish." She graduated in women's studies from the University of California, Santa Cruz and has worked for more than a decade in feminist and progressive organizations. Currently, she works for the Public Media Center, a San Francisco–based nonprofit public interest advertising agency.

KAREN SU is an assistant professor of English at Mills College in Oakland, California. In 1996–97, she was a Post-Doctoral Faculty Fellow in the newly established Asian/Pacific American Studies program at New York University. Her research and teaching interests focus on American literature, Asian American literature, multicultural education, and feminist/antiracist pedagogy.

GRACE ELAINE SUH was born in Seoul, Korea, grew up in Watertown, Wisconsin, and attended Barnard College. She is a poetry editor of *The Asian Pacific American Journal*, a contributing editor and former book editor of *A. Magazine*, and a writer for the *New York Times* Syndicates New America News Service. She lives in Brooklyn, where she is at work on her first novel.

RENEE TAJIMA-PEÑA is an Academy Award–nominated filmmaker whose work has premiered at the Cannes Film Festival, the London International Film Festival, the Sundance Film Festival, and other venues around the world, and broadcast on PBS, Home Box Office, ABC, BBC, Lifetime, and Fuji-TV. She is the director of the new documentary *My America . . . or Honk If You Love Buddha* (PBS), *Who Killed Vincent Chin?*, *The Best Hotel on Skid Row, Jennifer's in Jail*, and others. Tajima-Peña was formerly a film critic for *The Village Voice*, editor of *Bridge: Asian American Perspectives*, a commentator for National Public Radio, and the director of Asian Cine-Vision in New York City.

DANA Y. TAKAGI teaches sociology at the University of California, Santa Cruz. She is also the author of *The Retreat from Race* (1992) and various articles on Asian Americans and racial politics. Her current work is on race relations and sovereignty. She has a slight preference for riding rather than making waves.

TRINH T. MINH-HA is a writer, filmmaker, and composer. Her books include *Framer Framed* (1992), *When The Moon Waxes Red* (1991), *Woman, Native, Other* (1989), *En minuscules* (1987). She has made five films: *A Tale of Love* (1995), *Shoot for the Contents* (1991), *Surname Viet Given Name Nam* (1989), *Naked Spaces* (1985), and *Reassemblage* (1982). Trinh is Professor of Women's Studies and Film at U.C. Berkeley.

Born in Laos in 1973, KA VANG immigrated to the U.S. with her parents and five brothers and sisters when she was three years old. After spending her early childhood in Providence, Rhode Island, she attended Miss Porter's School, an exclusive boarding school in Connecticut. She graduated from Wellesley College and now attends the University of Minnesota School of Law. Ka plans a career in criminal or civil litigation.

LILIA V. VILLANUEVA is co-author of *Philip Vera Cruz: A Personal History of Filipino Immigration and the Farmworkers Movement* (1994). She has published articles and short stories and is currently working on a novel. She has served as president of the board of directors of Asian Women United of California since 1993. Villanueva lives in Berkeley with her husband and son.

MITSUYE YAMADA is author of *Camp Notes and Other Poems* and *Desert Run: Poems and Stories*. She co-edited *The Webs We Weave: Orange County Poetry Anthology*, *Sowing Ti Leaves: Writings by Multicultural Women*, and *Scaling the Chord* (forthcoming). Yamada founded Multicultural Women Writers; she chairs Amnesty International's International Development Committee, which promotes and funds human rights development efforts in the Third World; and she teaches creative writing.

An award-winning journalist, writer, and editor, HELEN ZIA is a contributing editor to *Ms.* magazine. Her work has appeared in numerous publications and anthologies. The daughter of Chinese immigrants, Zia is a long-time feminist activist for social justice issues. Her leadership in the Asian American anti-violence movement is documented in the Academy Award–nominated film, *Who Killed Vincent Chin?* Zia resides in the San Francisco Bay Area with her life partner.

ACKNOWLEDGMENTS

Asian Women United of California is deeply grateful to all the members of the editorial advisory board, without whose devoted and voluntary commitment there would be no *Making More Waves*. For their valuable contributions, we also wish to thank Chitra Divakaruni, Julie Ha, Gail Kong, Allan de Souza, and the Asian Pacific American Community Fund essay contest organizers, Karen Joe Laidler, Eithne Luibheid, Joan Varney, and Vin Wolfe. For her enthusiastic support and guidance, we thank Marya Van't Hul, our ever creative and helpful editor at Beacon. Other acknowledgments include:

Marilyn Chin's "Portrait of the Self as Nation, 1990–91" was published in *The Phoenix Gone, The Terrace Empty* by Marilyn Chin (Milkweed Editions, 1994). Copyright © 1994 by Marilyn Chin. Reprinted with permission from Milkweed Editions.

A longer version of Sumi K. Cho's "Asian Pacific American Women and Racialized Sexual Harassment" was published under the title "Converging Stereotypes in Racialized Sexual Harassment: Where the Model Minority Meets Suzie Wong" in *Critical Race Feminism*, ed. Adrien Wing (New York University Press, 1997).

Elaine H. Kim's "'Bad Women': Asian American Visual Artists Hanh Thi Pham, Hung Liu, and Yong Soon Min," appeared in slightly different form in *Feminist Studies* (Fall 1996).

Sophronia Liu's "So Tsi-fai: Memories from a Hong Kong Primary School" appeared in *Hurricane Alice* (Fall 1986), *Ourselves Among Others: Cross-Cultural Readings For Writers* (St. Martin's Press, 1988), *Points of Departure: A Thematic Reader* (McGraw-Hill, 1993), *Making Connections Between Reading and Writing* (Wadsworth, 1994), and *The Macmillan Reader*, 4th ed. (Allyn and Bacon, 1995). Reprinted by permission of the author.

Chandra Talpade Mohanty's "Defining Genealogies: Feminist Reflections on Being South Asian in North America" appeared in *Our Feet Walk the Sky: Women of the South Asian Diaspora* (Aunt Lute Books, 1993).

Lisa See's "Anna May Speaks" appeared in her book *On Gold Mountain: The One-Hundred-Year Odyssey of a Chinese-American Family* (St. Martin's Press, 1995).

Dana Y. Takagi's "Maiden Voyage: Excursion into Sexuality and Identity Politics in Asian America" appeared in slightly different form in *Amerasia Journal* 20, 1 (1994), and *Asian American Sexualities: Dimensions of the Gay and Lesbian Experience* (Routledge, 1995).